Breaking Through Depression

PHILIP GOLD

Breaking Through Depression

New Treatments and Discoveries for Healing

ALLEN LANE
an imprint of
PENGUIN BOOKS

ALLEN LANE

UK | USA | Canada | Ireland | Australia
India | New Zealand | South Africa

Penguin Books is part of the Penguin Random House group of companies
whose addresses can be found at global.penguinrandomhouse.com

First published in Great Britain by Allen Lane 2023
001

Set in 10.5/14pt Sabon LT Std
Typeset by Jouve (UK), Milton Keynes
Printed and bound in Great Britain by Clays Ltd, Elcograf S.p.A.

The authorized representative in the EEA is Penguin Random House Ireland,
Morrison Chambers, 32 Nassau Street, Dublin D02 YH68

A CIP catalogue record for this book is available from the British Library

ISBN: 978-0-241-65905-2

Dedication text [TK]

CONTENTS

Contents

PREFACE

Over the years, people have often asked how I can bear to study depression. How is it that I can digest all of that sadness without becoming overwhelmed by it? The explanation is as simple and as complicated as this: When I was young, I experienced my own depression, and due to a supportive family, many friends, close colleagues, effective psychotherapy, and effective antidepressant treatment, I was able to develop resilience, which helped me to bear the enormous distress of my patients and to live without despair.

My father was born in Tiberias, in northern Palestine. His father was an orthodox Rabbi, and my father was raised to strictly honor his father and mother. When he was thirteen, his mother died in childbirth. Two years later, his father remarried a woman who did not like his children. When my father was sixteen, his stepmother threw him out of the house. Afterward, my father asked his father to give him his blessing to go to America. His father initially refused, but then agreed to take the case to Rabbi Kook, the Chief Rabbi of Jerusalem. Rabbi Kook would decide whether my father should be able to start a new life in America. After spending two days with my father and grandfather, Rabbi Cook decided that my father should leave for America. His father accepted the decision.

Preface

Shortly thereafter, my father and a friend were attacked on the street. My father saw his friend's throat slashed right before his eyes. He was plagued by nightmares for the rest of his life. He was further traumatized by not being able to obtain a visa to go to America, which effectively put his life on hold. Eventually, after sojourns in Alexandria, Marseilles, and Calais, he stowed away on a ship and arrived in Providence, Rhode Island. Two years later, he married a woman who went on to have an affair with his boss. He was devastated, and they divorced soon thereafter. Because of his experiences as an adolescent and in his marriage, my father, who was a strong man in many ways, had a palpable, lifetime dread of abandonment.

My mother was born in what was Slonim, Lithuania, now located in Belarus. She told me she lived in several different countries without ever having moved. When, in 1913,, her father emigrated to America, and planned to bring over the rest of the family as soon as possible. World War I broke out, however, and my mother and grandmother could not embark for America until 1919, when my mother was fourteen. My mother remembers that during the war years, she and her sister would run across potato fields at night dodging the bullets of invading Russian soldiers. In addition, her family had to endure pogroms that often threatened their lives and destroyed their property.

When the war ended, my mother, her sister, and their mother obtained visas to come to America. My grandmother's eyesight was sufficiently poor that she worried that the whole family would be sent back from Ellis Island to Eastern Europe. My mother proudly remembers standing behind my grandmother and prompting her with the correct answers to the eye test. However, when my grandmother finally made it to America, she quickly discovered that her husband had married another woman and had started a new family. My grandmother had no choice but to try to build a life for her family without a husband. She settled the family into a tenement house on Hester Street in the Lower East Side.

Preface

My parents met at a Hebrew teacher's convention in New York City and made their way to Newport News, Virginia, where they started a Hebrew academy. My brother was born there, and I came along three years later. I was born during the period between the Jewish New Year and the Day of Atonement. My mother told me that this placed a responsibility on my shoulders for a lifetime of good works. My parents organized their lives around nurturing my brother and me in the hope that we would live up to our potential.

When I was six, the lives of our family were changed forever. My brother, Chip, suddenly lost the capacity to talk or swallow. I'll never forget the late Friday afternoon when the ENT doctor told my parents that my brother was seriously ill with a life-threatening condition called bulbar polio.

Bulbar polio invades the brain stem rather than the spinal cord and ultimately interferes with the respiration and cardiac functions the brain stem controls. Bulbar polio carried a mortality rate of 80 percent. My brother's doctor rushed him by ambulance to a special hospital across the James River Bridge twenty-five miles away. Anything across the seven-mile span of the James River seemed to me a world away, and I could only imagine what my brother was enduring. I had no idea how he was going to eat or communicate. I anticipated the worst.

My parents were shattered. My mother remembers being so distracted that at times she forgot to feed me, even though both of my parents were very loving and committed to my welfare. Both my mother and my father cried frequently. I vowed to myself not to cause them any trouble. I felt guilty that it was my brother who was so sick rather than me, and that my parents were so often distraught. I felt helpless because I could not lighten their burden. I loved them very much, and it was excruciating for me to see them in so much distress.

Miraculously, my brother recovered almost completely in eight months. According to the Jewish tradition, when a child recovers from a life-threatening illness, his middle name is changed to Chaim, the Jewish word for life. My parents often called him lovingly by that name. Overall, he was left with a slight difficulty in swallowing and an unusual, high-pitched sneeze. Because the area affected was near the sleep center in the brain stem, he slept for only five hours a night for the rest of his life. However, my parents' lives were changed forever. After, they were always anticipating catastrophes; they became overprotective of my brother and me, and we were very careful never to worry them. In many ways, we felt responsible for their emotions, as if those were something under children's control.

A year after my brother's recovery, he developed a severe case of scarlet fever and, again, seemed near death. Our cousin, a pediatric resident at Johns Hopkins, came down immediately with a very small amount of penicillin, which was not yet generally available. He administered small doses daily and extracted what had been excreted in my brother's urine to administer the next day. My brother survived. His nurses felt it was a miracle. The second so far in his life.

At eighteen, my brother decided to go to William and Mary college in Williamsburg and then later to the Duke University School of Medicine, where he ultimately graduated first in his class. When he was a junior there, I was ready to go off to college. I did well in high school, and was accepted by Williams College, but my parents persuaded me to go to Duke to be with my brother and to be close to home. My brother and I saw each other frequently and developed a very close relationship. I never regretted going to Duke.

When I was in college, I metHelen. She was a friend of my brother Chip's friend, Jennifer who was a senior at Duke. Jennifer was the daughter of an Episcopalian minister, and Chip knew he couldn't marry a non-Jewish girl, so rather than date, they remained good friends.

Helen was beautiful. She had a great sense of humor and a lovely Southern drawl. Her speech was like music. Helen and I were together continuously throughout my junior year at Duke. Not infrequently, we had dinner together with my brother and Jennifer My brother liked Helen a great deal, and she grew close to him. I was sure then and am sure now that our meeting in the context of my brother's friendship with Jennifer, and our sharing these relationships together, played a large role in my capacity to let down my ordinarily firm boundaries with Helen. We fell in love. On the nights we saw each other, I would go home to my dorm and think how wonderful it was to be alive.

At the end of the school year, Helen invited my brother, Jennifer, and me to spend a few days at her home in rural Gerogia. Soon after we arrived, Helen's parents spoke with me and were very clear that they did not want their daughter to marry a Jewish man. I said that I understood. Helen and I, astonishingly, never talked about my encounter with her parents. In retrospect, we were only children.

From that time on, and over the summer, Helen seemed to withdraw from me. Initially, she seemed less warm on the phone. After a while, she began to tell me of other boys she had met, and to whom she was attracted. I now find it extraordinary that I didn't tell her dating others was a deal breaker and that I was not willing to pursue the relationship with her under such circumstances. However, I hadn't yet thought through whether I could make a commitment to her because of the religious issue. Therefore, I felt, I had no claim on her.

I began to ruminate about the situation and tried to understand what was happening and why Helen was so ambivalent about me. I decided the problem was my appearance. I was neither athletic nor notably handsome. As I continued to ruminate, I decided that the only thing standing in my way of a relationship with Helen were superficial but critical factors. I thought I looked weak, and I certainly felt weak and ineffectual. I gradually became convinced that I would be alone for the rest of my life because of this insurmountable difficulty.

I broached none of these issues with anyone. These feelings grew over time, and after a month or two, I became increasingly depressed. I woke every morning at two and was unable to get back to sleep. My appetite diminished. I lost weight. My self-esteem was severely damaged.

Over the Christmas break, during my senior year as an undergraduate, I received a letter from Duke telling me that the medical school wanted to offer me early admission and would give me a full four-year scholarship. That evening, my father was admitted to the hospital with severe chest pains. I learned from a nurse that one of my former high school English teachers had met Helen and knew we were going together. She thought Helen was partying with a lot of boys and told my father. He never mentioned it to me. In retrospect, he likely felt that I was headed down the same path he'd been down in his first marriage. His fear for me manifested itself physically. Again, I felt responsible for his emotions. The guilt I felt was enormous.

I limped through the summer and the next semester. My depression continued to intensify. My sense of self continued to worsen. Over Thanksgiving, I had the idea that my parents were ashamed of being seen with me because I was so unattractive. I continued to awaken early. I struggled with maintaining my weight. I could enjoy nothing. My depression was deepening. I knew this, and yet I felt powerless to snap myself out of it.

In January, soon after the second semester began, a friend pulled me aside and told me that Helen had started dating someone else and that they had had become very close. For the first time during this ordeal, I was able to access my anger. I walked over to Helen's dorm, went up to her room, took the ring I had given her, and threw it over the roof of her dorm. The week thereafter, my depression literally ceased.

Prior to this event, I had been reexperiencing the full loss daily, and each day felt like the first day of a heartbreaking event. My preoccupation with my appearance and weakness vanished. I could approach my studies with a clear mind and had a very successful semester. Later, I could not decide whether this recovery reflected my capacity to face reality, or whether I was biologically cycling out of my depression, providing me with the capacity to act effectively on my own behalf with Helen. And though depressive disorders are often recurrent and tend to increase in frequency and intensity over time, this is not always the case. I have never had another depression, which I believe indicates that the cycle can be ended, and the damage not only repaired but harnessed for growth. But I also take an antidepressant now, which I believe insulates me from my natural susceptibility.

In retrospect, it is clear to me that I hadn't yet tackled any of the issues I would need to in order to live a satisfactory life and to feel like a strong human being. I hadn't separated from my parents, and I felt responsible for their welfare. I didn't have the freedom to be in touch with my own needs and to speak my mind. I had not yet learned to protest mistreatment, to get angry when I was provoked, nor was I able to grieve a great loss and walk away from an untenable situation. I also hadn't developed the capacity to be openly assertive on my own behalf. These skills developed slowly during many years of outstanding psychotherapy, for which I am very grateful. They also have protected me from experiencing another depression.

Yet, however hard my depression was, I am grateful I experienced it. I learned what a cruel illness it is, and how traits that help define our identity and upon which self-esteem rests are grievously affected. I learned to be humbled by the power of depression and to, under no circumstances, underestimate its strength. More than that, I felt a responsibility to fight it and to ensure that those suffering never had to experience the stigma, the alienation, and the shame I once felt.

It has been the fight of a lifetime.

INTRODUCTION

I first came to the National Institutes of Health in suburban Washington, DC, as a thirty-year-old. I was a freshly minted MD full of excitement and energy, fascinated by and intent on discovering more about how biology and lived experience intersect in the brain to create the disease we call depression and what we can do to alleviate it. Almost fifty years later I'm still here at NIH, and I'm still captivated by the same topics—and thankfully, in the intervening years our understanding of depression and how to best treat it is on the verge of major advances, to my satisfaction and gratitude.

Going back a bit further: As a college student in the late 1960s, I majored in English. When I decided to go on to medical school, I did so with the intention of training in psychiatry. My wish to study psychiatry reflected a belief that it represented a form of applied literature, where what I came to understand about the world could be expressed therapeutically. What good was our knowledge, I wondered, if we couldn't help someone who had lost the will to live to find a way back into the world? Even if I would never understand the meaning of life, I knew that pain mattered, that we all experience pain, and that a purposeful and worthy goal is to attempt its alleviation. For these reasons, I chose to pursue training in psychotherapy in the treatment of psychiatric illness, especially depression.

Introduction

I did my residency training at the Massachusetts Mental Health Center, which was closely affiliated with the Harvard Medical School. During that residency, my fellow residents and I spent three years of intensive training in the use of psychotherapy. I met with numerous patients and mentors for many hours each week over the course of those years. As I sought to help my patients work through their struggles with depressive illness, it became increasingly clear to me that although depression was clearly related to painful memories, life stresses, and traumatic experiences, there were biological factors that we needed to take into account as well. Data emerging at this time indicated that there were genetic components to depression. We also knew then that hormonal disturbances could trigger depressive episodes, and cyclical patterns of depressive episodes seemed to involve alterations in biological rhythms. I saw that if I was going to truly understand what depression was all about, I needed to understand more about these underlying biological changes.

I began a fellowship at the Clinical Center of the National Institutes of Health to study the neurobiology of depression when I was thirty years old. I have been at the NIH ever since. The Clinical Center, located on the NIH's 310-acre Bethesda campus, is the largest clinical research hospital in the world. It has more than three hundred beds totally devoted to clinical research (no other institution has more than forty research beds). Rather than a sole focus on treating and releasing patients, research hospitals look more deeply into the fundamental causes of disease and for new ways to treat them. This approach resonated with me.

The NIH is filled with laboratories where researchers design experimental studies that often parallel and inform clinical studies on some of the world's most difficult diseases. Multiple Nobel laureates spent their entire careers on the NIH campus. More than forty have received Lasker Awards, the top American prize given to those who have made outstanding findings that have changed medical practice.

Introduction

The NIH Clinical Center allows physician-scientists an unprecedented amount of freedom because we do not have to write traditional grants to get funded. We are thus encouraged to tackle projects that scientists on "the outside" might avoid because they need quick results to secure support. We are encouraged to stretch our imaginations and pursue high-risk ideas that may lead to major clinical discoveries—or to a dead end. In many ways, working at the NIH is the ultimate goal for scientists interested in big ideas.

After my fellowship I became a researcher, where I focused my energies on the neuroendocrinology of depression, eventually moving on to head one of the country's leading clinical and basic science research laboratories and to serve as the Chief of Neuroendocrine Research and Chief of the Section on Neuroendocrinology. It has now been forty-seven years since I first walked into the offices at the NIH—and I am still not ready to leave.

My transition from psychiatric training in Boston to becoming a neuroscientist required an initial steep learning curve that, in a way, continues to this day. There are numerous similarities between biological research and psychoanalytic psychiatry that I have uncovered along the way. Each is looking for a truth that is not apparent on the surface in the service of relieving pain. In fact, both find that the underlying source of pain can frequently be the opposite of what we had assumed it to be—and that efforts at self-protection, either psychologically or biologically, are often highly counterproductive, generating more problems than they solve. Each requires the capacity to bear frustration, loss, and failure without being overcome by shame or demoralization. Each also requires rigor, discipline, and the capacity to undertake formidable tasks, even though the chances of failure grow when the number of unknowns rises. Finally, both biological research and psychoanalytic psychiatry ultimately show that demanding circumstances, in fact, help us to realize ourselves most fully.

In recent years, a number of publications have disparaged the slow pace of biological depression research and the limits of anti-depressant treatment. I understand. It is hard not to feel discouraged at times by the true health crises that depression represents: We now know that 20 percent of the population will suffer from depression at some point in their lifetimes, and that depression can reduce a person's life expectancy by as much as ten years. But in the face of these grim statistics, it should be noted that an explosion of new knowledge about depressive illness and the emergence of more than thirty new, effective, rapid-acting antidepressants contradict these foreboding sentiments.

On the contrary, we are entering a truly remarkable time in terms of breakthroughs in our understanding of the biology of depression. For example, we now know that depression is a neurodegenerative disease associated with losses of tissues in key sites in the brain's stress system—the part of the brain that helps us manage and mitigate all kinds of threats to our safety. The parts of the brain impacted by this neurodegeneration are the very ones that help us estimate the likelihood of punishment or reward, that help regulate our levels of anxiety, that influence our self-assessment and self-esteem, and that strongly influence our capacity to anticipate and experience pleasure. Now that we know this, we've begun to learn how this loss of tissue can be halted, and we are now working to see if it can be reversed.

We also now know that depression disturbs important connections among nerve cells and inhibits the birth of new neurons in the brain—and that production of new neurons does not end in young adulthood, as long believed. We can create new neurons and neural pathways throughout our lifetimes, if the brain is appropriately stimulated. These findings, among others, have led to the development of powerful new families of superior antidepressants that are revolutionizing how we treat depression.

We recently learned beyond a shadow of doubt that depression is a total body illness. It is associated with premature coronary artery disease, premature diabetes, premature stroke, and premature osteoporosis. Overall, patients with depressive illness can lose approximately ten years of life, independent of suicide, hypertension, obesity, or smoking. The same changes in the brain that bring about the changes in mood and cognition in depression produce these systemic manifestations, in part, by broadly influencing hormonal and autonomic regulation all over the body. We know a great deal about how these systems work, and we have many tools that can halt the advance of these illnesses or treat them. In the meantime, these medical complications of depression represent a public health emergency, given the 20 percent incidence of depression around the world. With this in mind, and given the devastating effects of depression on mood, interrelationships, and work, the World Health Organization has declared depression as the second greatest cause of disability worldwide, and the leading cause of disability in individuals under the age of forty-five.

One of the purposes of this book is to alleviate current misunderstandings and underestimations of depression research and to communicate to readers the realistic hope that is embodied in the emergence of new, exciting advances in understanding depression and the development of new antidepressants based on these findings.

In a two-part series in the *New England Journal of Medicine*, I wrote that depression represents a stress response that has run awry. This premise has been confirmed by multiple studies. The stress system, a group of interconnected modules closely connected in the brain, encodes an adaptive response that is necessary for our survival. When the stress system is thrown out of kilter, depressive illness develops. Autoimmune disease is another example of a disease caused by an adaptive response system that has run awry. In autoimmune disease, the immune response that is supposed to protect us starts attacking our own tissues and organs, often causing serious illness or death. In a similar fashion, when the stress system becomes dysregulated, we become depressed.

Stressful experiences can imprint themselves on the brain

and change the structure and the function of the stress system. These stressful events are encoded in emotional memory and often reemerge during crises or danger. These emotional memories serve as fuel for the onset and continuation of depressive episodes. Their precipitation of depression occurs when we are faced with similar stressors or traumas to those we experienced in the past. The only way to modify these emotional memories is through psychotherapy. Scientists are working to find pharmacological means that could potentially help to extinguish these emotional memories or make them more accessible so they can be effectively treated. For now, however, psychotherapy is an indispensable component in the treatment of depression and is likely to remain so.

Ultimately, the frequency and intensity of stressful or traumatic events in our lives, coupled with genetic vulnerabilities, defines a person's predisposition to depressive illness. Think of susceptibility to depression as analogous to susceptibility to coronary artery disease. As with coronary artery disease, both genetic vulnerability and a predisposing environment confer susceptibility to depression. Factors like smoking, obesity, lack of exercise, and poor diet contribute to the likelihood of a heart attack. For depression, the predisposing environmental factors are early loss or trauma, unavailable or hypercritical parenting, and recurrent, often inescapable stressors throughout life. My book details what I consider to be thrilling new findings about core features of depression that show how psychotherapy is essential to its adequate treatment. I also introduce readers to breakthroughs in pharmacology that we've achieved thanks to a new understanding of the biological origins and manifestations of depression.

Depression distorts our perceptions and expectations. For many, it is really a "cancer of the self" that erodes our dignity and self-respect while it erodes our bodies. This book helps make clear this terrible reality. At the same time, there is reason for hope. We are getting closer and closer to truly understanding core aspects of depressive illness and are developing new families of rapidly acting antidepressant agents that bring even the most severe depressions under control. I hope this book adds to the growing awareness that depression is not a sign of weakness or inadequacy, but rather an illness beyond our control, and that surviving it takes courage, determination, and the capacity to bear enormous pain.

I have spent decades grappling with how our biology might influence the very traits that help define our humanity, and it is only now, late in my career, that I am beginning to understand how the interplay between biology and experience contributes to susceptibility to depression. Over the course of nearly fifty years of studying depression, I have learned a great deal about science and human nature, and it has been an education that has been inspired and nourished by many extraordinary people—my patients, fellow researchers, colleagues, and trainees. This book is an effort to repay these many kindnesses.

CHAPTER 1

William's Anguish

In July 1969, Dr. William Cummings began waking up at three o'clock every morning filled with worry. Not long after, his anxiety became virtually continuous, accompanied by a corresponding fear that encompassed almost everything of importance in his life. William became convinced that his family no longer felt close to him and that soon his wife and children would abandon him. He believed he was no longer a good researcher and that it was only a matter of time before his illustrious career would meet its end.

William was a successful physician at the Creighton University School of Medicine in Omaha, where he was working to unravel the biological mechanisms underlying leukemia and to develop improved medications for its treatment. But no matter how great his accomplishments, they could not insulate him from what was coming. It wasn't long before the anguish that resulted from these unrelenting thoughts evolved into a five-year depression and the end of life as he had known it.

His anxiety broadened to many aspects of his self-respect. He no longer was proud of his past accomplishments and felt thoroughly worthless. He began to question the extent to which any of his friends or colleagues really liked or respected him. Ordinarily generous, he became very cautious and guarded; he felt, uncharacteristically, that in his depleted and fearful condition, he could not afford generosity when his own resources were so limited.

In addition to his despair about himself, William was unable to experience pleasure in his work or usual recreational activities. He no longer looked forward to pleasurable events. He lost the capacity to appreciate sunshine and clear skies. He once had a deep interest in art and painting. Now, his depression entirely submerged any interests.

William noted increasing difficulty in thinking clearly, in concentrating, and in remembering. Although his short-term memory was diminished, his recall of painful, unpleasant memories unfortunately increased. He often felt assaulted by memories like those of his grandfather's death or his mother's depressions. When beset by sad thoughts, he could not disengage from them. He knew intellectually that he had felt energized and happy in the past, but he could not truly recall the emotional tone of these brighter times.

In addition to his dread of the future, William's memories gave him no comfort. He described a perpetual bombardment of painful, emotional memories of loss and failure. He took no pride in a prestigious research prize he had won. In fact, his depression began soon after he received the prize.

He vividly recollected the breakup of his first romantic relationship in high school, which, in all likelihood, had triggered an initial episode of depression. Scores of other negatively charged memories emerged that painted an unrealistically dim view of his life. It seemed he had preferential access to negatively charged emotional memories: He could easily recall instances of hurt or sadness, but not of joy or satisfaction. In essence, his depression erroneously crystallized a view of his life as one long, traumatic episode from which he could not find relief.

By the time William came to my office, I was already highly

invested in knowing the content of his pain so that he would not have to be alone with it. "Dr. Gold," William said, when I asked him to help me understand what he was going through, "I can't imagine that you don't look down on me as someone who was not strong enough to build a successful life. You can't imagine how deeply ashamed I am that I didn't have the strength to pull myself out of this depression." Looking away, he said, "I am convinced that the more you know me, the less you will respect me. It is only a matter of time until you lose interest in what I have to say and give up any hope that I might get better. I used to be afraid of death. Now it's life that frightens me."

Sitting in my office, William withered under a tweed jacket and khaki slacks, which he probably wore during his job as an academic physician at the university medical center. He was quite handsome, I imagined, when not so burdened. We met in my office on the third floor of the NIH Clinical Center with its windows overlooking the people enjoying the sunshine below. There is enormous energy and activity all around the Clinical Center, and its hallways are often as crowded as Penn Station. On any given day, there are thirty to forty formal lectures going on attended by large numbers of physicians, scientists, nurses, fellows, and students.

Despite the bustle and activity around him, William scrupulously avoided any eye contact, and when I did catch his glance his eyes had the dim quality I associated with people who had been abused or mistreated. From another perspective, he reminded me a bit of a diligent, painfully shy teenager at the top of his class who felt mortified by having been sent to the principal's office for discipline. We had only just met, but somehow, I intuitively felt that my colleagues and I could help him. I began intensive psychotherapy with him and grew to understand his pain intimately.

In addition to his anguish, William was beset with an insomnia that presented as an early-morning awakening. He was usually up at one or two a.m. and could rarely get back to sleep. His appetite floundered and he lost twenty pounds. His depression was most severe in the morning, when the stress response was at its peak, and diminished somewhat in the evening, when the stress response was somewhat dormant.

William had come to me hoping that a new antidepressant, imipramine, for which we were then administering trials, could make a difference in his mental state. The discovery of imipramine was the culmination of centuries of work trying to understand and treat depressive illness. In a lucky accident, the drug had been found to alleviate the symptoms of disturbed sleep, loss of appetite, and anhedonia (the inability to experience pleasure) in depressed patients. We wanted to study if these effects meant that imipramine addressed the underlying depression or merely caused the symptoms to subside, and if the results were widely replicable and sustainable.

There are two major clinical subtypes of depression: melancholic and atypical depression. William suffered with a melancholic depression. Melancholic depression often contradicts the word *depression* in that it is often a state of hyperarousal and anxiety rather than one marked by a suppression of thought and feeling. Melancholic depression includes feelings of worthlessness and an incapacity to anticipate or experience pleasure. Patients with melancholia have a distinct pattern of early-morning awakening, often with trouble getting back to sleep. They have significant decreases in slow wave, restful sleep, and increased REM sleep episodes.

Melancholic depressed patients have significant decreases in appetite and often lose weight. This can be life-threatening in frail, older patients with severe depressions. Sex drive is reduced, and depressed women often lose their menstrual cycles. Male depressed patients often have reductions in testosterone levels. Most melancholic patients lose interest in sex or are unable to enjoy it.

Patients with melancholic depression also have abnormalities in multiple hormonal, metabolic, and physiological functions that impinge on many brain regions and in virtually every tissue and organ in the body. The secretions of corticotropin-releasing hormone (CRH), and the stress hormones cortisol and norepinephrine are substantially increased in melancholic depression. Melancholic depression is, to a greater extent than most other illnesses, a total body disease.

Overall, the anxiety, increased arousal, sleep disturbances, substantial increases in stress hormones, and multiple physiological abnormalities ordinarily associated with stress indicate that melancholic depression represents a stress system that is locked in the "on" position.

A Brief History of Depression

There is a long history of humans trying to understand depression and how best to treat it. More than two thousand years ago, Hippocrates wrote that the most catastrophic illnesses occurred in the context of an increase in "black bile," one of four "humors" that dominated medical thinking at the time. Black bile, the most ominous of the humors, stems from the Greek words *melan chole*, the root of our word *melancholy*, denoting a great sorrow. Accordingly, black bile was associated with two of mankind's most dreaded scourges, cancer and depression, which I think of as no less than a cancer of the self that devours without always killing.

During the Middle Ages depression was termed *acedia*, which was a mortal sin—a turning away from God, punishable by damnation. This was contrasted to a venial, bodily sin, which is only a minor violation of God's will. Acedia was associated with an inability to relate to others, the world, and, perhaps most grievously, to God. It meant that people who were afflicted with depression were treated with the same contempt as those who had tried to enact their own deaths. To admit to being depressed was tantamount to admitting that you were going to Hell. Thus, depression became an affliction associated with immense shame.

In subsequent centuries, beliefs in depression as a moral failing persisted. Families sequestered their depressed relatives in basements or in attics and often chained them up to keep them from mingling with the townspeople and revealing to all the depravity of their conditions. The Mr. Rochesters of the world were not as rare as Charlotte Brontë might have had us believe when she dreamed up her character centuries later.

In the Middle Ages and early Renaissance, the relationship between morality and depression became even more extreme. Depression became associated not just with sin but with possession by the devil, who was, through the depressed individual, enacting a hatred for life. As a result of this belief, large numbers of depressed individuals were burned at the stake to free them of their demonic possessions.

By the eighteenth and nineteenth centuries, mentally ill patients were kept in warehouse-like asylums, which might have seemed like an improvement. But even if those with depression were not being chained and burned, this treatment still revoked their access to full lives. They were left to wander aimlessly among an entire population of individuals with all sorts of mental illnesses and dementias, in many cases exacerbating their feelings of worthlessness and sorrow.

Psychiatrists during this time began to court the idea that depression was not a moral failing, but rather a biological disorder. They suspected that all mental illness reflected neurodegeneration. Their work focused on trying to identify changes that occurred in the brains of any patient who had mental illness during their lifetime. Not unexpectedly, this effort proved to be an abysmal failure. Lumping patients with depression, schizophrenia, and the various forms of dementia together into one group diluted the findings that might have been discovered if patients with depression were studied as a separate group.

In the late nineteenth century Emil Kraepelin, a German psychiatrist, changed all of that. He developed a diagnostic system that differentiated patients with depression from those with anxiety disorders, schizophrenia, and dementia. Kraepelin's diagnostic system represented a major turning point in biological psychiatry, and it would later be refined by George Winokur, Samuel Guze, and their colleagues at Washington University in St. Louis in the twentieth century. For the first time, depression could be studied in isolation from other illnesses with different biological abnormalities and, thereby, be better understood.

This diagnostic system led to understanding subtypes of depression, and significantly increased our understanding of the meaningful differences between depressed patients and people without any depression.

Thanks to Kraepelin's work, we now understood depression as unipolar or bipolar. Unipolar, or major depression, is marked by recurrent episodes of depression alone, punctuated by periods of remission.

The second classification, bipolar illness, represented an illness associated with episodes of both depression and mania, also interspersed with periods of apparent remission. Melancholic and atypical depression could occur in patients with either unipolar or bipolar depression. Kraepelin considered schizophrenia and the dementias to be separate entities unrelated to depressive illness.

The formation of distinct subgroups of patients with depressive illness, and the serendipitous discovery of imipramine fifty years later, led to the beginning of a shift of the public's view of depressed people. Instead of failures in need of moral stamina, they were now seen as individuals beset by a serious illness and in need of intensive treatment.

What Depressi, on Is, and What Is It Not

Major depression is associated with persistent feelings of hopelessness, and, as noted, feelings of worthlessness, loss of interest in activities once enjoyed, disturbances in sleep and appetite, and broad changes in physiology.

The *Diagnostic and Statistical Manual of Mental Disorders* (*DSM-V*) outlines the following criteria to make a diagnosis of depression. The individual must be experiencing five or more symptoms during the same two-week period, including:

1. Depressed mood most of the day, nearly every day.
2. Markedly diminished interest or pleasure in all, or almost all, activities most of the day, nearly every day.
3. Significant weight loss when not dieting, or weight gain, or decrease or increase in appetite nearly every day.
4. A slowing down of thought and a reduction of physical movement (observable by others, not merely subjective feelings of restlessness or being slowed down).
5. Fatigue or loss of energy nearly every day.
6. Feelings of worthlessness or excessive or inappropriate guilt nearly every day.
7. Diminished ability to think or concentrate, or indecisiveness, nearly every day.
8. Recurrent thoughts of death, recurrent thoughts of suicide without a specific plan, or a suicide attempt or a specific plan for committing suicide.

To receive a diagnosis of depression, these symptoms must cause the individual clinically significant distress or impairment in social, occupational, or other important areas of functioning. The symptoms must also not be a result of substance abuse or another medical condition, which poses a challenge as depression is often intertwined with other illnesses.

It is also important to note that none of the criteria for diagnosis yet includes biochemical or genetic components, even though there is ample evidence for both. There has been no biological marker yet verified that occurs only in medication-free patients when they are not depressed. Moreover, depression is an illness associated with abnormalities in multiple genes, and no clear genetic abnormality stands out. While scientists hope this is coming soon, until that day arrives, the features of depression the DSM describes will be purely behavioral.

Sadness Versus Depression

The cardinal manifestations of depression are feelings of worthlessness, hopelessness, and, hence, a dread of the future. Many depressed patients feel abandoned and alone. They consider this state of affairs to be their own fault. They are convinced that these feelings will be permanent features of their lives. Depressed patients have difficulty in feeling truly sad because their range of feelings is constricted and focused on their anguish and the futility of their lives. True sadness is often associated with cherished, loving memories of, for instance, a lost loved one, combined with grief over their loss, and, at times, a bittersweet feeling encompassing both the bounties of life and the harsh reality that all relationships must come to an end. However, many severely depressed patients often cannot feel this kind of sadness or even cry. Anger is often inaccessible to them as well.

To depressed individuals, the complex components of sadness are often out of their reach. In this regard, severe depression is one of the cruelest illnesses of all because it can restrict focus to a deadening litany of self-excoriation and hopelessness. Depressed individuals often experience a profound alienation that sad individuals do not. From a biological perspective, antidepressants such as imipramine do not cure sadness. But they can help to abate depression. We hoped imipramine would be able to help William.

CHAPTER 2

When Psychiatry Met Biology

At various points in history, we have gone back and forth between thinking depression arises in the physical body or that it is all in one's mind. The discovery of one drug, imipramine, revolutionized our thinking about the biology and treatment of depression, and it all occurred entirely serendipitously.

In order to understand the breakthroughs we are now making concerning the biology of depression and how to treat it effectively, we must revisit the 1960s when a new sedating antihistamine called Thorazine, developed by pharmaceutical giant Geigy, was found to make lower doses of anesthesia effective and safer. What does this have to do with depression? It turned out that Thorazine had effects that not only made surgery safer, but also had significant calming effects. This led psychiatrists to attempt to use it to treat schizophrenic patients, who are often agitated, terribly afraid, paranoid, and psychotic. Thorazine was remarkably effective in alleviating schizophrenia and for many years was the principal pharmacologic agent used in its treatment. Unfortunately, Thorazine proved not to be useful in the treatment of depressive illness.

Roland Kuhn, an Austrian psychiatrist at the Münsterlingen Institution, contacted Geigy with the hopes of conducting some trials of Thorazine. Many pharmaceutical drugs were then and still are quite expensive, and the cost of this drug was prohibitive for Kuhn. But Geigy sent him a cheaper compound taken off the shelf to try, one that differed from Thorazine by only two atoms. This other compound was called Geigy 22355, or imipramine.

When Kuhn administered imipramine to his schizophrenic patients, he found that rather than calm them, many of his patients became manic; in fact, they appeared sicker than ever. This prompted Kuhn to consider an intriguing thought: What if, rather than providing a calming effect, imipramine was a euphoriant? If there was one group of patients in need of euphoria, he thought, it was those affected by depression.

Kuhn administered imipramine to his depressed patients and discovered something profound: An incredible 60 percent of them achieved remission from their depressive symptoms, but only after taking the drug for two to four weeks. Kuhn observed that the patients who best responded had disturbed sleep, early-morning awakening, and loss of appetite. We now recognize these as core symptoms of melancholia, which responds very well to imipramine.

It was unbelievable to many that after two thousand years of treating patients with depression by chaining, burning, isolating, and warehousing them, there could be an effective oral treatment that was simply manufactured in a lab. What this meant from a clinical perspective cannot be understated: For the first time, it appeared depression turned out to have a physiological component. Kuhn thought he was opening a door, but he was in fact releasing a floodgate, one that would change the way we thought of depression forever. We were getting closer to understanding how depression worked and, by extension, how we could help alleviate it. Imipramine was just the beginning of psychopharmacological treatment for depression, but it was a promising start.

William's Response to Imipramine

My patient William had been on the ward for twenty-one days of evaluation. Now he could begin a therapeutic imipramine trial. He would receive three weeks of a placebo and three weeks of imipramine, in random order. It was designed as a double-blind, placebo-controlled trial. This meant that neither William nor I, nor the nurses rating the severity of William's depression three times a day, would know when he was receiving either imipramine or the placebo at any given point in time during the trial. This meant our objectivity would not be swayed by knowing whether he was taking a placebo or the active drug. We learned, moreover, that patients rarely responded to imipramine sooner than two weeks after starting the drug. We could have quite a while to wait before seeing any results—which also weren't guaranteed.

William felt worse for the two weeks after we started the trial. We didn't know whether this state reflected a side effect of the drug or his disappointment about having shown no response. William remained depressed for another three weeks. He generally awakened at about two thirty a.m. during the first month of the trial. However, by day thirty-five, his sleep had lengthened to three thirty a.m. He evidenced no change in his feeling tone, appetite, energy, or capacity to experience pleasure.

By day forty, William reported a slight improvement in mood. By day forty-five, he awakened feeling refreshed for the first time in almost six years. Most notably, the feelings of worthlessness and self-disparagement had virtually ceased.

What did it mean that over the course of forty days, without real reorientation in his way of looking at the world, a drug had snapped William out of his depression? Though I'd have a long time to ponder this question in the days and years to come, at the time my initial reaction was to be overjoyed. William had been my first patient at the NIH. I'd never seen a patient respond to an antidepressant before. On some level, I couldn't believe it.

William reported that his feelings of well-being were not foreign, nor a drug-induced high. They instead felt like an emotional state he once knew before depression. This indicated to me, and to him as well, a restoration of prior wellness, rather than a masking of unwellness.

As William continued psychotherapy with me, the tenor of our sessions changed dramatically after he responded to imipramine. We were at last able to begin in earnest to unravel the psychological factors that contributed to his depression.

It could be argued that William's experience on the ward significantly contributed to his remission rather than the imipramine. William, however, had been depressed for five consecutive years. It is highly unlikely that he would have experienced a spontaneous remission after two to three weeks on imipramine.

How Did Imipramine Work? The First Hypothetical Model of Depression

Understanding the mechanism of imipramine's antidepressant effects was crucial to helping us begin to unravel the neurobiology of depression. My colleague at the National Institute of Mental Health, Dr. Julius Axelrod, won the Nobel Prize in Medicine and Physiology in part for his work related the basic mechanisms of norepinephrine's synthesis and metabolism and its mode of action and role in depression.

Axelrod found that imipramine raised norepinephrine levels after one day of administration and produced an antidepressant response, while reserpine, an antihypertensive that lowered norepinephrine, induced depression. Thus, scientists later concluded that depression was associated with a reduction of norepinephrine in the brain, and drugs that increased norepinephrine in the brain treated it effectively. This norepinephrine hypothesis of depression not turn out to be strictly true upon further study but this hypothesis represented the first biological model for the role of neural mediators in what causes depression, and gave rise to the modern era of biological psychiatry.

Julius Axelrod (or Julie, as we called him) was born in 1912 on the Lower East Side of New York City. He once said that he had hoped to go to NYU for college, but when interviewing he pronounced Houston Street as "Howston"—which is what the kids from the neighborhood called it—and the admissions director corrected his pronunciation, Julie knew that he wasn't going to be accepted. Instead, he became of one several Nobel Prize winners to graduate from City College of New York in the 1950s and '60s.

After Julie finished his master's at George Washington University, he landed a job at the NIH, thus beginning a journey that would have profound effects on the future of psychiatry and medicine. Julie's work at the NIH was widely known among the world's researchers. When he retired, several people were offered his lab space but refused—the story went that they didn't think lightning would strike twice in the same lab, and they were gunning for a Nobel Prize. I gladly took the space, since I am not superstitious, or at least not very superstitious, and did not go about my research with an idea of the prizes I might win.

In the latter years of his career, Julie's lab (the one that I took) was on the D2 corridor of the Clinical Center. But much of his work was done in Building 3, a structure the size of a small elementary school that was also home to the labs of five other Nobel Prize–winning scientists over the next forty years: Arthur Kornberg, 1959, for elucidating the mechanism of the synthesis of DNA and RNA; Chris Anfinsen, 1972, for exploring the basics of protein structure; Marshall Nirenberg, 1979, for cracking the genetic code; Michael Brown, 1985, for unraveling the intricacies of cholesterol metabolism; and Stan Prusiner, 1997, for discovering prions.

Julie's work on imipramine took place in 1964. Before that time, however, Julie had already made several important discoveries. In each, he showed his capacity for asking the right question and pursuing simple strategies for getting an answer. He was interested in how synthetic drugs were broken down into simpler compounds in the body despite the fact that they were foreign substances. He discovered a group of enzymes in the liver that were in charge of breaking down more than 75 percent of synthetic drugs known at the time. Today, with thousands of new drugs on the market, these enzymes still serve that role.

Julie discovered the putative mechanism of imipramine's action through a series of elegantly simple experiments. As noted, he discovered that imipramine rapidly increased norepinephrine neurotransmission and that reserpine, an antihypertensive drug that often led to depression, depleted norepinephrine in the central nervous system. The norepinephrine hypothesis was first published by William Bunney in the late 1960's. Norepinephrine is involved in many components of the depressive syndrome including anxiety, level of arousal, emotional memory, stress hormone secretion, appetite, and sleep so it seemed to be a natural suspect for contributing to the symptom complex of depression. Because imipramine also increased serotonin neurotransmission, deficient serotonin was added as another potential cause of depressive illness.

Virtually all the antidepressants developed during the next forty-year period were designed to affect the levels of norepinephrine and serotonin. William Bunney, one of Julie's colleagues, spearheaded many of the clinical studies that led to the norepinephrine hypothesis of depression and was a key player in the history of biological psychiatry. Known as Biff to almost everyone, he had a distinguished twenty-year career at the NIH Clinical Center. He made many contributions to our understanding of the clinical features of depression and to our elucidation of the early concepts of the basic biological mechanisms underlying depressive illness, especially those involving norepinephrine. As I detail later, he was also instrumental in evaluating dopamine and serotonin in depression. He was one of the first people I met at the NIH, and I grew very fond of him.

Biff helped develop a number of strategies to examine norepinephrine secretion in depression. With Fred Goodwin, my first mentor, he also studied the effects of starting and stopping lithium treatment. Biff and Fred repeatedly found that patients responded positively to lithium, relapsed when the drug was withdrawn, and then responded again when the drug was restarted. This was the first convincing validation that lithium worked.

Biff gradiated from Oberlin, went on to Penn for medicine, and was accepted at Yale for his residency but hesitated. He contemplated going to Colorado to work in an ER, ski on weekends, and finish his novel. The Chief of Psychiatry wrote that he had turned down 131 people for the position currently offered to Biff, and that Biff needed to decide in twenty-four hours. Biff thought it over and felt that maybe he could get good material for a novel during a psychiatric residency, so he wrote back and accepted.

Biff never finished the novel but he fell in love with his residency and got to work with such luminaries as Tom Detre and Danny Friedman, both icons in American psychiatry. When Biff later went to the NIH, he ran the Depression Clinical Research Unit where he got the most severe depression cases. Many were highly suicidal. He remembered one subject who was a highly suicidal physicist. After several weeks, he was released on a day pass. He dutifully followed the instructions of the staff to regularly collect urine in specimen bottles in order to record cortisol secretion. Then he went to a bridge 150 feet above the Potomac river and jumped in. There was a note: "Please return this bottle to Dr. Bunney at the NIH." Fortunately, there was a man in a rowboat who saw him jump and saved his life.

Biff finally left the NIH in 1982 to go to the University of California at Irvine, which had one of the best neurobiology departments in the country. He was both Chair of the Psychiatry

Department and head of its research program. He had a very successful career there, training in molecular biology and in the neurobiology and molecular aspects of biological rhythm disturbances in depression.

Evaluating the Biology of William's Depression

We evaluated norepinephrine function in William via infusions of norepinephrine itself and via measurement of norepinephrine in his cerebrospinal fluid. The data revealed that William's norepinephrine function was at the upper limits of normal. As noted, norepinephrine is involved in many components of depressive illness including anxiety, the level of arousal, emotional memory, appetite, and sleep. Dopamine levels in his CSF were also low. Since dopamine is instrumental in promoting the capacity to anticipate and experience pleasure, low levels contribute to the anhedonia of depression. William's seratonin levels were also low, in keeping with evidence from studies of low levels of serotonin in depressed patients. Serotonin is a key neurotransmitter that restrains the amygdala and that activates the pleasure and reward center, but serotonin deficiency is not directly correlated to depression, and the premise of serotonin deficiency in depression is not fully established.

Since melancholic individuals often seemed stressed and anxious, we measured the levels of stress hormones in William's and others' blood around the clock. We found them elevated continuously, even throughout sleep. This finding suggested that William's biological abnormalities were unlikely to be due to conscious distress over the disorder.

Melancholic patients typically have insomnia, characterized most often by early-morning awakening and difficulty falling back asleep. We conducted multiple sleep EEGs on William. They consistently showed a decrease in deep sleep and overall insomnia. They also showed high levels of REM sleep, the kind associated with dreaming. REM sleep occurs normally at the end of the sleep cycle, signaling that a person is close to a waking state. We all require some amount of REM sleep, which is tightly coupled to the activity of the stress system. When too large a proportion of our time asleep is spent in the REM state, it means that the stress system is activated.

Parenthetically, conducting these studies is time-consuming, and I participated in them firsthand. I performed the infusions, spinal taps, drew blood around the clock, and set people up for sleep EEG studies. My own sleep rhythms surely suffered at this point in my life!

We studied William and many others like him during the time they were on placebo, during treatment with antidepressants, and after their antidepressant-induced remission from depression. We found an association in remission with normalization of the levels of compounds like norepinephrine, dopamine, and serotonin. In addition, the levels of stress hormone secretion and sleep EEG patterns returned to normal in almost all patients after antidepressant-induced remission of depression.

William was among the fortunate individuals who had a positive response to imipramine. Unfortunately, however, antidepressants are not an instant cure. Imipramine and all other standard antidepressants of that era could induce remission in depression and fully or partially resolve biological abnormalities, but they did so less than 60 percent of the time. In addition, patients must continue to take imipramine or other antidepressants indefinitely to improve their chances of remaining in remission, and even many who continued to take the drug indefinitely eventually relapsed. A recent major article reported that the relapse rate was greater if imipramine or other antidepressants were stopped at twelve months rather than being continued indefinitely. These drugs also do not bring immediate relief and instead take at least two to three weeks to work. Imipramine is not a magic pill, but it did bring relief to millions of individuals.

Questioning the Norepinephrine Hypothesis of Depression

I later challenged this hypothesis, in part by showing that patients with melancholic depression had elevated norepjinephrine levels in blood and cerebrospinal fluid taken hourly around the clock. I also found that the chronic administration of imipramine in animal experiments caused a marked decrease in levels of norepinephrine. These findings were not unexpected since norepinephrine produces anziety and arousal, two of the cardinal manifestations of melancholic depression. We also know that imipramine does not improve depression as soon as it rasies norepinephrine levels, but, rather, requires at least three to four weeks to work. So what was really going on? What was the true link between norepinephrine and depression?

More than forty years after the discovery of imipramine, scientists began to see that depressed patients routinely had abnormalities in the structure and function of many components of the stress system in the brain. Some areas showed clear signs of neurodegeneration and were significantly smaller than the same areas in nondepressed patients. They also discovered disruptions in connections among nerve cells, in the structure and function of synapses, and in the birth of new neurons in a specialized component of sufferers' stress systems. Most antidepressants ameliorated most, if not all of these abnormalities in two-four weeks, but not through norepinephrine. Rather other factors contributed to the deficits in structure and function noted above, as well as to resolution of these deficits through antidepressant treatments.

Research over the past few years has revealed that brain-derived neurotrophic factor (BDNF), a growth factor that nourishes neurons, is a key molecule involved in the mechanism of action of the tricyclics (imipramine and other drugs) and SSRIs. Both classes of drugs stimulate BDNF actions after the three weeks it takes them to work. BDNF addresses and corrects a number of factors in depressive illness, including issues with loss of tissues, synaptic integrity, the interconnections among neurons, and the birth of new neurons (i.e., neurogenesis), and it decreases the premature death of neurons and the cells that support them. In fact, inactivating the BDNF system abolished the antidepressant efficacy of imipramine and the SSRIs. This discovery meant that we needed to construct a new conceptual model that explains what these processes are and how their dysregulation encodes the depressive syndrome—a huge part of my research and of what I aim to do in this book.

At the end of the twentieth century, we knew that standard antidepressants helped some patients but were not reliably effective, and that patients often relapsed on them no matter how long they had taken them. The agenda for the twenty-first century was to develop new families of antidepressants that acted more quickly, were effective in well over 60 percent of patients, had fewer side effects, exerted long-term effects, and could be safely taken by depressed individuals of all ages. Such drugs are now a reality and are discussed in great detail in later chapters.

CHAPTER 3

Stressed and Depressed

Stress is a word and a sensation with which all of us are familiar; it's a natural and unavoidable part of life. However, the amount of stress we now experience in our modern, day-to-day existences is enormously different from what our ancestors encountered—yet our basic physiology has remained the same. This mismatch affects all of us but some of us more profoundly than others. About 20 percent of the population has vulnerable stress systems. For these individuals, exposure to trauma or significant stressors early in life or throughout adulthood leads to depression, in which all the responses of the normal stress system become disordered and pathologically expressed.

The normal stress response involves two principal modules, one relating to the limbic system, and one involving the prefrontal cortex. Understanding the general features of these two structures and showing how each responds to stressful or threatening situations can then help us understand what happens when the stress system goes haywire, as it does in people dealing with depression.

It is one of the principal assertions of this book that depression represents a stress response that no longer functions properly and produces harm. The stress response involves multiple sites in the brain, and stress responses impact every tissue and, indeed, every cell of the body. This helps to explain why, to a greater extent than almost any other illness, depression is a total body disease.

Hippocrates wrote that we are all beset by disturbing forces that upset our balance. Today we call the disturbing forces stressors, the healing forces adaptive responses, and the balance homeostasis. Stressors are imminent or perceived challenges to homeostasis. Stress is almost always accompanied by heightened vigilance and anxiety, and the response is strongest when the stimulus is seen as highly unpleasant and uncontrollable. Like other adaptive responses, such as the immune response, the stress response is essential for survival.

Depression represents one way that the stress-response system can go awry. One of the ways it can gets thrown off-kilter is when the stress system does not resolve to a previous baseline state after the stressful stimulus has passed, but rather transitions into a melancholic depression, an exaggerated, highly distorted version of the healthy stress response.

Let's first consider a normal stress response. Imagine that a small group of individuals are hiking in the woods as night approaches. A wildfire is spreading rapidly nearby. The hikers are anxious, highly vigilant, and entirely focused on the threat. Their collective mood fixes in a distressed and fearful mode. They clearly feel that their lives are endangered. To keep them focused, the stress response lowers their distractibility. In particular, they aren't drawn to pleasurable stimuli. During a threatening situation, they won't stop for food, to sleep, to have sex, or to view a pretty scene. This inherent component of the stress response means that we have tremendous difficulties experiencing pleasure if the stress response doesn't resolve appropriately (for instance, in the context of depression).

Our hikers' brains push the pause button on complex thinking about anything beyond finding their way home. Accompanying their behavioral responses are physical responses. Their hearts race and their blood pressures increase. The levels of CRH, the principal stress hormone in the brain, increases. CRH then stimulates cortisol and norepinephrine secretion, activates inflammation, and sets into motion multiple behaviors such as anxiety and cautious avoidance. Inflammation during stress increases substantially to protect against a potential anticipated injury. Similarly, blood clotting systems activate and go on high alert to prepare for a possible hemorrhage. Blood sugar rises to provide extra fuel for stressed brains. Notably, these behavioral and physiological manifestations occur during psychological stressors, such as public speaking, as well.

When the hikers reach familiar territory by morning, they feel much better and can think more clearly. They can enjoy a beautiful scene, and their breathing, heart rates, immune systems, clotting, and their blood sugar levels return to normal. If these phenomena do not resolve, a depression will emerge; I'll describe how that happens in a moment.

Let's step back for a moment to consider the parts of the brain where the stress system is housed. The stress system is controlled by the prefrontal cortex (which includes the controller) and the limbic system. The prefrontal cortex is located in the area behind our forehead; the limbic system lies deep within the brain. Three of the limbic system's key structures are the amygdala; the hippocampus, which I will call the emotional memory center; and the nucleus accumbens, which I will call the pleasure and reward center.

Over the course of evolution, the prefrontal cortex has enlarged to a much greater extent than other portions of our brain and is the most highly developed among all living things. Indeed, it encodes most of the features that define our humanity, including abstract thinking, personality traits, our assessments of our pasts, and our anticipations for the future. It is not random that depression infiltrates many of these features as well.

When we are not stressed, the prefrontal cortex coordinates

the brain's activity to effectively regulate behavior, thought, and emotion. One of the prefrontal cortex's most critical functions is to regulate a host of executive functions. These include flexible thinking, planning, effective decision-making, and organization. In the nonstressed state, the prefrontal cortex significantly influences self-assessment in the direction of promoting self-esteem. It restrains our amygdala, which controls our fear system, so we are not unduly anxious. The prefrontal cortex also significantly enhances our capacity to anticipate and experience pleasure by priming the pleasure and reward center. It orchestrates self-control, restrains impulsivity, and prevents an obsessive search for reward and pleasure. It is important in our assessments of the quality and meaning of our pasts and the anticipation of our futures.

One particular area, the subgenual prefrontal cortex, modulates so many components of the stress system response that I call it the controller. The controller plays a huge role in depression and interacts with many structures in the limbic system. It is the controller that restrains the excessive secretion of the brain stress hormone CRH, as well as the stress hormones in the bloodstream: cortisol, norepinephrine, and adrenaline, keeping them in a tight normal range. CRH also serves to restrain appetite and sleep during a stress response, since these would be maladaptive during dangerous situations. As noted, it also contributes to the regulation of inflammation.

When we are stressed, the prefrontal cortex's regulation of the limbic system shifts as the brain transitions into a more rapid response mode. As I mentioned, three key structures of the limbic system are the amygdala; the hippocampus, which I call the emotional memory center; and the nucleus accumbens, also known as the pleasure and reward center. The amygdala is necessary for the conscious experience of anxiety and fear, which can be intense when the amygdala is highly activated. The emotional memory center stores and releases positive and negative emotional memories based on circumstances. Stressful experiences can imprint themselves on the emotional memory center and change its structure and function. The pleasure and reward center is essential for the anticipation and experience of pleasure.

The limbic system and its close connections to other brain sites play a vital role in emotions such as pleasure, fear, and rage, and in the fight-or-flight response.

The Normal Stress Response

We used to think that the brain was incapable of manufacturing new nerve cells, but we now know that the adult human brain has neurons that can divide to produce new cells, a process called neurogenesis. A related process, neuroplasticity, is the capacity for nerve cells to increase connections with one another as we face a complex, changing environment. Both neurogenesis and neuroplasticity are essential to maintain a healthy, nonstressed state and to respond effectively to stressors, while being markedly suppressed in depression.

We also now know that neurons produce substances called neurotrophins that are like tonics for brain cells that keep them healthy and resistant to damage or death. A key member of this family is brain-derived neurotrophic factor (BDNF). The principal sources of BDNF in the central nervous system are the emotional memory center, followed by the amygdala. BDNF is essential for maintaining healthy neurons and protecting them from damage or death, successful neurogenesis and neuroplasticity, and hence, a normal stress response. BDNF also supports brain cells during stress and counters anxiety. BDNF levels are increased during stress and markedly decreased in depression. Interestingly, environmental enrichment in children increases BDNF's concentrations. Thus, children in impoverished environments are more likely to be anxious or depressed during childhood and afterward.

In thinking about our hikers, we see that various components of the stress system react in response to the dangerous situation they encountered. The controller's function is modestly decreased during the hikers' brush with danger. This leads to worry and fear, which are essential for survival. A modest decrease in the controller's function also diminishes the capacity to antici- pate and experience pleasure because, as noted, the controller primes the pleasure and reward center to respond positively. This restraint of the pleasure and reward system is essential for pre- venting unwanted distractions during threatening situations. This restrained response to pleasurable stimuli is markedly accentu- ated in a depression, which is often associated with anhedonia, or the incapacity to experience pleasure. It's one thing to maintain a singular focus when there is a dangerous wildfire raging nearby, but in normal life the inability to appreciate any pleasurable stim- ulus is a great burden. This inability to experience any pleasure or feeling of well-being or efficacy interferes with the depressed individuals' capacity to combat their depressions.

The hikers will also experience an increase in emotional mem- ories laid down during previous brushes of danger that may aid them in surviving the present situation. In addition, the control- ler restrains the alarm center, so when the controller's activity is diminished, the hikers' alarm system rings more loudly. The hikers' alarm system, located in the brain stem, is the key site for synthesis and storage of norepinephrine. When the alarm system sounds off loudly, it prevents actions such as eating or sleeping. With fire gaining on our hikers, eating and sleeping are not the number one priority; fleeing the scene is their main focus. The stress-related activation of the alarm system leads to a palpa- ble sense of being in the midst of an emergency. The modestly decreased function of the controller during stress leads to activa- tion of the hikers' cortisol, norepinephrine, and adrenaline secre- tion, and an additional dose of anxiety.

Increased CRH in response to stress leads to increased levels of plasma cortisol in each of the hikers. Cortisol is essential to their stress response: It raises blood sugar levels during stress, improves the responsivity of heart muscle, and activates the coagulation system. In the brain, cortisol stimulates the amygdala while modestly suppressing the controller and the pleasure and reward center. In high concentrations for prolonged periods of time, cortisol causes neurodegeneration.

Norepinephrine plays as important a role in the stress response as CRH. Rising norepinephrine levels are a key component during a stressful episode, increasing anxiety and arousal, blood pressure, heart rate, and inflammation. Norepinephrine also contributes to the storage and release of emotional memories and increases the oxygen consumption of the brain. Norepinephrine diminishes the propensity to sleep and eat.

Increased inflammation in the body and the brain is associated with the secretion of a host of inflammatory promoters called cytokines, which stimulate white blood cells and specialized brain cells called microglia to release compounds that support the inflammatory response. The inflammatory system is activated, in part, to ready the immune response in case of injury during a fight-or-flight situation. Blood clotting also increases during stress as a potential stay against a possible hemorrhage during a threatening situation. As noted, these phenomena occur during psychological stress as well.

During the stressful event, the hikers' moods are relatively fixed in a distressed, fearful mode, but this does not reach sufficient levels to interfere with their ability to function during a normal, healthy stress response. Their cognitive processes shift from complex, ordered thinking about cause and effect to relatively instinct-driven thinking or reliance on memories laid down during prior experiences of danger.

Neurotransmitters That Support the Stress Response

Looking at the deeper reasons for the stress response and what occurs in the brain during a stressful episode, we see that multiple neurotransmitters are also participating. Norepinephrine levels increase, producing many effects including, among other phenomena, increased arousal and anxiety, while levels of dopamine, essential for the experience of pleasure, are diminished to prevent distraction. Serotonin plays two clear roles during the stress response. The first is to restrain the amygdala from overresponding. Second, serotonin helps prevent the control center from becoming so suppressed that a normal stress response cannot occur. Both of these actions help to control anxiety.

The neurotransmitter glutamate also plays multiple roles in the stress response by influencing physiology, thoughts, feelings, and behaviors. Glutamate is the most plentiful neurotransmitter in the brain and is involved in neurotransmission in 50 percent of all neurons. Glutamate is an excitatory neurotransmitter that stimulates the firing of the nerve cells it influences. On the other hand, the activity of the system Gamma-aminobutyric acid (GABA) is decreased during stress. In contrast to glutamate, GABA is an inhibitory neurotransmitter and places the nerve cells it influences into a state of rest. It serves as a principal brake on the glutamate system. Drugs that stimulate GABA activity are often used as effective antianxiety agents or sedatives.

How the Stress Response Can Morph into a Pernicious State of Anguish and Despair

The normal stress response and depression mirror one another in multiple ways. The defining behavioral features of each consist of fear, anxiety, and alarm.

During *stress*, sufficient anxiety promotes substantial efforts to avoid being hurt without interfering with effective functioning. In *melancholic depression*, fear, anxiety, and alarm are profoundly greater than during stress, and produce anguish and hopelessness

During stress, each hiker's self-esteem is modestly diminished in the context of being up against something so much more powerful than they. In melancholic depression, self-esteem falls profoundly, and depressed individuals often feel worthless.

During stress, cognition shifts from complex reasoning to automatic instinctual actions, or actions that have previously worked in dangerous situations. In melancholic depression, cognition is virtually limited to obsessive, ruminative preoccupation on the deficiencies of the self and the likelihood of a bleak future. Depressed individuals are often bombarded by negatively charged emotional memories of past traumas to produce hopelessness and anguish.

During stress, there is a modest decrease in the propensity to experience pleasure to avoid unwanted distraction from coping effectively with the present threat. This decreased capacity to experience pleasure does not lead to a demoralization that might interfere with such coping strategies. In melancholic depression, the decrease in the capacity to experience pleasure is pervasive and profound. It is associated with the inability to enjoy anything, hopelessness, and anguish.

During stress, there is a tendency toward a decreased appetite and the propensity to sleep as a means of maintaining focus and decreasing distractibility. In melancholic depression, appetite can be so markedly diminished that weight loss occurs, while sleep is significantly diminished, with early-morning awaking and an inability to fall back asleep.

During stress, our bodies prime themselves for potential injury, including things like anticipatory inflammation and increased clotting to prepare for possible hemorrhage. Blood sugar levels rise modestly to supply increased fuel to the stressed brain. In melancholic depression, inflammation is pronounced in the body and the brain, contributing to illnesses such as premature coronary artery disease, diabetes, stroke, and osteoporosis. Blood sugar rises to levels that can cause tissue damage despite the fact that they remain within the normal range. Clotting is increased to protect against a possible hemorrhage, but also potentially contributes to the propensity of myocardial infarction and stroke.

During stress, neuroplasticity and neurogenesis increase in a pronounced fashion. In melancholic depression, neuroplasticity and neurogenesis are profoundly decreased.

Overall, while a normal stress response is highly adaptive, depression represents a distorted, prolonged, pernicious version of the stress response.

Back to the hikers for a moment. Once they escaped danger and had a chance to recover from the trauma of the experience, most of them transitioned from a state of stress to being able to feel safe and relaxed. But let's say Jennifer, one of the hikers, did not recover in this way. Rather, her appropriate behavioral and physiological responses to the wildfire not only persisted, but became much more pronounced, distorted, and prolonged.

Her anxiety and fear increased enormously, and she was terribly afraid of even innocuous things. She felt intensely vulnerable. Her self-esteem plummeted, and she was beset with feelings of not being good enough.

Like other depressed patients, Jennifer's attention was strongly biased toward sad stimuli, and she could not ignore or dispel them. Jennifer had persistent ruminative thoughts, especially those that reminded her of her perceived flaws. Her rumination was associated with activity in the limbic system involved in the recall of negatively charged emotional memories. Jennifer could not "forget" or extinguish these negatively charged emotional memories, and she has great difficulty in accessing positive memories. She vividly recalled the feeling tone of past losses and embarrassments, and she was beset by memories of previous ruminations about her deficiencies, helplessness, and dread of the future. These emotional memories were virtually constant and contributed significantly to the feeling tone of her depression.

Jennifer's capacity to anticipate or experience pleasure virtually ceased. She could not enjoy any of the things that had previously brought her pleasure, and instead had fallen into a state of anhedonia.

Jennifer's appetite was significantly diminished, and her sleep was disturbed by early-morning awakening at about two a.m. She was often unable to go back to sleep.

The inflammation the she experienced during her stress response became markedly accentuated and was sufficient to potentially lead to premature systemic diseases and a progressive intensification of her depression. Her blood clotting was also much more pronounced than when she was stressed, and this raised her vulnerability to myocardial infarction and stroke. Her blood sugars were increased and, if sustained, could contribute to an increased risk for developing type II diabetes.

Based on extensive studies of the impact of stress in experimental animals, it was likely that her neuroplasticity and levels of neurogenesis were highly diminished. In addition, recent data from the brains of patients with depression who had committed suicide have revealed that neuroplasticity and neurogenesis are markedly decreased in such individuals.

As noted before, Jennifer's stress response morphed into a state that superficially mirrored her stress response but was much more pernicious both behaviorally and physiologically.

In addition to the stress response running awry, let's say Jennifer had a strong family history of depressive illness. Her mother had bipolar illness and her father had sustained multiple major melancholic depressive episodes. Her maternal grandmother was bipolar and had committed suicide. What was going on in Jennifer's brain and body after the stressful incident passed? How could she be helped?

The Prefrontal Cortex and Limbic System During Melancholic Depression

Overall, during depression, there is a profound decrease in the controller's capacity to perform its multiple tasks. In fact, Wayne Drevets discovered that the actual volume of the controller is reduced by as much as 40 percent during a depressive episode! Glial cells are most affected. Glial cells play key roles in protecting neurons from a variety of stressors, provide immune protections, and aid in their nutrition. Neurons in the controller do not die during a depression, but their connectivity is significantly reduced and their size is diminished. Jennifer showed evidence of a controller that was clearly reduced in volume.

Wayne and I often met to have discussions about the role of changes in brain structure in depressive illness and how the stress system might contribute to these abnormalities. (Wayne was born and grew up in the South. Because I was a Southerner and was born and raised in Tidewater, Virginia, we shared lots of experiences in common and enjoyed discussing them.) He confirmed my hunch that the depressions that were most often associated with loss of volume of the controller had prominent melancholic features.

Wayne trained with Marcus Raichle at Washington University in St. Louis, the dean of American neuroimagers. Their discovery of a marked reduction in the size of the controller required an exquisite mastery of the nuances of neuroimaging and would have been missed by most people in the field. After their pioneering work, it has been replicated multiple times, so the defect is beyond a shadow of a doubt.

The controller ordinarily restrains the amygdala; thus, in the context of a controller that is so much smaller and less functionally active than it should be, the amygdala is exceedingly hyperactive. In keeping with an increase in its size, neuroplasticity in the amygdala is substantially increased, which further contributes to the amygdala's capacity to generate anxiety. Jennifer's amygdala was also clearly increased in size, commensurate for it to be highly active during melancholia.

Jennifer's emotional memory center was also significantly reduced in size, and she easily slipped into recalling the fear and dread she felt at the time of the incident. On the other hand, her memory of positive emotional memories virtually disappeared. In addition, her pleasure and reward center was increased in size and responded very sluggishly to pleasurable stimuli.

The stress hormone CRH is oversecreted in melancholic depression, setting into motion multiple behavioral and physiological processes associated with stress and depression. On the other hand, Jennifer had very low levels of BDNF in her blood and cerebrospinal fluid. BDNF is essential for neurogenesis and neuroplasticity, adequate synaptic function, and effective connections among components of the stress system.

Jennifer's body and brain also showed evidence of inflammation. Her blood levels of cytokines were highly elevated, including plasma IL-6 levels that were elevated around the clock. She had increased cytokine levels in her cerebrospinal fluid. In addition, a PET scan designed to quantify inflammation in the brain revealed significant inflammation in multiple areas of the prefrontal cortex, including the controller, as well as in the emotional memory center.

Jennifer was suffering from a full-blown depression following the traumatic, near-death experience she encountered in the woods.

An Overview of Inflammation in Melancholic Depression

Our evolutionary and biological roots have fostered the close connection between stress, depression, and inflammation. Almost all stressful situations that mammals encountered in our distant past had to do with being hunted or competing for a mate. Our inflammatory systems were primed to anticipate possible injury and infection, and respond. The risk of pathogen exposure and a consequent infection was high in ancient environments, and thus the connection between the *perception* of stress or danger activated responses of the inflammatory and coagulation systems.

CRH, or corticotropin-releasing hormone, a hormone related to the stress response, is among the most potent inflammatory triggers thanks to its involvement with mast cells in the brain. Mast cells are filled with compounds that are toxic to bacteria and viruses that assist in the disposal of damaged or dead cells. Activation of the CRH system during stress also leads to the release of CRH from terminals outside of the brain in tissues like the skin. This provides an explanation for the mechanism of stress-induced skin disorders that occur as a consequence of stress, including hives. CRH is also the brain hormone that stimulates cortisol secretion and norepinephrine release into the bloodstream. High norepinephrine levels also contribute to inflammation, as well as activation of what is called the acute phase response, a stress-mediated activation of proinflammatory mediators released from the liver.

Women have a greater behavioral response to inflammatory mediators than men. This may be due to the fact that women's enhanced inflammatory responses during pregnancy help in coping with infection, healing wounds, and subsequent exposure to pathogens. On the other hand, inflammation also inhibits fertility. This may have protected women from unwanted pregnancies during times of adversity.

I have suggested, based on significant study, that the form of inflammation most present in depressive illness appears to be parainflammation. This is a low-level, persistent inflammation characterized by high levels of the inflammatory marker c-reactive protein (CRP), well-known to be a predictor of heart disease. CRP is elevated in patients with depressive illness. The difference between classical inflammation and parainflammation is that the latter does not occur in response to bacteria, viruses, or tissue damage, but arises in response to stressors that alter baseline functioning of things like metabolism, endocrine regulation, and the activity of the sympathetic nervous system.

Parainflammation occurs in response to stressors such as overfeeding or aging that were not present during our early evolutionary history, and for which we are not adequately prepared. Other triggers include changes in the light-dark cycle imposed by artificial lighting, and exposure to processed foods or chemicals. In my research and study I have suggested that the kind of frequent daily psychological stressors we encounter, including the markedly increased social interactions we experience in our modern lives, were not present in our early evolutionary history and contribute to parainflammation, which in turn leads to the prevalence of health issues such as coronary artery disease and depression.

Multiple studies have found anti-inflammatory agents useful in the treatment of depression. Patients with major depression exhibit increased peripheral blood inflammatory biomarkers, including inflammatory cytokines, compounds produced by immune cells that activate other immune cells to encode a significant inflammatory response. These peripheral cytokines have been shown to access the brain and are produced by the brain itself. In the brain, these cytokines interact with virtually every domain known to be involved in depression. These include neurotransmitter metabolism, neuroendocrine function, neurogenesis, and neural plasticity. In addition, activation of inflammatory pathways within the brain is believed to contribute to a decrease in the birth of new neurons and decreased neuroplasticity, as well as oxidative stress, leading to the destruction of neurons and loss of glial elements, cells that provide nutritional and other support to nerve cells.

Glutamate is a potent stimulus to the central nervous system inflammation and affects many areas of the brain thought to be involved in depression, such as the controller and the amygdala. Glutamate also has powerful effects on neuronal firing, and increased glutamate neurotransmission can result in firing rates so great that neurons deplete their energy stores and die. While glutamate function is generally decreased in depression, increased glutamate activity is found intermittently during severe stress in depression.

Microglia are brain cells that are best known as the immune

cells of the brain, but emergent data indicate that they also influence brain development, synaptic plasticity, neurogenesis, memory, and mood. Microglial activation due to infections, stroke, neurodegenerative disease, aging, or psychological or physical stress can lead to depression. BDNF and, hence, antidepressants suppress microglial activation as well as stimulation of cannabinoid (marijuana) receptors, melatonin, and drugs that inhibit the angiotensin system, a key player in blood pressure regulation. While almost all cytokines promote inflammation, IL-4 and IL-10 block inflammation and can inhibit microglial activation. Two antibiotics, minocycline and rifampicin, suppress microglial activity.

Consider the context of giving a speech, a situation that causes many people to exhibit a fight-or-flight response, characterized by temporary increases in cortisol, other stress hormones including norepinephrine, increased inflammation, and increased coagulation. A full blown pro-inflammatory response often occurs with activation of the secretion of multiple cytokines, and a host of other inflammatory mediators. In essence, the body mounts an immune response not against a virus, bacteria, or an injury, but against a threat to the subject's self-esteem, a source of great psychological stress.

Neurotransmitter Function in Depression

We found that norepinephrine in blood and spinal fluid is clearly elevated around the clock in melancholic-depressed individuals. These elevations in norepinephrine induce many effects, including hyperarousal and anxiety. As noted, Jennifer's plasma and cerebrospinal fluid levels were highly increased around the clock.

Dopamine activity plummets during melancholic depression. This clearly contributes to the anhedonia experienced during melancholia. Serotonin activity may also be deficient in melancholic depression, though data are mixed regarding the role of serotonin in this disorder. Jennifer's cerebrospinal-fluid dopamine levels were on the low end of normal but not significantly reduced, while her serotonin levels were normal.

Glutamate is the principal excitatory neurotransmitter in the brain. It is released into 50 percent of the synapses in the central nervous system. Its levels are decreased in many brain areas during melancholic depression. Paradoxically, sustained elevation of glutamate activity in these sites during severe stress leads to the death of glial cells and damage to neurons.

High glutamate in selected brain areas during severe stress, high levels of CRH and norepinephrine, inflammation, and low BDNF production are some of the factors that cause cell death in depressive illness.

The Default Mode Network in Depression

The default mode network engages in introspection, self-referential processing, thinking about the past and the future, and ultimately, reaching conclusions regarding the value of the self. It begins forming at around the age of six years old. In this way, extreme stress or trauma during childhood can influence an individual for a lifetime and lay the seeds for the onset of depression years later.

The overall activity of the default mode network is increased in depression, and connections among the various regions involved in it are significantly abnormal. Given the involvement of the amygdala fear system, activation of the default mode network leads to feelings of worthlessness.

Jennifer's PET scan revealed evidence of a hyperactive default mode network.

Atypical Depression

So far, I've mostly referenced melancholic depression, which accounts for up to 40 percent of major depressive episodes. Melancholia often seems the antithesis of the other major form of depression, atypical depression, which affects about one-third of depressed patients. Atypical depression is associated with increased fatigue, sleep, and appetite and weight gain. Instead of being bombarded by painful feelings and memories, patients with atypical depression often feel out of touch with their feelings, their pasts, and with others. Hence, they often feel lonely and empty. They rarely seek out advice and reassurance, but rather keep to themselves.

Unfortunately, much more is known about melancholic depression than atypical depression, and reliable data about the biology of atypical depression is quite limited. My group has shown that atypical depression is associated with decreases rather than increases in stress hormones such as CRH and cortisol. I still remember distinctly the case of one of my patients, Rachel Dawson, who suffered from atypical depression.

In 1981, Rachel came to the Clinical Center with a depression that had not responded to previous treatment, including three separate trials of medication. I met her on the second floor of the Clinical Center in my office, right next to my basic science laboratories. I sat down with her right after we finished morning rounds.

Rachel had been depressed for almost three years. Unlike William, her depression was not characterized by a heightened state of anguish about herself and anxiety. Rather, Rachel reported being exhausted all the time, sleeping too much, having no motivation and an increased appetite that had caused her to gain twenty pounds. She reported feeling better in the morning, when the stress system is activated, and worse in the evenings, when stress system activity is relatively dormant.

When I asked Rachel what caused her the most pain in her depression, she replied, "The worst part is feeling disconnected from everyone and everything. I even feel disconnected from myself and my past. Sometimes, I feel that I am locked in a transparent chamber that keeps me from reaching others, and that keeps others from reaching me. On the other hand, even brief interactions with anybody exhaust me. I've forgotten what it feels like to be happy."

Rachel had quit her job as a college professor because of her severe depressions. "My teaching provided a source of my contact with others, and I miss it. It's made worse by the fact that I even feel remote from my beautiful children. I know my husband is at the end of his rope. He hasn't mentioned divorce explicitly, but I know that it has crossed his mind. What would I do if I were all alone and still severely depressed? I don't think I could bear to go on living."

I asked Rachel if she was suicidal at that moment. She told me that she had no active plans, but often wished that she would develop a fatal illness that killed her quickly. "That would solve all my problems," she told me. In addition to increased sleep, increased appetite, and profound fatigue, we found that her CRH and cortisol levels were very low (low cortisol levels are associated with inflammation, since cortisol suppresses inflammation). Rachel had several signs of active inflammation.

Rachel was the oldest of three children. Both of her parents were physicians. When Rachel was four, her mother had her second child, who turned out to be autistic. He became the focus of her parents' full attention. He had many behavioral abnormalities, but his parents were committed to keeping him at home.

Rachel recalled that after his birth, she never saw her parents happy. She felt helpless because she could do nothing to cheer them up, and she felt overlooked. Rachel scrupulously avoided causing her parents any distress and would never reveal any concerns or distress to them. She tried to function as self-sufficiently as possible and did not develop the capacity to ask friends or relatives for help when she needed it. She rarely brought friends home because the household was often disrupted by her autistic brother, and she felt she did not have a safe place to comfort herself. She felt sad during much of her childhood and adolescence but didn't remember a depressive episode similar to her current depression.

Rachel believed that the precipitant for her depression was her failure to find a publisher for her book. On a certain level, she felt ignored and abandoned, similar to the way she felt when she was growing up. That feeling never really left her.

Four years before Prozac was released to the public, we decided to treat Rachel with an experimental SSRI, zimelidine, given in a double-blind crossover design. We later discovered that she was given the active compound first, and she showed a significant remission three weeks after starting the zimelidine. But zimelidine had to be taken off the market after Rachel started taking it because of significant side effects. We received frequent follow-ups from Rachel, who remained well on zimelidine. After it was taken off the market, her therapist prescribed an MAO inhibitor, which continued to sustain her remission. MAO inhibitors are potent antidepressants reviewed in detail in a subsequent chapter.

Compared to melancholic depression, atypical depression has an earlier onset and is more frequently chronic. Patients with atypical depression have a significantly higher incidence of childhood and adolescent trauma than those with melancholia, which may in part explain the separation they feel from their bodies.

The eminent developmental psychiatrist René Spitz studied infants in orphanages where they received little care. Initially, most of the infants cried bitterly for hours until attended. Subsequently, they withdrew and ceased crying altogether, even if they were left alone or had gone without eating for many hours. In addition, they lost apparent interest in the environment around them. It was as if the trauma of their early deprivation had led to a virtual shutdown of their stress response and affective existence to protect them from enormous distress. Subsequent studies in nonhuman primates who were removed from their mothers and raised by peers reveal a similar behavioral withdrawal. These nonhuman primates raised by peers also had low cortisol levels. These may represent very severe forms of atypical depression.

While melancholic depression appears to be associated with a stress system that is locked in the "on" position, atypical depression appears to be associated with a stress system locked in the "off" position. The distinction in types of depression leads to different approaches in treatment, which we will investigate further. Ample data confirm that the treatment of atypical depression is significantly more effective when pharmacology is complemented by psychotherapy.

Stress has always been an element of the human experience, whether it arises while fleeing a predator on the savannah or preparing to deliver a keynote presentation in front of a crowd of distinguished experts. How we handle our response helps to determine the long-term effects on us, and whether we recover fully from a stressful incident or it permeates our lives to the degree that it transforms into a case of depression. No matter the underlying cause or trigger, psychotherapy is an essential component of treatment that I believe is required in any full and lasting recovery from any type of depression, stress induced or not. Often, the most effective treatment for pernicious depression is a combination of talk therapy and drug therapy.

I now want to describe some of the first generation of drugs on which we have depended for the last fifty years, and which laid the foundation for a new generation of drugs arising out of recent research.

CHAPTER 4

The Brave New World of First-Generation Antidepressants (1960-2010)

Deciding which drug will work best for a specific patient and their unique circumstances is like trying to decode an encrypted message. This was certainly the case for Ellen Jenkins. I first met Ellen when she came to the NIH Clinical Center in 2005 for treatment after a long history of severe depression, which was often associated with serious suicidality. Ellen was fortunate to already have an excellent therapist whom she saw three times a week and who had been a lifeline to her for several years previous. She had tried many different antidepressants, but all failed to produce a response. This was not entirely surprising.

Like many people who suffer from depression, Ellen's history reflected serious trauma, which had likely triggered her illness. When Ellen was fifteen her brother coerced her to participate in an incestuous relationship. While in the beginning this was nonconsensual, as with many such cases, over time, the lines between consent and complicity became blurred for Ellen such that she felt responsible. Three years after the assault began her brother committed suicide.

Ellen was shattered by the loss of her brother. She felt guilty for having potentially contributed to his death and also about the incestuous relationship itself. Her therapist had been masterful in her efforts to help Ellen understand the meaning of all of this but the trauma was so profound that she would need considerably more time to forgive herself and regain her self-respect.

Ellen suffered a severe atypical depression. She slept up to fourteen hours at night, experienced significant daytime fatigue, and had an increased appetite. She felt remote from herself and others, and hence, felt extremely lonely and abandoned. She completely lost her capacity to anticipate or experience pleasure, and was totally anhedonic. She had tentative plans to take her life by hanging herself, the way her brother had ended his life.

When Ellen came to stay at the NIH she was twenty-four years old and highly suicidal, so she was placed on one-to-one observation, twenty-four hours a day. However, as she got to know me and to form some bonds with the nursing staff, and as she began to observe that other severely depressed patients with depressive illness do in fact get well, her suicidality diminished. After seventeen days she no longer needed one-to-one supervision.

I met with Ellen three times a week. During that time, I got to know her well enough that she felt understood. This was a challenge in no small part because I was a man and a figure of authority. In the past, a male figure in a position of authority had taken advantage of her. Yet we overcame this. We were able to build off the work she had already done with her regular therapist so that I could help her continue to gain insight about her troubled life.

Because of the failed attempts to treat her with psychiatric drugs in the past and given the severity of her depression, we decided to treat her with a monoamine oxidase (MAO) inhibitor, Parnate. Parnate is significantly more effective than other traditional antidepressants, but can produce dangerous side effects. If a person taking Parnate ingests any foods that contain tyramine (including aged cheeses and meats, pickled herring, etc.), their blood pressure rises precipitously to potentially dangerous levels.

We administered Parnate in a double-blind, placebo-controlled manner while we closely monitored Ellen. This especially involved meticulous monitoring of her blood pressure and her diet.

For almost thirty days, Ellen showed no response, We hoped she had been given the placebo first, but we had no way of knowing. This is the nature of a double-blind, placebo controlled trial. Neither I or the nurses who rated the level or her depression knew if Ellen were taking the parnate or the placebo. If Ellen were given the placebo first, she would receive it for twenty-one consecutive days before switching over to the MAO inhibitor. This would mean that on day thirty, she had received only nine days of Parnate. We were afraid that if instead she had in fact been given the MAO inhibitor first and there was little else we could try to alleviate her depression other than electroconvulsive treatment, which I describe in chapter 13.

On the thirty-fourth day, however, Ellen began showing subtle signs of a response. Her sleep improved and fell from fourteen hours per night to eleven. Over the next several days, it normalized entirely. Her voracious appetite subsided. She began taking notice of her surroundings and was able to experience them as pleasant. She seemed less thoroughly demoralized, more in touch with herself and others, but still deeply troubled about her relationship with her brother and his suicide.

We found some of the same biological markers that William had. Her norepinephrine levels were at the lower limits of normal. Her cortisol levels were significantly lower than in controls for the early morning hours, but otherwise were in the low normal range. Her sleep EEG studies detected that she slept excessively, though she had reduced deep sleep and reduced rather than increased REM sleep.

Overall, while William demonstrated many featured of a stress system that had become pathologically activated, which is characteristic of melancholic depression, Ellen showed signs of a sluggish stress system at or below the normal range, which is characteristic of atypical depression. Since reduced thyroid function predisposes a person to depression, we augmented her with a small dose of thyroid hormone to get her into the mid-normal range. Her sleep EEG revealed, as expected, excessive sleep, but a decrease in deep sleep. She also had reduced rather than increased REM activity. Successful MAO inhibitor treatment reversed these abnormalities.

A month after significant improvement in her profound depression, she was discharged from the hospital on her MAO inhibitor and with her thyroid hormone level titrated closer to the middle of the normal range. We both knew she had a long way to go, but I believed with time, skillful psychotherapy, and effective antidepressant treatment, she could effectively rebuild her life.

A Brief Overview of the First Generation of Antidepressants

The antidepressants available between the 1960's and the turn of the century represent the first generation of antidepressant drugs, and most were designed for their capacity to safely modify norepineph-rine and serotonin levels in brain.Thus, though most are labeled as norepinephrine or serotonin uptake inhibitors or inhibitors of the uptake of both neurotransmitters, I previously noted that they all actually seem to rely on a capacity to augment the availability or actions of BDNF. Since knowledge that their effects on BDNF are required for efficacy has been only available for the past two months, most practitioners will still attribute their primary mode of action as uptake inhibitors of norepinephrine, serotonin, or dopamine. I should like to note that these neurotransmitters may play roles in the pathophysiology of deoression and its response to treatment, though they are not the principal mediators of antidepressant efficacy.

Imipramine and Other Tricyclic Antidepressants

Imipramine is a tricyclic antidepressant; others include, Norpra-min, and Elavil. The latter drugs are structurally very similar, and are as effective as imipramine, but not more so: imipramine induces remission in patients less than 50 to 60 percent of the time, and the other tricyclics perform no better. These drugs do differ in their side effects: Elavil is very sedating and causes a dry mouth, and in a small number of patients, urinary retention. Imipramine is less sedating, causes less of a dry mouth, and is less likely to cause urinary retention, and Norpramin is relatively free of sedating effects and causes little or no dry mouth and urinary retention. We now know that imipramine and the other tricyclics are more effective in treating melancholia as compared to atypical depression, where it induces remission in only ten percent of patients. Tricyclic antidepressants have cardiac effects such as increasing pulse rate and blood pressure, thus have the dangerous potential to push people with substantial cardiac disease into congestive heart failure. They can also cause cardiac rhythm disturbances.

Specific Serotonin Reuptake Inhibitors (SSRIs)

SSRIs generally have fewer side effects than tricyclics, and influence serotonin neurotransmission, but not that of norepinephrine or dopamine. They have no adverse cardiac effects, so they can be safely given to older adults, and even substantial overdoses are not fatal. They can, however, cause sexual side effects and weight gain. Like the tricyclics, they induce remission only 50 to 60 percent of the time. There are several SSRIs available now. Each drug has its benefits and drawbacks.

We conducted clinical trials with the first SSRI, zimelidine, in the early 1980s. Though our early experience found it to be an effective antidepressant, it unfortunately had serious side effects and had to be taken off the market. The next SSRI, Prozac, was not developed until the late 1980s. Like imipramine, it was effective only 50 to 60 percent of the time. Other SSRIs include Zoloft, Paxil, Cipralex, Cipramil, Lexapro, and Brintellix. Despite the fact that these are all SSRIs, if an individual does not respond to one, she may respond to another.

SSRIs are effective in treating both melancholic and atypical depression, but are not as effective as MAO inhibitors in treating atypical depression.

Viibryd is another drug that possesses SSRI properties, and it simultaneously stimulates a serotonin receptor similar to an anti-anxiety drug, Buspar. Thus, Viibryd possesses antianxiety effects, and in addition to depression, it is indicated in the treatment of generalized anxiety disorder. It is still effective only about 50 to 60 percent of the time.

A newer antidepressant, Trintellix, is a multi-modal antidepressant. It is unique in that it affects multiple neurotransmitters and claims to be helpful for the cognitive symptoms of depression. A principal side effect is gastrointestinal upset and for some it is less likely to cause sexual side effects.

Recent data indicate that if you inactivate key components of the serotonin system in a neuron, the SSRI's still work. Thus their antidepressant efficacy is not dependent on their effects on the serotonin system, but like the tricyclics, on BDNF levels and actions.

I shall later review data that a new generation of antidepressants rapidly induce remission form depression, often within 24 hours, and have much more powerful effects on promoting BDNF release and actions, as well as possessing other properties that make them exceptionally effect. Later in the book, I will review these drugs and their mechanisms of actionin a separate chapter.

Other Classes of Drugs

In addition to the SSRIs, there are drugs that block the reuptake of both serotonin and norepinephrine, and are designated as SNRIs. Cymbalta is one such agent. It is effective in treating both melancholic and atypical depression, though not as effective as MAO inhibitors in treating atypical depression. It has unique analgesic properties and is effective in ameliorating what we call neuropathic pain, whose origin is in nerves themselves. People with neuropathy from agents such as anticancer drugsor because of diabete experience a significant reduction in pain when given Cymbalta. Mbalta also has some efficacy in a syndrome known as fibromyalgia, characterized by diffuse pain and fatigue.

Dopamine is a neurotransmitter that is essential to experience pleasure. Activating the dopamine system in the brain can help combat depression. Only one available antidepressant currently activates the dopamine system: Wellbutrin. In contrast to the other classes of antidepressants, Wellbutrin has few or no sexual side effects and does not cause weight gain. It often increases energy levels in those who take it, and it may have efficacy for some patients with attention deficit disorder. Again, the response rate in depression is only 50 to 60 percent of the time.

A drug that affects both norepinephrine and serotonin systems, not as an uptake inhibitor but rather as a complex blocker of multiple receptors, is Remeron. It is ideal for patients who both have lost a great deal of weight and have severe insomnia, since it significantly increases appetite and promotes sleep. This may be a disadvantage for many patients, which is unfortunate, since Remeron is such an effective antidepressant, inducing remission about 75 percent of the time

The first generation of antidepressants are not perfect by any means, but they definitely provide helpful options in the treatment of some patients with depression. They do ameliorate depression in more than half of individuals who take them. Thus, they are important drugs and serve important functions, and despite their limitations, they have revolutionized the treatment of depression. Responses are better if combined with psychotherapy. A troubling fact is that the majority of depressed individuals who would be great candidates for antidepressants go untreated.

CHAPTER 5

The Art of Therapy

Addressing the underlying biological contributions to a person's depression is important. I also firmly believe that psychotherapy is a meaningful and important way of dealing with environmental factors that contribute to depression, such as interpersonal conflict or traumatic events.

Studies consistently report that a combination of medication and either cognitive behavioral therapy or psychodynamically oriented therapy works better than either drugs or therapy alone. Cognitive behavioral therapy concentrates on how thoughts, especially negative rumination, can produce depression and how addressing these thoughts can help to treat it. I prefer psychodynamically oriented therapy instead, because using it considers how a patient's past experiences and interpersonal relationships affected how they felt when they were young and helpless, and how these emotions recur in their adult life to produce a sense of worthlessness, fears of abandonment, and, hence, a depressed mood. Many depressed patients organize their lives around avoiding such feelings, and banish the emotions associated with loss and disappointment, about which they feel ashamed. Thus, they cannot grieve losses and move beyond them. Their defenses do not protect them but rather impoverish them.

Complex illnesses like depression and coronary artery disease reflect both genetic vulnerability and a predisposing environment. For an analogy, take coronary artery disease. The predisposing environment includes smoking, obesity, poor diet, and lack of exercise. For depression, the predisposing environment includes early neglect or loss of a parent, sexual or physical trauma, poverty, or unrelentingly demanding parents. In either case, significantly changing the predisposing environment can lower susceptibility to the development of depressive illness.

One of the major premises of this book is that depression represents a stress system run awry. Since stressful experiences imprint themselves in our emotional memory in the stress system and change its function and structure, the burdens of stressful experiences influence our susceptibility to depression. Psychotherapy is the best strategy we have available to address these emotional memories and their impact on mood and behavior. If such issues are not addressed, they are likely override the positive response that patients like William experienced during his trial of imipramine.

I was fortunate to do my psychiatric training at the Massachusetts Mental Health Center, which was closely affiliated with the Harvard Medical School. It had previously been named the Boston Psychopathic Hospital and was often referred to as the Psycho, or Mass Mental. In contrast to its nickname, it was a hospital characterized by deep respect and compassion for the patients we attempted to help. At the time, the Mass Mental offered an extraordinary program in psychotherapy training. The inpatient population of two hundred and the outpatient population of a thousand were selected for their potential to benefit from psychotherapy. Twenty-five residents per year, chosen from several hundred applicants, had the experience of working intensively with a limited caseload. We had the privilege of daily sixty-minute teaching conferences and eight to nine hours of weekly individual tutorials with very experienced and skilled clinicians. We often met with our patients for two or three hours per week or more over a period of three years.

Despite all the training and expertise, we were faced with what seemed like at times an overwhelming task: to help bring individuals whose lives had fallen apart back into a meaningful encounter with themselves and the world. At the time, there were no fully documented, reliable drugs or dramatic procedures that led to rapid improvement in our patients. The going was slow, and at this point in the past we knew virtually nothing about the principles of psychotherapy.

The heart of the program was Dr. Elvin Semrad, a caring, sad-eyed man born on a farm in Nebraska. Dr. Semrad was a genius at condensing complex concepts into understandable lessons. This learning was not theoretical. The patients were to be our guides and mentors, and we owed much to them for allowing us to become a meaningful part of their lives. Our task was to get to know them and their suffering very well, to form an emotional bond, and to uncover the layers that prevented them from being true to themselves. Exceedingly empathic, Semrad proved to be of inestimable help in these tasks. Semrad had a special ability to evoke feelings that the patients or any of us might try to keep at a distance.

I first met Semrad in an interview for admission to the training program. At the outset, he asked me to describe the most difficult situation I had ever faced. I told him that I greatly upset my immigrant family by falling in love with a girl of a different religion. He looked at me with a sad smile and said, "You must love her very much." At that point, I burst into tears and told him more of the story. This experience and Semrad's response to my retelling of it convinced me of the path I should take in the study of psychiatry.

Semrad was the Director of Training at Mass Mental. Our first year was on an inpatient unit, and any patient we saw that year remained in treatment with us until the remainder of our three years of training. Semrad felt that in order for us to become therapists, we needed to refine and extend our capacities to help our patients encounter and communicate their pain in the direct face-to-face engagement with the therapist. Their reluctance to do so often reflected earlier experiences of having been rejected, punished, or abandoned for not keeping their troubling feelings to themselves. We needed to demonstrate to our patients that we had the stamina to stay with them in the midst of their sadness, anger, and fears of abandonment. In the short run, this meant not deserting them either by changing the subject, interjecting brief, unrelated comments, or providing glib reassurance. In the long run, it meant refraining from sending nonverbal signals of disinterest, frustration, or fear. Thus, much of my training at Mass Mental was focused on learning about people's mental strategies when confronting fears, loss, and disappointments in their lives—all key psychological issues that affect the brain's stress response system.

Why did our patients benefit by gaining access to their feelings and reexperiencing them in our presence? By avoiding the sources and meanings of their feelings previously, they had lost an opportunity to grieve the losses that have occurred over a lifetime. Grieving must occur in the context of conscious awareness over what one has lost, and it is greatly aided by expressing the content of the pain to an understanding individual who, as it were, bears witness to the ordeal. Losses that have not been grieved are sources of great stress. By recalling their deeply buried feelings over and over and looking at them from multiple perspectives, patients can reawaken from a kind of sleep and feel more like their real selves. One of Semrad's simple phrases has stayed with me for a lifetime. "The best way to forget is to remember." By remembering what has been suppressed, the patient has a chance of beginning to process a lifetime of sadness and losses that has been buried beneath the surface, causing enormous stress and untold suffering. My patient William had spent a lifetime trying not to remember.

During my years of training, I became progressively more aware of the enormous price our patients or any of us pay for isolating ourselves from any of our feelings, including our sadness and remorse over the major losses and disappointments in our lives. One of the greatest stressors in life is not knowing ourselves and the feelings that help define our identities. Keeping such feelings at bay prevents us from coming to terms with the inevitable suffering that our lives entail and the healing process of grappling with sadness and ultimately neutralizing some of it by acknowledging and grieving what has been lost.

Many of our patients are only dimly aware of these feelings, perhaps for many reasons. Some may not have had the support of nurturing parents to help them encounter their sadness and struggle to come to terms with it, and, hence, neutralize some of it. Others may be constitutionally wired to react so profoundly to the experience of disappointment and hurt feelings that they find the distress and sadness generated by these experiences simply unbearable. We found our patients to be highly invested in suppressing sadness, especially those who are sufficiently burdened to gain admission to a psychiatric hospital. Many do not know how to deal with sadness, and when it breaks through, they are overwhelmed. Others, who are better defended, will literally organize their lives around the avoidance of sad feelings. As an example, we all know individuals who will never again take the chance of feeling overwhelmingly sad after experiencing an agonizing breakup. Often, many end up living alone. Others lose themselves entirely in their work or avoid feelings by becoming distracted by dangerous activities such as substance abuse. Some withdraw into a state where all emotion is blunted. They are not true to themselves or their feelings, and their lives are impoverished because of it. It did not (and does not) help that our culture also discourages people from being too open about their sadness.

Patients with depression also often have a long-term difficulty in expressing their anger and are much more likely to blame themselves for their suffering. When they identify this pattern and search for reasons, we find that our patients expect their anger to either damage someone or to provoke hatred, abandonment, or both. Individuals pay a high price for the conscious or unconscious exclusion of anger from their lives. They become handicapped in responding to anyone who provokes them or treats them badly. They cannot readily look after their own best interests or come to the aid of friends. In essence, they cannot be true to themselves. It is like they are literally slicing off a part of themselves. They often feel ineffectual in any conflict or struggle. This leaves them feeling weak and helpless. Hopefully, in the relative safety of the hospital, our patients can learn that they will not be punished or abandoned for revealing their anger. They can learn that the angry feelings do not destroy the good ones, that the two can coexist simultaneously.

Patients who have a hard time dealing with anger also frequently develop the means to deny or shield themselves from assertiveness and competitiveness. They procrastinate, avoid showing their mastery over important concepts, and shy away from any confrontation or lively disagreement. The purpose of these defenses is relatively similar to those defending against anger: to avoid hatred and abandonment. In this case, envy of others would be an instrument that could potentially injure them.

We all know very talented individuals who cannot get anything done, as if to say to us, "Don't worry about me, I'm no threat." Camouflaging their competitiveness takes several other forms. Some never enter the race and stay in the background as much as they can. Others may seem outwardly less competent then they are or fold when they are close to winning a competition. Once again, their true selves get buried under the weight of efforts to protect themselves. These efforts at self-protection actually damage them seriously.

Semrad challenged us to approach therapy in this way: "The only truth that you have is your patient. In addition, the only thing that interferes with that truth is your own perception. You may want to turn away and not observe what there is to be observed, chiefly because it evokes feelings in you that are so troublesome that you quit looking. The only way to get through avoidance behavior is through feelings. The technique is to talk of emotions, let the patient know she has them, and stay with her even though the pain you are hearing about is virtually unendurable for you." Semrad elevated this capacity to the level of a sacred obligation.

We also learned that it was critical to help our patients diminish the impact of their shame over being imperfect. Perfectionism impedes the patient's task enormously. Patients sadly feel ashamed because they are depressed, a state they feel they could have avoided if only they were not so grievously imperfect. They develop this equation: "If you are not perfect, you are worthless." Hence, they feel humiliated by their depression.

In addition to being ashamed of their depression, many patients feel this way whenever they experience a loss or a disappointment. It is critical that individuals develop the perspective that loss is an everyday part of life, and that if we accepted this, we could better grieve our losses rather than feeling ashamed. The capacity to bear loss and disappointment is essential for a life not saturated by depression. Losses are inevitable, and it is a handicap not to be able to grieve them.

One of my explicit goals is to help patients enhance their capacity to bear disappointment without despair or shame. In addition, by interfering with the key elements of expressing sadness, pain, and anger, perfectionism makes it difficult to learn from past mistakes. The perfectionist is ashamed about what he doesn't know, and therefore becomes guarded, even to the point of not asking simple questions whose answers he feels he should have already mastered. Thus, perfectionistic individuals are rarely good students of their lives. Perfectionism also impedes acknowledging and learning from mistakes. We can, of course, only learn from mistakes if we can bear to acknowledge them.

Individuals arrive at this perfectionistic stance in various ways. One common pathway is indifference or hostility from parents on a systematic basis. A young child is incapable of saying to herself, "My parents are burdened and that is why they are unavailable or so critical." Rather, implicitly, she reaches the conclusion, "I can win them over only if I am more appealing or really perfect."

Semrad and others tried to help us maintain our poise when some of our patients expressed how much they cared about us. He found these expressions critical to helping our patients learn in the here-and-now about how some of life's strongest feelings affect them. Often the patients felt love for us and expected that we would find it absurd that they dared to love someone so "lofty." Semrad asked, "How are you going to bring patients back to life if you don't let them love you? Nothing is enacted. But talking about what that love means and helping the patient to bear the grief that the love is to be understood but not enacted is the key. The patient learns to grieve the most difficult thing of all to grieve, not having the love of another person in their lives."

Although we admired Semrad enormously, we did not idealize him. Semrad was no means immune from having his own embarrassing missteps. He was a creature of the '50s and '60s, when medicine was still fundamentally, unquestioningly, dominated by men. There were only three women in my medical school class of seventy at Duke, and only four female residents out of twenty-five at the Mass Mental. I recall one incident when a third-year female resident gave a well-executed presentation on a patient with whom she had worked at the Psycho (we call this "presenting" the patient—even though they are not in the room). I thought she showed great skill and maturity in her talk. Semrad asked how long she had been the patient's therapist. "Three years," she said. "Three years," he shot back. "When I was your age that would have been unheard-of. We finished our own analyses in less than a year. Why, mine only took eleven and a half months." With complete composure she said, "It seems to me, Dr. Semrad, that you could have used at least another two or three weeks."

The residents at the Psycho formed close bonds, and we frequently presented our patients to one another to compare notes. As we approached the end of the residency, we shared regrets that we might never again experience such a concentrated period of learning and growth. We had each worked with patients with whom we had met for our entire stay during the residency, at times seeing them in as many as three or four sessions a week in psychotherapy.

None of us were prepared to imagine that such sadness and despair existed in the world. This was even beyond what I had seen at Boston City Hospital, where I was a medical intern.

I remembered one patient whom we lost who I always felt should have survived his depression. He was an eighteen-year-old freshman at Yale University with bipolar illness who, in the midst of a severe depression, had made a serious suicide attempt. After six or seven weeks in the hospital he seemed to be doing much better, and his attending physician had given him a pass from the hospital for the weekend. I ran into him on his way out and politely inquired about his plans for the weekend. He told me that he was most looking forward to seeing *The Man of La Mancha* that evening. He loved its premise of dreaming the impossible dream and endlessly searching for it. Later that evening, all of the residents on our service received calls informing us that he had fatally overdosed on his medications.

During our chance brief meeting before he left the hospital to take his life, I was not able to decode what he was telling me about his tortuous dilemma. What he had told me indirectly was that he himself was on a quest to achieve an impossible dream, and that he could not imagine living unless he achieved it. Thus, his perception of the distance between his real self and his ideal, perfected self was enormous, a discrepancy that was a good marker for the severity of his depression and his enormous fragility. Now, forty years later, even though I was not his physician, I still fervently wish that I had sat down with him and asked him to tell me more about what so captivated him about impossible dreams, and how he felt when he despaired of ever reaching them. I might have cancelled his pass that evening until his musings could be more thoroughly explored. Subsequently, I bridled at any reference to impossible dreams and overcoming impossible odds. My colleagues objected, feeling that we should never discourage someone from having a dream. Rather, we should emphasize that such dreams required a highly developed capacity to grieve disappointments without shame and despair. I appreciated this advice and thoroughly agreed with it.

As I reflect on the three years I spent at the Psycho, I see that I took many steps to begin my own process of becoming a person in order to better help my patients become truer to themselves and, hence, more alive. I shared many of the tasks and challenges my patients faced. I had to better recognize my own sadness and not let the enormous sadness of my patients overwhelm me or get me to look the other way. I had to become more familiar with and comfortable with my own anger, and to never discourage my patients from expressing anger toward me. In some ways, I needed to model that hatred and love often coexist, and that one does not destroy the other. I had to overcome my own fears about competitiveness and encourage my patients to not shrink away from challenges. Most of all, I had to overcome my own perfectionism.

The slow pace of my work with my patients discouraged me. I found this particularly troublesome after my medical internship at Boston City Hospital, where things moved so quickly. One month into my psych residency, I required a root canal for a tooth that was very painful, and in the aftermath experienced almost immediate relief. I remember thinking, "Oh Lord, why didn't you let me become a dentist?"

I struggled with imperfection in a number of other ways. I

inevitably said the wrong thing, and overly sharp self-criticism intermittently led to demoralization. I had to better understand that many of the most important matters in life are, at heart, ambiguous. Early on, I felt deficient when I was unable to identify a clear-cut solution to a patient's problem or difficult situation. I invariably encountered material in the course of my study that I simply couldn't yet understand, and I was, at times, unduly distressed by this inevitable part of the work. I am not likely to be able to help every patient and should not condemn myself for failing. To effectively learn from my mentors, I had to accept criticism without shame or anger, but to accept disagreement as alternative ways of analyzing phenomena. This kind of interchange promotes growth, but perfectionism can interfere with progress in expanding our knowledge and range.

It has always been important to me to be well liked, and earlier in my career I carefully avoided confrontations that might have elicited anger or disapproval. I wanted my patients to like me as well. This proved to be an impediment, since it neutralized any chance that they might express their anger to me and learn that it did not damage the relationship but was rather an ordinary part of communication that others would tolerate in them. I tended, in my early therapeutic efforts, to be reassuring to minimize the patient's distress, not knowing that this would leave them alone with their pain. I initially was often quick to prescribe medication before I thoroughly knew my patient as a way of trying to hasten the relief of their suffering. I might have made better medication choices if I'd known my patients better. I initially had trouble setting limits, which left many of my patients unsettled because they needed structure and had not internalized certain controls on behavior that caused them difficulty in relationships and work. I certainly had a lot of work ahead of me to improve my capacity to be an effective therapist.

In becoming more capable of dealing with sadness, anger, competitiveness, and perfectionism, I had to work on the same things I was trying to work on with my patients. In the process, I learned that we share most attributes, and that the differences between us are subtle. We are all in this together.

During and after my residency, I was in psychotherapy four times a week with a senior training analyst over a period of six years. It was of immeasurable assistance in freeing me up to be appropriately assertive, resolving unrealistic guilt, and in tempering my perfectionism so I had reasonable expectations of myself. It increased my capacity to relax and enjoy myself with family and friends and to diminish my obsessive focus on work. At the same time, my work improved because I was less distracted by inner conflict and more capable of assertively pressing forward. I became a better psychotherapist and a more effective investigator as I grew through the therapy. It improved my capacity to make commitments and diminished my tendency to judge others too sternly. It helped me to become a better husband, father, brother, and friend. The psychoanalytic process was accelerated considerably when I started using imipramine in the last two years of my analysis, largely resolving the biological component of my depression. The medication strengthened me to look beneath the surface and uncover material that made me uncomfortable but needed to be broached.

I like to think that as physicians we hold up a mirror to our patients and show them an image of themselves lit with compassion and empathy. At some point when they are ready, we pass off this mirror to the individual so they too can see themselves in a new light.

When my patient William began psychotherapy with me (a short while before his therapeutic trial of imipramine began), I was thirty-two and relatively new to the Clinical Center. We met three times a week. I tried to be warm and accessible and to convey that we would all do our best to treat his depression. For the first several days, I attempted to carefully work at understanding William's suffering so he would not be alone with it. I met twice a week with a senior clinician and reviewed my notes in detail to get a better understanding about what I might be doing to foster or slow down our progress and to refine my strategies for effective treatment. These sessions, though always informative, could be quite stressful.

Over time, I developed an understanding of what William was experiencing and the content of his worst fears. I was able to couple this information with numerous details about his childhood, his adolescence, and the years leading up to the onset of his current depression five years before. We meticulously reconstructed what had happened prior to the onset of the depression that brought him to the NIH.

William had led an extremely stressful life. He was a long-awaited child, who was born when his mother was forty-one. She cherished him above all else, a fact that was not lost on his father, who resented him. William's father had been a star football player in college; William looked like his mother, and preferred books to sports.

His father criticized his wife for pampering and protecting William excessively. He warned that she was impeding his self-sufficiency and assertiveness. He feared that William would grow up to become a "weakling" if she weren't careful. On a certain level, his mother understood that her husband resented her devotion to William. She kept silent. She feared his rages and threats of abandonment.

When William was ten, his mother experienced a severe depression after her own father died suddenly. From then on, William's mother worried that tragedy could strike at any time without notice, and she became very overprotective. William saw he could do nothing to help her as she woke up in the middle of the night, avoided her friends, stopped going outside, and he felt like a failure for his inability to come to her aid.

William recalled the difficulties he had in asking his parents for help—for instance, after a difficult breakup with a girlfriend as a teenager. Had he confided in his father about his distress, he would have been ridiculed and disparaged. Had he confided in his mother, she would have become overwhelmed by anxiety. My line of questioning around this surprised him a bit, because it never occurred to him that he could ask anyone for help. Feeling helpless himself and unable to go to others for assistance, he was left feeling hopeless and alone.

For as long as he could remember, William had wanted to become a physician. He attended college and medical school in the town in which he was born so he could be close to his mother, whom he felt was fragile. He excelled in medical school, and soon after graduation he married a woman whose self-sufficiency, competency, and quiet modesty were among the traits that allowed him to feel completely at home with her.

It was not lost on William that in medicine, the physicians who had achieved success as scientists were most highly esteemed, and he decided to pursue a life as a medical investigator. He chose oncology because cancer biology seemed the most important and challenging area in medical research. He acknowledged that he would only be satisfied with reaching the highest echelons of his profession. I asked him why his only choice was to be the best in a highly competitive field. The question took him aback, because he assumed that it was only natural to want to be the best. I suggested, however, that not every physician thought that the only way to earn self-respect was to become a renowned researcher. William had no ready answer to this question but promised he would think about it. At the same time, he wondered what difference it would make, since he was still deeply depressed and feared that the imipramine was not going to work.

Gradually, multiple publishing deadlines and a hectic professional schedule left little time for relaxation and time with his wife and children. His explicit aim was to work himself up to the top of his field. Nothing else would do. On rare getaways with his family, he found the slower pace monotonous and often spent time on the phone with his colleagues at work. "I felt as if I were wasting my time if I were not at work." He was exhilarated when he won a large five-year research grant that helped to build an even more high-powered laboratory. Two years later, he won a prestigious award for his research. But the award brought him surprisingly little pleasure, and it was soon afterward that his depression began.

It was around the time when William was discussing this overworking when he responded to the imipramine. His response came rapidly, almost like a switch from one state into another. One week he was as depressed as ever and the next week he felt virtually well. He marveled at how refreshed and alert he felt and could imagine enjoying himself on a trip outside the hospital with his wife. We were cautiously optimistic but did not want to take a chance that the remission would be brief, and that he might be despondent should a relapse occur. We waited for more than a week before we felt it was safe for him to leave with his wife on a pass.

I spent the sessions after his remission getting a sense of the differences he felt in this new state compared to during his depression. William was struck by how the depression had intruded into every aspect of his self-concept, way of thinking, and emotional state. He was virtually astonished at the extent to which his self-disparagement resolved. He was simultaneously aware that his losses were enormous. In particular, he was acutely aware of the extent to which the depression had damaged his relationships with his wife and children. He acknowledged how lonely his wife must have felt when he disappeared into his work, and how preoccupied he became with himself during his depression. He remembered how happy they had been when they were first married and during their first years together. He was able to recall the joy he felt when his daughters were born and the wonderful times they shared during their childhoods. He recalled magical vacations, wonderful birthday parties, and the sheer pleasure of being at home with them for a quiet evening. By the time they entered grammar school, William had become steeped in his work on the wards and in his lab. He spent less and less time with his children and lost contact with the day-to-day details of their lives. They were now entering their adolescence and he barely knew them. William wept as he considered how much of his daughters' lives he had missed. He acknowledged that their childhoods were over, and that the time lost with them was irretrievable.

William soon after decided his first priority was to rebuild his relationship with his family. As an oncologist, he had frequently encountered patients who had recovered from a life-threatening cancer and felt they had been given a second chance at life. As a consequence, they would value every day. Apart from the trepidation that he might become depressed again, William felt that he too had been given a second chance and pledged he would try to value the days one at a time.

In subsequent sessions, William freely acknowledged that his father had never fully respected him and, in fact, had disparaged him throughout his life. The phrase, "You'll have to do better than that to impress me" was seared into his emotional memory. I had the sense that William could not yet appreciate what a severe wound his father had inflicted. It was my impression that he had organized his life to win his father's approval in order to heal the wound. He felt his father's dismissal was likely to have contributed to his drive to excel, but he wasn't clear exactly how.

I suggested that as a child or an adolescent, it is difficult or impossible to step back and observe that one's father is carrying burdens from the past or is too flawed and self-centered to accept their child for who they are. Instead, the child concludes that they can win over their father only by being extraordinary, or perfect. The more the child's father disparages them, the more extraordinary they feel they have to become. Being an outstanding student, going on to medical school, and becoming a researcher pleased William's mother. She built her life around him, and his success was enormously important to her. It is hard to imagine that he wouldn't have felt driven to make extraordinary contributions in his work.

William wondered why his father was so antipathetic to him. As we reconstructed the details of his relationship to his mother, it became clear that William was the center of her life rather than his father. I wondered aloud if his father were jealous of him and resented the extent to which his mother valued him most of all. William thought this made sense, but that he would have to think about it. He found it hard to believe that a father could be jealous of his own child.

Later on in therapy, I asked William if he thought there was a relationship between his winning the most prestigious prize in his field and the onset of his depression shortly thereafter. He didn't have a ready answer. I told him about a case that I heard about when I was a resident in training—a Nobel Prize winner had become depressed soon after receiving his award, like William. He was an exceptionally bright person and sailed through his schooling with top awards. He did brilliantly as a scientist and won every prize in his field. When he won the ultimate prize, he could not escape the nagging feeling that he had carried all his life: that he was not cared for as a person in his own right, but rather as the superachiever. When this nagging feeling that had plagued him for so long failed to resolve with the Nobel Prize, he abandoned hope that he would ever really feel fully well. He became depressed. William found this idea intriguing but was unsure if this scenario related to his experience.

William and I discussed some of the meanings of our work together. He felt increasingly clear that he had organized his life around trying to win his father's blessing, and we both felt it was critical for him to stop running after unattainable relationships. No matter how successful he might be, he would never win his father's love. His father might become even more jealous if he succeeded brilliantly. William acknowledged that his drive for success was not purely out of love for the work, but was, in part, an attempt to heal a long-standing injury. After this, he felt freer to be himself, and that included investing an important part of himself in his wife and family and leaving time for himself to become more engaged with the world around him. I pointed out to William that he was also freer to express his anger toward his father, and to even acknowledge some anger with his mother. I noted that this constituted another way for him to be true to himself. He no longer had to keep this part of himself hidden. He noted that he hadn't yet become comfortable with his anger, and he felt surprised at how assiduously he avoided acknowledging such strong feelings.

These psychological issues, had they not been discovered, would have left Dr. Cummings in a very vulnerable position. He would have continued a life devoted to the singular goal of chasing recognition and fame and being prone to depression. He would have continued to ignore his family, resulting in further alienation from his wife and children. It is possible that his wife would eventually have left him if he did not direct his focus back to the family, and that he would remain alienated from his children. This scenario would have been likely to produce sufficient stress that his response to the medication would be overridden, plunging him back into depression.

I did not take it for granted that William could relinquish his quest for achievement easily. For years he had devoted his life to outstanding scientific accomplishment without regard to other facets of his life. He and I agreed that he had a good deal of grieving ahead of him to integrate his losses without becoming demoralized. I recommended that he continue with psychotherapy after he left the NIH to further probe the issues we had discussed and uncovering new issues that we had not yet covered. He heartily agreed to follow this course of action. I took the responsibility of finding him a sophisticated therapist in his hometown.

When we were finishing our work together, I spoke with

William about unexpected struggles he might anticipate after recovering from such a lengthy siege of depression. Some patients feel that they may have lost the instinct of taking a proactive stance in their lives. The fact that depression had been able to take them over so fully created a fear that in the future they couldn't count on themselves to do what they needed to do in critical situations. Some also experienced a measure of disorientation. The depression had been a virtually constant companion, and now they would encounter the world with an entirely different set of assumptions and expectations. William wondered how long he would fear that he might wake up depressed the next day. Although less shattered by what he had lost, his life was totally different from what it had been before he became ill.

William, his wife, and I met before he was discharged. His wife remained fully committed to working at rebuilding their marriage. Hopefully, the girls would have their father back at a crucial age and enjoy the benefits of a united family.

I don't believe it was a coincidence that William got in touch with his sadness and anger soon after responding to imipramine. It has been my experience that successful antidepressant treatment improves the quality and quickens the pace of psychotherapy. Many individuals feel less anxiety about loosening some of their long-standing defenses and more capable of bearing difficult feelings after responding to antidepressants. Patients can still feel sad on antidepressants but can also get in touch with their anger appropriately; rather than feeling constricted within a narrow range of feelings, they feel liberated to experience a broader and deeper range than when they were depressed. Thus, they free up the capacity to allow the expression of a larger repertoire of thoughts and feelings that seem similar to what they experienced before they became depressed.

Over the years, as I accumulated more experience with depression, I began to feel that individuals who have recovered from depression seemed particularly resilient in the aftermath. During episodes of depression, William and others had to develop the capacity to grapple with intense anxiety about their deficiencies, hopelessness, inability to experience pleasure, and virtually unending pain. Yet they survived, day after day, implicitly learning how to get through the most difficult times imaginable. Once they were able to emerge from depression, their steps then seemed lighter at times, as if they were buoyed by a strength they had acquired under duress then helped them through the inevitable stresses and frustrations of everyday life.

During one- and two-year postdischarge follow-ups, William continued to respond to imipramine. He got to know his adolescent daughters very well, and reestablished a loving relationship with his wife. He also found himself capable of enjoying many things that he had valued in the past, including his passion for art. He decided not to attempt to rebuild his research career, and he instead built a full-time clinical practice in oncology and continued to teach at the medical school as a valued full professor.

William's journey through depression and into recovery inspired me to believe that I could help others find their way as well. Watching William suffer and then recover and thrive against great odds also further instilled in me the strong belief that psychotherapy and drug therapy combined are the most effective way to treat depression.

CHAPTER 6

Genetics, Destiny, and Depression

I was impressed by how much William's early life experiences and the subsequent stressors he faced played a role in contributing to the onset of his depression and its long course. At the same time, for as long as we have had a sense of what depression is, we could see that it runs in families. Even so, studies have established that there is no single gene for depression and that the genetics give you a propensity, not a prediction, that depression will develop in your lifetime.

In the general population worldwide, the overall incidence of major depression is estimated to be 15 to 20 percent, though the incidence varies somewhat by culture. Some people develop depression largely on the basis of genetic inheritance and some largely on the basis of psychological or physical stress. That said, individuals with a sibling or a parent with depression have a two to three times greater chance of having depression, or a rate of 40 to 60 percent. If one parent has a recurrent form of depression with multiple episodes over time, the risk is four to five times greater than the average person, or 60 to 75 percent. In identical twins who share 100 percent of their genes, if one twin has depressive illness, the other has only a 60 percent chance of having the disorder. This means that environment contributes 40 percent of the risk.

Despite our relief at discovering that there is no genetic "sentence" to having depression, genes still play a key role in predicting whether a person will suffer from the disease, so it's worth understanding the genetic component of depression.

Nowadays there are two major strategies for conducting genetic studies in depression. The first is the screening of patients with depressive illness for mutations in candidate genes for abnormalities, and looking at postmortem studies of brains taken from patients with depressive illness, especially those who died by suicide. Candidate genes are those identified through repeated study that we know encode demonstrable abnormalities. As an example, we know that CRH, corticotropin-releasing hormone, a hormone related to the stress response, is involved in depression. Therefore, CRH and its receptors are candidate genes.

The second strategy explores the genetics of depression as one of a group of complex diseases such as Alzheimer's or Crohn's disease, and depression that can involve abnormalities in as many as one hundred genes. We are addressing diseases like these by scanning large components of the whole genome. Such scanning studies are not hypothesis driven, but rather "work backward" by looking for affected genes that turn out to be linked with the complex illness.

Genomics already allows personalized therapy in patients with depression based on their unique DNA sequences: a branch of genomic science related to this fact is called pharmacogenomics. Specific DNA sequences have been linked to positive responses to specific drugs, and research is underway to identify a specific genetic fingerprint to isolate those with depression who are highly likely to respond to a specific medication. Such approaches promise the advent of personalized medicine in which drugs are optimized for each individual's unique genetic fingerprint, a major breakthrough in psychopharmacology.

As I mentioned, your genetic structure does entirely predict your susceptibility to a complex disease like depression or coronary artery disease. A predisposing environment is also required, even in the context of 100 percent shared genes. For coronary artery disease, the predisposing environment includes factors like obesity, poor diet, smoking, a sedentary life, and stressful lifestyles. For depression, the predisposing environment consists of factors including negatively charged emotional memories, early abandonment, sexual abuse, chronic inescapable stress, or other traumas.

The fact that genetic susceptibility to depression involves perhaps hundreds of genes means on the positive side that no one automatically inherits depression from their mother or father. On the negative side, this makes the process of identifying the genetic fingerprint of these illnesses profoundly more difficult. No one has isolated an entire repertoire of genes reliably responsible for any complex disease. Given the twenty thousand genes in the genome and 3.2 billion base pairs, it is no wonder that the search for contributing genes requires study of hundreds of thousands or millions of patients to obtain reliable data.

There have been several recent notable studies of the genetics of depression. A study that included findings derived from surveying the whole genome found associations with genes that play roles in neuronal development, synaptic structure, immunologic function, neurotransmitter metabolism, and regulation of gene expression in the brain. Some of the clinical features of depression—including early onset, recurrence, and severity—were tied to events in the prefrontal cortex of the brain. Current genomic findings hold promise for the development of new depression medications, many of which we are primed to develop in the very near future.

The Search for Candidate Genes in Depression

We have a big challenge ahead of us in isolating exactly how genetics influences susceptibility to depression. On the bright side, extraordinary advances in the ability and speed of scientists to decode DNA sequences means that we can more accurately and rapidly identify candidate genes, genes that are clearly involved in the physiology of a disorder or disease process. Candidate genes for depression include CRH, BDNF, the cortisol receptor, and the enzymes involved in synthesizing or degrading serotonin, norepinephrine, and dopamine. For these studies, the candidate genes are fully sequenced and examined for possible mutations.

We are also combing the genome for associations, meaning we are looking for patterns in the genetics of complex diseases caused by multiple genes, where each gene individually plays a relatively small role in the overall inheritance of an illness. For multifaceted disorders like depression and coronary disease, up to one hundred genes may be working together to create the matrix of biological alterations that encode a depression or a case of coronary artery disease. This means finding up to one hundred base pair substitutions throughout the genome to get a handle on the genetic architecture of a complex disease, and to determine which combinations of genes are responsible for the disorder.

Contributing to the difficulty of study is the fact that two individuals having some of the same core symptoms of depression may differ from one another considerably. In fact, no two cases of depression are exactly alike. One patient may have a single episode of depression, and another seven or eight episodes. Different patients vary with respect to subjective mood, cognitive function, appetite, and sleep. Another problem is that some genetic variants may play a significant role in the illness and others only a minor one. Finally, some mutations may affect more than a single trait, further complicating the search for the specific combination of genes and their relative impacts on susceptibility to depressive illness and its overall course.

Environment also clearly plays a role in the propensity to depressive illness. Although depression can be found everywhere, substantial national and regional variations in frequency exist. Diagnostic procedures to identify depression may also vary widely from site to site. That makes differences in frequency hard to interpret. Furthermore, high risk for depression has been documented for people who deal with long-term difficulties (e.g., taking care of a disabled partner, persistent unemployment, being the victim of chronic bullying) or in the aftermath of stressful short-term life events (e.g., acute illness of child, estrangement from a good friend). The latter, short-term factors are often the last straw, an event that can push a susceptible individual across the threshold to clinical depressive illness. Another complicating factor is that genetic background may also have environmental implications (e.g., some genetic features may predispose individuals to be risk-takers, increasing their exposure to stress).

A most informative genetic study of depressive illness was published in May 2021. It encompassed over a million subjects, making it the largest genome-wide association study yet undertaken. The authors, Dr. Daniel Levey and others, fine-mapped 178 mutations. The lead mutation from their primary analysis was neuronal growth factor. Inactivation of the gene related to the production of neuronal growth factor in mice creates irregularities in several brain regions, including decreased brain volume in the emotional memory center, and is related to abnormalities in social behavior and nonsocial interest. Another study of these mice identified a variety of depression-like and anxiety-like features in behavioral assays that assess depression severity.

An important dopamine receptor called the D2 dopamine receptor, heavily involved in the capacity to anticipate or experience pleasure, was found to have significantly decreased expression in the pleasure and reward center of depressed subjects.

Thus, depression-like behavior in animals and depression in humans both seem linked to the reward system and to symptoms of anhedonia. It is remarkable that this gene and brain region of known biological significance has emerged from a hypothesis-free gene-wide association study, and points to the value of other key findings in other large-scale investigations.

Another genetic-related line of inquiry involves epigenetics. Epigenetic changes are experience-based alterations in the expression of genes, without involving how your genes are sequenced—meaning that they do not cause mutations in the genes themselves, and that they are reversible. Epigenetic changes seem most prominent after stressful experiences and are more likely to occur in children than adults. After a stressful event, stress-responsive genes are surrounded by molecules that alter their capacity to produce the protein they encode, without changing the structure of the gene at all. Thus, they change the expression of the gene rather than its content. Many believe that epigenetic changes contribute a great deal toward the lifelong vulnerability of children who have been mistreated or abused.

Mice can be made more resilient or more vulnerable to stress by blocking or inducing epigenetic modifications to certain genes. Michael Meaney and his colleagues at McGill University found that positive postnatal care in rats, as assessed by increased licking, grooming, and breast feeding, led to a reduction in the actions of cortisol, which, when excessive, contributes to depressive illness. These rats were more resilient than rats who had not been nurtured in the same way. Some epigenetic changes can last for a lifetime, even though they are technically reversible.

These same phenomena occur in humans. Researchers saw that the genes identified in the rat-grooming studies were analogous in humans. These findings indicate that epigenetic changes could produce depressive-like symptoms and biological effects associated with depressive illness.

BDNF is a compound of major importance in the pathophysiology of depression. Mistreated baby rats showed BDNF gene silencing in their prefrontal cortex, without a change in the sequence of the BDNF gene. The offspring of female rats who had been mistreated early in their lives also experienced increased epigenetic changes that increased their susceptibility to depression-like illnesses. Since there was no mutation involved, but rather a change in how much gene product was produced, gene-wide association studies would not pick up a key change that was contributing to the rats' depressive symptoms.

Epigenetic changes may be one factor explaining why it is so hard to find genetic markers for depression. Maternal care as well as childhood mistreatment or trauma can lead to epigenetic changes that influence the stress hormone systems or important compounds such as BDNF that either contribute to the development of a depressive episode or protect from it. The good news is that in contrast to the DNA sequences of genes we can't yet reliably change or correct, we can reverse or promote specific epigenetic changes with antidepressants.

I noted earlier that only 50 to 60 percent of depressed patients show remission after treatment with standard antidepressants. The delayed response to antidepressant treatment could reflect long-term adaptations like epigenetic changes. For instance, imipramine produces epigenetic changes, but only after a three- to four-week latency period. It makes sense that these changes in the expression of genes take time to manifest.

I am confident we will see extraordinary advances come about as a result of genomic medicine. Identification of a network of genes involved in depressive illness provides clues for treating depression through drugs known to affect the function of these genes, as well as by gene therapy, when it becomes available, to replace or repair mutant genes. This is an exciting new frontier in pharmacology related to depression, and could provide relief for millions.

Identifying and understanding the epigenetic changes that influence susceptibility to depression is a critical frontier for preventing or successfully treating depressive illness. We already know that the mood stabilizers lithium and Depakote undo unwanted epigenetic changes. New agents that have recently become available or will emerge in the near future can also play similar roles in undoing pathogenic epigenetic change related to depression, perhaps more quickly and with fewer side effects.

We have also identified strategies to identify mutant genes through gene-wide association studies that will provide us with opportunities to significantly enlarge our knowledge about underlying causes of depressive illness and the action mechanisms of antidepressant agents. When gene therapy becomes available, we will be able to treat depression by correcting the genomic abnormalities in multiple genes that contribute to the susceptibility to depression. A remarkable procedure has already been developed that allows us to replace a single mutated letter in a gene, in the way a word processor can correct a spelling error.

Genomics is not necessarily a discipline of its own so much as a technology to expand our ability to address the manifestations of depressive illness and its underlying causes, and to cure it. In the next chapter, we see how the identification of CLOCK genes that control circadian rhythms, for instance, will ultimately allow us to repair circadian abnormalities in depressed patients as a way of promoting their recoveries.

CHAPTER 7

Darkness Visible

We live in a world of light and darkness. We are deeply attuned to the rhythms and patterns that correspond to these two states. Most organisms have developed rhythms to anticipate daily variation in light intensity, ambient temperature, and humidity. Many mammals have monthly, seasonal, and yearly rhythms that affect behavior, physiology, hormone secretion, and in gene expression that have helped us adapt to changing conditions. Synchronization of multiple rhythms is necessary for health, and desynchronization can be associated with severe illnesses.Depressed patients have many abnormalities in biological rhythms, including in circadian rhythms, which occur every twenty-four hours. These produce insomnia and oversleeping, the timing of switches into depression or into mania, the twenty-four-hour patterns of hormonal secretion, and the time of day that depressive symptoms are most severe in different subtypes of depressed patients. Longer-term rhythms such as those that cycle monthly or with the season also occur in patients with depressive illness. The monthly menstrual cycles of depressed women are also either irregular or disappear altogether.

The most apparent rhythmic disturbance in depressed patients is the disruption of the twenty-four-hour sleep-wake cycle. Virtually 90 percent of patients with depressive illness have alterations in their sleep-wake cycles. Insomnia is a common symptom of melancholic depression, most often characterized by early-morning awakening. In contrast, patients with atypical depression sleep excessively at night and often complain of daytime sleepiness. Depressed patients also have variations in the severity of symptoms over the course of a day. In melancholia, patients feel at their worst in the morning and report some relief as the day progresses. It is in the morning when the stress system is most active, thus worsening the manifestations of melancholia. Patients with atypical depression feel best in the morning, and their depression worsens as the day progresses. In the evening when stress system activity is at its lowest, the severity of atypical depression symptoms intensifies.

In some patients with depressive illness, interfering with circadian rhythms, such as total sleep deprivation, can produce a temporary recovery—or can provoke manic episodes in bipolar patients. During a manic episode some patients can remain awake for thirty-six to forty-eight consecutive hours without feeling fatigued. The mechanism by which sleep deprivation causes mania is unknown. One possibility is via the activation of the thyroid axis. During sleep, the stimulus to thyroid hormone secretion falls. During sleep deprivation, the stimulus to thyroid hormone does not fall but, instead, rises substantially. Thyroid hormone is well known to promote the emergence of mania.

One depressive subtype, seasonal affective disorder, is associated with depressions in the winter, during the period when daylight is limited. Later, we will see that these individuals are in fact light deprived and respond to bright-light therapy.

Let's consider some of the synchronizers of biological rhythms in healthy individuals that either become disturbed in patients with depressive illness or are processed abnormally. Light is the most potent synchronizer of day-night (or diurnal) rhythms. In humans, these various rhythms cue that we are safe, help prime us for productive activity during the day, ensure adequate sleep at night, and prepare us for the transition from sleep to wakefulness. A master clock in the brain that is sensitive to light monitors the timing of the day-night cycle. Light reaches the master clock from the retina via a pathway that does not feed information to the visual centers of the brain, but rather to the master clock itself. The master clock is located deep in the brain in an area called the hypothalamus.

One of the most important processes controlled by the light-dark cycle is melatonin secretion. Melatonin is produced in the pineal gland, which also lies deep within the brain, and which receives information directly from the master clock. Melatonin secretion begins immediately after exposure to darkness at night and falls abruptly with the onset of daylight. Next to light exposure itself, melatonin is the most potent synchronizer of daily rhythms. Physicians often prescribe melatonin as an aid to sleep or to resynchronize rhythms after travel through multiple time zones.

We secrete more melatonin during long winter nights and less during the short nights of spring and summer. Melatonin influences many physiological processes, including acting as a potent suppressor of the reproductive system. With a prolonged period of melatonin secretion during the late autumn and winter months, characterized by long, dark nights, the reproductive axis is shut down in many animal species. The reproductive axis reinvigorates when nights are relatively short, and melatonin secretion is significantly diminished. The inhibition of reproduction during late autumn and winter months protects many mammals against conception that would lead to births during the harsh conditions of winter.

Although there are innumerable physiological processes related to circadian rhythms, let's consider the time of sleep onset (using ten p.m. as our marker) and two other closely linked markers: the time of night when the stress hormone cortisol rises, simultaneous to a rise in body temperature. These latter two phenomena are tightly linked, occurring normally around five a.m. (if we are talking about ten p.m. as our bedtime). The time of night when cortisol and temperature begin to rise are markers of stress system function, and they occur to prime us for waking in the morning. Cortisol promotes arousal, increases blood sugar levels, and stimulates heart contractions and the activity of the sympathetic nervous system. A higher body temperature is associated with a more rapid metabolic rate and prepares us for the day. We now know that once the cortisol levels and body temperature begin to rise, it is very difficult to go back to sleep.

There is normally a seven-hour period that separates the time of going to sleep and the time that cortisol levels and temperature begin to rise. When this seven-hour separation is intact, these rhythms are appropriately synchronized.

In patients with melancholic depression, the cortisol and temperature levels begin to rise at around two a.m., only four hours after going to sleep. Since it is hard to stay asleep when cortisol levels and temperature begins to rise, this means melancholic patients often have early-morning awaking. For them, rhythms of arousal are set to occur after a shorter period of sleep.

In the late 1970s, Dr. Tom Wehr, who worked on the same unit where I conduct my research, wondered if he could resolve a person's depression by reestablishing the seven-hour latency between the time of going to sleep and the time of rising cortisol and temperature levels. He theorized that correcting this desynchronization could be a means of treating depression.

One of his patients was Jane Blair, came to the NIH with a long history of recurrent depressions that were resistant to medications. Her first depression had occurred twenty-five years prior, when she was twenty years old. After that they recurred about three times a year and characteristically lasted three to six weeks, when she would spontaneously recover. Her depressions were associated with early-morning awakening and anxiety, especially on arising. She was bitterly upset with herself for not being more available to her close-knit family, who nevertheless appreciated that she did her best to function well even when she was depressed.

During her episodes of depression, after Jane fell asleep, usually at ten p.m., her cortisol and temperature rhythms, which would normally peak at around six a.m., had jumped ahead five hours and were peaking around one a.m. Instead of occurring seven to eight hours after the onset of sleep, these rhythms occurred only three hours after the onset of sleep. Since it is hard to remain asleep when cortisol and temperature are rising, these phase shifts were accompanied by early-morning awakening, a hallmark of melancholic depression. Dr. Wehr named this phenomenon a "phase advance" and found it consistently during her depressive episodes.

Dr. Wehr decided that he would attempt to treat her depression by experimentally restoring the usual timing of sleep onset and the timing of the cortisol and temperature rises to the normal separation of seven to eight hours. To accomplish this task, he had Jane go to sleep at five p.m. and awaken at one a.m. This schedule restored the regular interval between sleep onset and the onset of the rise in cortisol and temperature to the usual seven to eight hours. After four days of this schedule, Jane was in recovery from her depression. Once she was in remission, Dr. Wehr slowly restored her usual sleep schedule by advancing the hour of sleep one hour per day until she was again falling sleep at ten p.m.

Jane remained in remission for three months. Unfortunately, she had a relapse. One week after the onset of another depression, Dr. Wehr repeated phase-advancing the onset of sleep for four days and induced another remission that lasted almost two years. Other investigators verified phase advance therapy as an effective mode of treating some patients with depressive illness, but it remains a research tool that has not received wide acceptance in the routine treatment of depression. This relates partly to the fact that it is so labor-intensive and requires a prolonged hospitalization; most hospital settings would not be equipped for the all-night monitoring required to document the time when cortisol secretion and temperature begin to rise.

Shift workers are obviously impacted by a disruption in natural rhythms. Say the shift worker goes to bed at nine a.m. and awakens at five p.m. Their melatonin levels will be low during the night when they are awake and exposed to light, and cortisol levels and body temperature will be rising at five to six in the evening, while they are still working. All these events occur while they are awake rather than several hours after sleep onset. This disruption of the time of sleep onset and the timing of arousal markers represents a state of internal desynchronization, and is often associated with .arousal and depression, and the onset of premature illnesses such as coronary artery disease.

We are not completely dependent upon light for synchronizing our rhythms. During constant light or darkness, the master clock relies on its own intrinsic rhythmicity. This rhythmicity is referred to as "free running" and follows a cycle frequency of 25 rather than 24 hours. Thus, free-running individuals go to bed at, say at ten p.m. on Monday, at eleven p.m. on Tuesday (25 hours later) and at twelve a.m. on Wednesday (another 25 hours later). Many free running individuals are depressed. Some 10 percent of people who are free running for various reasons will begin operating on a 40-hour day, which means that one sleep-wake cycle encompassed 40 hours, constituting one extremely long day and one extremely long night. These subjects are also desynchronized and almost all are depressed.

Many blind individuals are free running. They have rhythms in their sleep-wake cycle, and cortisol and temperature rhythms that are dictated by an intrinsic rhythm of twenty-five rather than twenty-four hours.

When free running, desynchronized blind individuals become depressed and fatigued, melatonin can help them resynchronize.

Al Lewy, who trained with me at the NIH, was the first to prove that blind people are free running. After experimenting with many patients throughout different times of the day, he found that a small dose of melatonin administration given at six p.m. synchronized their rhythms. This synchronization was associated with resolution of depression and fatigue. Al's 2005 finding was a substantial contribution to medicine.

Around the same time, investigators in Europe observed that some patients with depressions alone switched out of depression and into remission after a full night's sleep deprivation. For most, the remission was short-lived and recurred when the patient went back to sleep and had a REM episode. For recovered or depressed patients with bipolar disorder, one night's sleep deprivation often caused a switch into mania. Clinicians had long noted that sleep deprivation in patients with bipolar disorder often led to mania and warned their patients to get appropriate sleep.

Tom Wehr later found that if depressed patients were kept awake after four a.m., they also had a tendency to have a remission in depression, but again, the remission was short-lived. Groups in Europe experimented with partial sleep deprivation two to three times per week and were able to achieve some lasting remissions. To my knowledge, there are no controlled studies in large numbers of patients that formally demonstrate the effectiveness of multiple partial or full sleep deprivations on the course of depressive illness.

Dr. Wehr was also fascinated by the cycles of depressive illnesses including the timing of onset and offset. He was particularly interested in the extent to which some patients were cycling between mood episodes on a regular basis, and factors other than sleep deprivation that promoted switches from one state to another. He aspired to be like Tyco Brahe was to Galileo: Brahe first mapped the heavens so that Galileo could then forge his scientific observations. Dr. Wehr was convinced that until we understood what depressive illness was in the simplest of terms, namely in the timing of depressive and manic episodes, we would not be able to solve any more of the puzzle about its origins and effective treatment.

Over the years, Dr. Wehr noticed that a number of patients who had a major depressive episode and at least one manic episode switched into a pattern of relatively rapid, regular cycles of depression and mania or hypomania when they were given antidepressants. Hypomania is a state of mild to moderate elevated mood that does not last long enough or represent a deviation from normal behavior to a degree that would qualify it as mania (for instance, a hypomanic episode lasts a minimum of four days whereas true mania lasts at least one week). Antidepressants also led, at times, to hypomanic episodes in depressed patients who had never had them before. These observations established the idea that antidepressants could accelerate cycling in patients with bipolar depression and produce hypomania or mania in some patients who probably had underlying, undiagnosed bipolar illness. We now know to prescribe mood stabilizers like lithium to every bipolar patient given antidepressants.

Bipolar illness is very clearly associated with rhythmic phenomena. Some patients switch out of mania and depression at regular intervals, and this may be more apparent than we think as we study more individuals. As I mentioned earlier, the sleep-wake cycle is profoundly altered in patients with bipolar illness, and manic patients can stay awake for many days without seeming tired. Others sleep excessively during the depressed phase of the illness. The cyclic changes in bipolar disorder disrupt and ruin the lives of many individuals.

Rapid-cycling bipolar patients experience switches between depression and mania on a short schedule; in the case of one of my patients, Martha Jones, this happened every eight days. This form of bipolar disorder is generally resistant to lithium and most other treatments for bipolar disorder, but we found Martha responded to a new strategy for treating rapid cycling. This method, the deployment of anticonvulsants first utilized by Dr. Bob Post at the Clinical Center, brought relief to others as well. More on that later.

Martha Jones arrived at the NIH Clinical Center at the age of forty-six. She was married with two teenage sons. She knew that her mother had phases of rapid cycling during the course of her own bipolar disorder and her father had severe recurrent depressions. She first developed symptoms of bipolar disorder when she was twenty, and her first episode was one of mania that lasted for about three weeks. After several weeks of feeling reasonably well, she would often develop another manic episode or become depressed. She had experienced only partial responses to lithium and almost invariably shifted abruptly from depression to mania when put on antidepressant medication.

Dr. Tom Wehr also made the observation that antidepressants precipitated switches into mania and wrote a classic paper pointing out this phenomena, which led to a marked decrease in the use of antidepressants in bipolar patients. Tom is extraordinarily well educated, and he has a wide range of knowledge encompassing psychodynamics, history, music, and mathematics, and in multiple other intellectual areas. He is among the various gifted people at the NIH with whom I have been fortunate to work.

Martha did not begin rapid cycling until she was forty-four years old. There was no apparent trigger for the onset of her cycles or for any of her subsequent clinical episodes.

Martha's cycles soon established themselves as absolutely regular eight-day depressions alternating with eight-day manias. The depressions were severe melancholic episodes characterized by pronounced feelings of worthlessness, early-morning awakenings at around two a.m. without being able to get back to sleep, and loss of appetite with about a two- to three-pound loss of weight each depressive episode. She felt terribly vulnerable, was convinced that no one could love or respect her, and feared eventually being alone for the rest of her life. She was not actively suicidal but had wishes that she would contract a terrible illness and die. Her switches out of depression or mania were abrupt, often occurring around three a.m., when she was already up with the early-morning awakening of her depressions or the sleeplessness of her manias.

During her manias, Martha slept only two to three hours per night. She was sometimes irritable, verbally abusive, and often flirtatious with the male staff. She had never, however, acted out this hypersexuality at any time during her illness. She tended to gain back the pounds she lost during her depressions.

We noted that during her manias she could not remember feeling depressed, and that during her depressions she could not remember ever feeling well or manic. Elliot Gershon, another doctor on the ward, studied this phenomenon systematically. He also found that this selective memory extended to everyday events: patients who were manic could not remember where they lost their keys during a depressive episode, but could recall where they were when they switched out of mania into depression. He called this phenomenon state-dependent learning.

Martha was aware of the cycles' eight-day durations, so she could make appointments with her dentist or doctors when she knew she would be in a depressed state, since a manic episode could make these visits difficult or impossible

She was in regular psychotherapy with a skillful and devoted therapist who saw her alone two days a week and met with her and her husband on a weekly basis. This treatment was indispensable. It helped her to partially function during her depressions and provided her guidance that helped to tone down her impulsivity and irritability during her manias. This work seemed to stabilize the family considerably, though Martha was constantly afraid that her husband would give up, take the kids, and abandon her. While she was in either a manic or depressive episode, we also continued to help her cope with these states and had regular meetings with both her and her husband.

Martha tried multiple trials of lithium and various antidepressants, none of which led to significant improvement in her illness. On the basis of work done by Bob Post on the efficacy of anticonvulsants on rapid cycling illness, we decided to try a double-blind, placebo-controlled trial of Tegretol, an effective anticonvulsant for temporal lobe epilepsy, which often included some mood-disordered symptoms. She showed no response for two weeks. After that her depressions became milder, and a week later her mania also fell in intensity. She was virtually astonished and began to believe that perhaps this medicine would work. Indeed, within three more weeks, her cycling ceased and she felt well. She was discharged three weeks later, and after a three-year follow-up remained free of manic or depressive episodes.

Another patient of mine, Abigail Morris, came to the NIH Clinical Center with a six-year history of mild cyclic depressions and manias lasting one or two months at a time. She was married with four grown children. During her depressions, she often felt sad and detached, slept excessively, ate excessively, and felt extremely fatigued. She did not feel the anguish that many depressed individuals experience. When she was hypomanic, she was mildly elated, cheerful, sociable, and rarely if ever irritable, impulsive, or hypersexual. In contrast to sleeping nine or ten hours a night during her depressions, she slept five to six hours a night when hypomanic. She had had two trials of lithium at unknown doses without responding, and multiple unsuccessful trials of antidepressants.

I met with Abigail three times a week, in part to determine if there were environmental precipitants to her mood changes, to get a good sense of her day-to-day life, and to explore any underlying conflicts or pronounced disappointments that might be fueling her cycles. Abigail was fairly remote, and I was unable to definitively uncover significant ongoing issues that seemed to precipitate her mood changes. She, herself, however, almost always had an explanation for the switches. She would often identify as precipitants of her depressions such events as the discharge of a patient whom she had befriended, the failure of her children to call for several days, or her husband's disappearance into the rigors of a demanding occupation. On her switches into hypomania, she would describe making a good friend on the ward, the attentiveness and care of her family, or a nice gift or care she had received.

During her stay, Dr. Tom Wehr studied the chronology of her recurrent mood changes by conducting mood ratings with Abigail undertaken by our experienced nursing staff and his own daily observations. He developed algorithms that revealed a precise thirty-four-day cycle in Abigail's mood swings. He had suspected an underlying mood cycle but was astonished to find such a precisely systematic one.

Throughout the course of her illness, Abigail tried multiple antidepressants that only increased the frequency of her cycling. She had received two courses of lithium treatment at low doses. She responded to considerably higher doses of lithium, attaining blood levels at the upper limit of normal. Although by history, Abigail had failed to respond to lithium, she had a complete response when the dose was changed to produce truly adequate lithium levels.

Tom and I often discussed science together and our reasons for choosing the areas of science that we pursued. He spent several years attempting to make sense of the periodicity of patients who attributed their switches into or out of depression or mania to concurrent environmental events. (It is natural that patients would look for events that caused their mood to change, rather than thinking they might be subject to mood cycles of apparently indeterminate periodicity). One evening Tom and I were conducting a procedure together at night and had an hour's lull before the next intervention. I asked Tom what had gotten him interested in studying time, especially as it related to the dynamics and periodicity of rapid cycling bipolar disorder.

He relayed to me something along these lines:

> I think it was my father's unexpected death in a car
> accident when I was thirteen. At that moment time
> seemed to consist of two epochs. After his death, my
> carefree childhood came to an abrupt end. A radi-
> cal change occurred that I didn't choose, but rather
> happened to me. I entered another state consumed
> with a sense that I had lost my world. I dimly had
> the feeling that I was not a child anymore. Without
> thinking, I took on the role of trying to be supportive
> to my mother. I had the fantasy that I could bring my
> father back to life. That was, of course, impossible.
>
> Soon thereafter, I became obsessed about the
> past. I had an intense fascination with archeology,
> the digging up of the past and giving it new life. I
> didn't understand at the time that this preoccupation
> with archeology was a derivative of my lost child-
> hood and the fantasy of bringing my father back to
> life. At Yale, I loved my history courses. When I was
> a medical student, I thought that helping someone
> through a severe depression was like bringing them
> back to life and chose psychiatry.
>
> I got interested in rapid cycles because, unlike my
> father's death, they were predictable once you iden-
> tified the cycle length. The switch from depression
> to mania was like the switch I felt when my father
> died, and, like my patients, I became a new self. As
> a scientist, I could study the patient a week before
> she was going to switch and find out and define what
> happened premonitorily before the expected drastic
> change in mood state. Then I felt driven to figure out
> the timing of the switches and what biological mech-
> anisms were responsible for it.

Ultimately, after thirty-five years, I was able to assemble all of my accumulated data, learn astronomy, and link the switches in many rapidly cycling patients to the lunar cycle. Using the same novel methodology, I was able to link the menstrual cycle to the lunar cycle. One of the things that it required was studying individual patients daily for months or years. That way I could figure out the dynamics of their individual cycles. If you lumped twenty patients together, their individual linkages to lunar cycles would differ, and the data would be a smudge of different periodicities that would wash out any pattern. The NIH was probably the only place in the world where I could conduct these studies and pursue my passionate interest in time and expectability.

Tom has been fascinated by mood cycles and collected daily mood ratings from hundreds of patents for more than 3 years. He had daily mood ratings from hundreds of patients. In a select group of twenty-four patients who had regular mood cycles ranging from 2 months to 6 months, he had daily ratings spanning 2 to 4 years, or 600 to 1,200 data points per patient. He analyzed the cyclicity in each of the twenty-four patients separately. Extraordinarily, he found that each patient had his or her mood cycle that was strictly locked in to either the new moon or the full moon. In eight individuals, he found that the patient's cycle alternated between being locked into the new moon and switching to the full moon. These were the first data recorded in humans showing a lunar influence on a physiological parameter.

These were revolutionary findings and showed that we were tied to extraterrestrial forces. He could not now identify the organizing factor that supported this linkage, but several possibilities exist. One is cryptochrome, which is found in the master circadian clock in the hypothalamus. Cryptochrome is sensitive to electromagnetic waves and is utilized by birds in reaching desired locations. Another is polarized light. During the various phases of the moon, either polarized or unpolarized light is produced. During the full moon and the new moon, the polarized light is at a unique phase. Gravity is also a possible factor as well. Understanding what force is responsible for locking regular mood cycles on to specific phases of the moon could provide a powerful tool for abolishing manic-depressive cycles.

Tom and his colleagues also found that young women under the age of thirty-six had menstrual cycles which were also locked on to the new moon or the full moon. Individuals have been trying for decades to make this connection but failed. The reason for this failure is that they had only one data point per patient, and when they analyzed a group of, say, forty patients, the data would wash out and be all over the place. By analyzing each patient separately, they generated hundreds of data points over six months, and the signal could emerge.

Seasonal Affective Disorder

Tom along with Dr. Norm Rosenthal also first described seasonal affective disorder at the NIH in the early 1980s. One of their patients was Alfred Jones, a sixty-three-year old who had been followed at the NIH for two years with bipolar disorder. When depressed, he was highly self-disparaging, withdrawn, anxious, and incapable of experiencing pleasure. He slept and ate a great deal and felt slightly better in the morning. When manic, he was energetic, outgoing, required less sleep, and had racing thoughts. His mood swings began when he was thirty-five years old, and he became aware of a seasonal pattern eleven years later. He was diagnosed with bipolar disorder at the age of forty-nine. All efforts to treat him with antidepressants and lithium had failed.

Remarkably, after his diagnosis, he had kept a daily diary for fourteen years, documenting the onsets and offsets of every one of his depressions and manias. His depressions usually began in December or January and lasted for about three months. He usually became manic in June or July.

Shortly after his admission in the first week of December 1980, when dawn was at seven a.m. and dusk was at five p.m., Alfred was well into a depressive episode and was not due to switch out of it for at least fourteen weeks. Norm and Tom decided to treat him with bright artificial light between his time of awakening at five until nine a.m. Their rationale was that the short days were responsible for depression, and that if they could artificially change the photoperiod to one resembling that in spring, they would be able to effectively treat his depression. After four days, he switched out of depression into a remitted state. His activity levels doubled. On the last night of the study, he was awakened at two a.m. and exposed to bright light for two hours at the same intensity as his five-to-nine a.m. light treatment. They wanted to see if this intensity of light was capable of suppressing melatonin regardless of timing, meaning that the light itself was physiologically relevant. Blood samples drawn at two and four a.m. revealed that indeed it was, as they noticed a pronounced light-induced drop in plasma melatonin levels.

Another patient, Jan Smith, came to the NIH Clinical Center after a history of depressions that had invariably occurred every winter in November for the previous seven years. They would always remit by late March or early April. Her winter depressions had all the hallmarks of an atypical depression.

Jan was involved in the first double-blind placebo study of light therapy in patients with seasonal affective disorder conducted by Norm Rosenthal and Tom Wehr at the NIH. The placebo consisted of exposure to a light intensity just below the threshold for inhibiting melatonin secretion, while the "real" treatment occurred at levels high enough to affect melatonin levels. They recruited twenty-nine patients for studies of winter seasonal depression in the fall and winter of 1984. Typical of seasonal affective disorder, almost all experienced an increased appetite and a craving for sweets. Few enjoyed eating but felt a pressure to eat, a craving for food, describing it as a compulsion they could not resist. For almost all patients, symptoms of depression and fatigue were less severe in the morning than in the evening. Ninety-seven percent reported difficulties at work during their depressions, and all experienced interpersonal difficulties. Despite work difficulties, patients were able to keep their jobs, though some took sick leave when they felt particularly cognitively impaired and unmotivated.

Twenty-three patients had traveled north or south during the winter. Of these, more than 80 percent reported a change in mood. Those who traveled south to sunnier climes experienced improvement, with one patient becoming hypomanic. Three subjects felt worse upon traveling north, where daylight was shorter. From a clinical distance, we suspected this had to do with the amount of sunlight exposure patients received, which is obviously related to the length of the day.

Several patients themselves related their seasonal depression to day length or the quality of environmental light. Some recognized a light hunger during the dark months. One woman had been nicknamed "Lights" by her family because of her turning on all the lights in the house after she entered. Another patient went to the beach in Florida as often as she could, and when she was back home, she dreamed of sunbathing. Some termed their illness "the gray syndrome" and reported a lowering of mood after three or four cloudy days. It is noteworthy that 70 percent of the patients reported a history of major depression in at least one first degree relative. There was a family history of seasonal depression in only five cases.

As the winter approached, eighteen patients noted the gradual onset of mood disturbances with changes in appetite and sleep that preceded the mood changes.

Almost all patients experienced significant antidepressant responses to light therapy at a brightness level known to suppress melatonin secretion. They did not respond to light of a slightly lower intensity that did not suppress the levels of melatonin. In almost all cases, remission in response to the proper intensity of light occurred between the third and seventh days after light treatment began. After the lights were removed, relapse occurred in all but one patient. When bright lights were started again, their remissions resumed.

Norm and Tom next studied around-the-clock melatonin secretion in patients with seasonal affective disorder compared to healthy controls. They theorized that patients with seasonal affective disorder were relatively insensitive to ambient indoor light, and thus needed an extra dose of bright light in order to remit.

For most of their evolutionary history, humans lived according to the naturalistic day-night cycles of the seasons. Electricity changed all of this almost overnight. We now know that artificial light can influence melatonin secretion and biological rhythms. The implications of this artificial imposition on the natural order are not completely understood. Scientists have suggested that a form of inflammation occurs in the context of our exposure to stimuli that we did not encounter during our early evolution, and for which we are not biologically prepared. Patients with depressive illness have increased inflammatory phenomena that may be related to artificial light or other factors such as inactivity, overeating, overreliance on processed foods, and frequent exposure to chemicals that we now encounter in large quantities in our daily lives. Whether or not patients with depressive illness have not adapted to these stimuli has not been determined.

The extent to which abnormalities in the master clock or other mediators of circadian phenomena play a primary role in depressive illness is something we are still working toward understanding. The fact that depression is such an all-encompassing illness affecting many parts of the brain and multiple systems in the body suggests that such a fundamental abnormality might well be linked to the underlying cause. An alternative explanation is that depression arises due to dysregulations of the stress response. The rise in cortisol levels, temperature, and the increase in REM sleep are adaptive changes that occur during threatening situations. Given the fact that the rhythms of temperature and cortisol that start to rise at six a.m. are arousal producing and prepare us for awakening, their occurring at two to three a.m. in depressed patients falls in line with the idea that melancholic depression is a disorder of arousal, whose markers surface earlier in the evening than in those who are not depressed

Transcranial Photobiomodulation

In addition to patients' responsiveness to artificial light above a specific threshold of intensity, another kind of light has also been shown to exert antidepressant effects. Transcranial photo-biomodulation uses low-energy lasers to transmit near-infrared light through the skull into specific sites playing important roles in depressive illness. An emergent technique to promote healing in various parts of the body, photobiomodulation is believed to work by stimulating activity in mitochondria, thus boosting cellular energy production. In a trial involving fifty treatment-resistant patients, 62 percent responded, compared to an 8 percent placebo response. Patients with depressive illness, especially those with bipolar disorder, have a defect in mitochondrial energy production that leaves their neurons undernourished and subject to early deaths. Mitochondria are the enrgy producing component of cells, exist enclosed in sacs, and possess over thirty genes, several of which are easily mutated.

Circadian CLOCK Genes and Depression

Scientists have identified twelve circadian locomotor output cycles kaput (CLOCK) genes in the master clock cells of the hypothalamus. We have further discovered that every cell in the body has CLOCK genes that regulate some components of how cells behave in ways that are sensitive to day-night cycles and seasonal fluctuations. In patients with major depression, the expressions of CLOCK genes in the brain were significantly dysregulated. Some of the most significant changes were seen in CLOCK genes located in the controller region of the brain as well as the amygdala, the emotional memory center, and the pleasure and reward center.

The incidence of depression increases when circadian genes are dysregulated. The level of depression correlates with the level of desynchronization. As patients improve, abnormal circadian gene expression often normalizes. Recent research is providing detailed clues as to the mechanisms involved in phase shifting and resetting circadian rhythms. The identification of small molecules that modulate and rapidly reset cellular rhythms has motivated the evaluation of synthetic small molecules. These compounds allow more precise control of the circadian machinery and alter clock gene proteins. Effectively deploying small molecules to correct CLOCK genes would be a major breakthrough and one that seems to be on the horizon.

These discoveries are promising leads for the development of compounds to treat mood disorders and reset abnormal CLOCK gene machinery in order to normalize circadian rhythms and rapidly treat depression. Where standard antidepressants can renormalize these clock rhythms after a latency period of approximately two to three weeks, preliminary studies suggest that newly developed rapid-acting antidepressants can take effect within hours. This is an exciting breakthrough that could bring relief to many. In the meantime, regular sleep, access to sunlight, or light exposure at 10,000 lux or more (a bright sunny day is 50,000 lux) for at least thirty minutes a day is a good way to aid or help reestablish healthy circadian rhythms.

CHAPTER 8

Hormones and Depression

Hormones and depression are tightly linked. Many diseases associated with significant changes in hormone levels are linked to depression—and in these cases, depression resolves when the hormone abnormalities are corrected. Our ability to manipulate the release of brain hormones like CRH for use in the treatment of depression is currently in development, and this is a promising new area of treatment. Recently, neurosteroids—compounds that involve adrenal or ovarian structures but are made entirely by the brain—have also been successfully used to treat depression in lab settings, and a whole series of these substances is about to be tested for safety, efficacy, and speed.

In the meantime, we know that the brain synthesizes and releases hormones in a variety of situations, including in response to stress, and some of these hormones clearly play a role in depressive illness.

Hormones are compounds produced by a specific gland or site in the brain or body that circulate to distant sites which have receptors to recognize them. The location of these receptors allows hormones to orchestrate complex, interrelated patterns of behavior and physiology. A disruption of stress hormone secretion is associated with the stress response that runs awry to produce depression.

The effects of hormones depend on the sites that have receptors to respond to them. For instance, testosterone binds to receptors in the brain, muscle, larynx, skin, and testes. These binding sites constitute the physiological context for the role of testosterone in aggressive behavior, increased muscle mass and strength, a deep voice, prominent facial and body hair, and intact erectile function in men. Thyroid hormones bind extensively in the brain, skin, heart, muscle, and hair follicles. Thyroid hormone deficiency is thus associated with depression, dry skin, slowed heart rate, decreased muscle mass, and loss of hair. Levels of certain hormones in the bloodstream influence behavior and physlogy, and have the potential to cause the premature onset of systemic illnesses such as coronary artery disease, stroke, type II diabetes, and osteoporosis.

As noted, individuals with endocrine diseases are also often depressed—and then experience a remission of depression with correction of their endocrine disturbance. This is true of thyroid hormone deficiency. Cushing's disease, associated with very high levels of cortisol, is also often associated with a depression that resolves with the resolution of hypercortisolism.

The relationship between depressive illness and hormonal function in the brain and body fascinated me, and I spent my first two years at the NIH studying their interactions. My initial interest in endocrinology didn't come about because of any link to psychiatry, though. My initial contact with the endocrine group came about because of unexplained infertility with which my wife, Carol, and I had struggled for several years.

Both of us had gone through extensive workups to no avail. I decided to learn as much about reproductive endocrinology as I could. I began to go on rounds with the reproductive endocrinology group at the NIH three times a week. Lynn Loriaux, the head of the overall laboratory, was very supportive and welcomed me to the rounds.

Hormones and Depression

Female endocrinology is so complex that subtle deficits in their reproductive hormonal balance may not be picked up by ordinary tests. Carol agreed to participate in many rigorous studies, including my drawing of her blood for seventy-two consecutive days to search for subtle changes in reproductive hormone patterns that could impair fertility. Her patterns were entirely normal. Nevertheless, she forgave me for testing not only her blood but also her endurance.

Carol was diagnosed with a mild case of endometriosis, often associated with deposition of uterine tissue outside the uterus, especially in the fallopian tubes. Patients with endometriosis have a hard time getting pregnant because uterine tissue blocking the fallopian tubes obstructs sperm from reaching the ovaries. An earlier surgery revealed that Carol did not have any obstructing endometrial lesions, and only a few small scattered areas of endometrial tissue otside of the uterus. Neverthess, Carol agreed to have surgery to see ifr emoving these small patches would help resolve our infertility. Two months after the surgery, Carol became pregnant and gave birth to a healthy daughter nine months later. I measured her blood to see if she had hormone levels compatible with pregnancy, and she did. I came home from work with flowers and announced, "Carol, you're pregnant."

I was extremely impressed by the endocrine group and became fascinated by their work. I asked my boss, Fred Goodwin, for permission to take a three-year sabbatical in endocrinology. It proved to be one of the best and most important decisions of my career.

Fred was an excellent scientific and clinical mentor and one of the leading psychopharmacologists in America, instrumental in pioneering lithium treatment for bipolar illness and showing that lithium was an effective antidepressant. He spearheaded trials of the first SSRI in America several years before Prozac, and made significant contributions to the application of anticonvulsants in the treatment of refractory bipolar disorder. He also introduced biological rhythm research into depression research at the Clinical Center. Many of his trainees went on to establish distinguished labs and to run many of the leading departments of psychiatry in the United States. Fred himself went on to become the National Director of the NIMH itself.

On the endocrinology team, Lynn Loriaux and I developed a cordial relationship that grew into a long-term friendship. He was pleased to have someone in neurobiology as part of his group, as he was very interested in the brain and its role in orchestrating endocrine function throughout the body. We both compiled a list of psychiatric diseases that could reflect central nervous system hormonal alterations that included depression, anorexia nervosa, obsessive-compulsive disorder, and generalized anxiety disorder. Moreover, as noted, endocrine diseases such as hypothyroidism, Cushing's disease, and cortisol deficiency are associated with major depressive episodes. These diseases provided proof that depression was not all in one's head but was, rather, a disorder precipitated by known biological factors.

Around this time Wylie Vale at the Salk Institute isolated CRH, the key brain hormone that orchestrated many of the behavioral and biological components of the stress response. CRH is highly arousing and, as I noted, produces anxiety, fear-related behaviors, highly focused attention on anxiety-producing stimuli, inflammation (a key feature of depression), secretion of the stress hormones cortisol and norepinephrine, and inhibition of sleep, eating, and sexual behavior. All of these are characteristic of melancholic depression.

Wylie asked Lynn Loriaux to initiate studies regarding the regulation and roles of CRH in human health and disease. I was co-leader of -a small team asked to spearhead the studies. Over thirty years, my colleague George Chrousos and I developed a very close relationship and became more like brothers than collaborators. George is one of the most brilliant individuals I have ever met, and has multiple sophisticated intellectual interests he has cultivated over the years. In addition, his scientific knowledge is prodigious, especially concerning how complex processes become dysregulated in disease.

We introduced CRH to clinical medicine, developed the means to show that CRH regulated the secretion of the stress hormone cortisol in humans, and developed pioneering diagnostic tests to uncover the mechanisms of multiple diseases associated with CRH dysregulation. Many of the tests we designed remain central in depression and endocrine clinical care today. As an example, we developed a diagnostic test to identify depression associated with high cortisol levels from the hypercortisolism of Cushing's disease that caused a small, often hard-to-detect pituitary tumor. Prior to that, it was often necessary to do pituitary surgery to document Cushing's disease. George and I had to rotate on alternate nights for months to conduct studies that produced this diagnostic test.

In the midst of this intense period, while my wife and children went to visit her parents for a long weekend, I stayed home to finish a paper that I had promised to send out in the three days. On the last day, I stayed up all night to finish the paper. Suddenly I had the insight that depression reflected a stress response run awry. I was electrified by this idea, but also felt chilled, as if I were developing a flu-like syndrome. I discovered that the heat had gone off and the temperature in the house had fallen to the high forties. I was too absorbed in my work to check on that possibility.

About a year later, I first showed that CRH is oversecreted in melancholic depression. CRH contributes to multiple behavioral and biological manifestation of melancholia, including anxiety, fear-related behaviors, high cortisol and norepinephrine levels, inflammation, and decreases in sleep, appetite, and sexual function. CRH is also involved in stress-related or weight-loss-related cessation of menses. In addition, my colleagues and I showed that very high CRH levels could destroy brain cells. This finding was the first of several lines of data indicating that depression represented a stress response that had gone awry.

My work on the endocrinology team also included collaboration with the world-famous medicinal chemist Kenner Rice, who developed the first synthetic opiate, codeine. Kenner was born in Tidewater, Virginia, not far from where I was raised, and though we didn't know one another at the time, we had many shared memories of our experiences there. Together with George, we synthesized an important new agent we called antalarmin, which blocks the effects of CRH in the brain and in the body and might be useful for a variety of psychiatric disorders other than depression, including anorexia nervosa, anxiety disorders, and obsessive-compulsive disorder. We shared our findings on antalarmin freely with the scientific community. Today, more than 280 studies have been conducted with antalarmin to show the critical roles of CRH in multiple forms of stress, anxiety, and animal models of depression. The first trials of using CRH antagonists by others to treat depression failed, but they were poorly designed. We are now in the process of a large study exploring the role of CRH in depression with a protocol that has been meticulously designed to avoid the shortcomings of other studies.

Another important substance implicated in depression is cortisol, which we commonly think of as a stress hormone. Cortisol and its interactions with the amino acid glutamate are related to how the brain responds when dealing with repeated stress exposure. High cortisol levels produce arousal, raise blood sugar, incite activity in the sympathetic nervous system, increase the strength of heart contractions, and at high levels can destroy brain cells.

Mineralocorticoids are first cousins of cortisol and are produced in both the adrenal glands and the brain. Two studies have found that the mineralocorticoid fludrocortisone was found to enhance the efficacy of antidepressants and to improve memory and executive functions in young depressed patients.

Let's take a closer look at some of the hormones most linked with the biology of depression.

Hormones and Depression

Insulin in the Bloodstream and the Brain

One especially important hormone is insulin: As any diabetic knows, an imbalance can kill us. Little or no insulin is made in the brain even though insulin has many effects on it. Instead, insulin found in the brain is produced in the body and transported into the brain. Elevated cortisol levels inhibit insulin uptake into the brain.

Insulin receptor signaling correlates with the density of synapses, insulin receptors maintain synaptic density, and synapse density decreases when insulin receptors are removed or damaged. Insulin has been shown to play a key role in neuroplasticity in the emotional memory center and elsewhere.

Many lines of indirect data indicate that insulin signaling in the brain is decreased in depressed patients with increased blood cortisol and/or blood insulin concentrations. Insulin can be administered intranasally to test this hypothesis.

Estrogen and Progesterone

Estrogen levels are often decreased in depressed melancholic women. Some of the synaptic dysfunction associated with depressive illness in women is likely to be caused by reduced circulating estrogen levels. In contrast, activating estrogen receptors increases nerve fiber size and branching and is connected to improved performance in tasks handled by the emotional memory center. Estrogen increases the responsiveness of the pleasure and reward center, while stress decreases the biological effects of estrogen. Estrogen has also been shown to prevent neurodegeneration, reduce the inflammatory response of brain immune cells, reduce anxiety and depression, and promote cognition; it also modulates the plasticity of synapses in the emotional memory center of animals in studies.

CRH, along with the high cortisol levels it produces, inhibits estrogen. Depressed women often stop menstruating, an issue that usually resolves after recovery from depression.

Neurosteroids are compounds produced entirely by the brain but that are identical to many steroids produced in the adrenal glands. One neurosteroid, allopregnanolone, has emerged as the most potent therapeutic agent in the treatment of postpartum depression. Allopregnanolone is structurally similar to progesterone and exerts progesterone-like effects. Since many feel that postpartum depression is often associated with a substantial drop in progesterone after the baby is born, allopregnanolone makes logical sense in the treatment of postpartum depression.

Androgens

Androgens are a group of hormones that regulate the onset of puberty in males, contribute to growth and reproductive function, effect secondary sexual characteristics such as hair growth and muscular development, and have multiple effects on brain and behavior. Androgen receptors are widely distributed in the brain, but high concentrations of androgen receptors are especially found in the amygdala, the pleasure and reward center, and the prefrontal cortex, including the controller.

Testosterone's association with aggression reflects, in part, its effects on reducing the connectivity between the amygdala and a component of the prefrontal cortex that is part of the apparatus involved in impulse control, and in effective self-regulation.

Androgens have profound effects on the structure and function of the emotional memory center. Androgen deficiency in males is associated with its decreased size, while androgen administration increases neuroplasticity, in part, by stimulating BDNF.

High doses of testosterone, above the normal range, can treat depressive symptomatology in men, but these doses are too high to be administered safely for long periods.

Androgens also activate dopamine neurons in the pleasure and reward center in ways that could potentially lead to maladaptive, excessive searching for rewards, such as we see in mania.

Thyroid

Thyroid hormone binds to multiple sites in the brain, skin, hair, larynx, muscle, and heart and plays a large role in determining metabolic rate. There is a long history of findings that show how thyroid activity and regulation are involved in depression and can help in its treatment. Thyroid hormone is essential to the growth and health of neurons in the emotional memory center. In addition, thyroid hormone synergizes with serotonin in the brain.

A great deal has been learned about thyroid hormone effects on the brain from patients with hypothyroidism. Adult hypothyroid patients have an increase in cortisol receptors in the amygdala, associated with fear memory enhancement and deficits in the extinction of fear memories. These abnormalities are reversed with thyroid hormone replacement. As noted, hypothyroidism is associated with shrinkage of the emotional memory center, a likely contributor to its capacity to induce depression.

Overall, signs of hypothyroidism include depression, impaired memory, dry skin, thinning hair, hoarseness, muscle weakness, slowed heart rate, and decreased metabolic rate with weight gain.

Hyperthyroidism also significantly influences mood. Symptoms can include depression, anxiety, panic attacks, sleep disturbances, and irritability. More frequently, hyperthyroidism may also precipitate mania. The emotional memory center in patients with hyperthyroidism is significantly smaller than in healthy individuals. The connectivity between the emotional memory center and the controller is also significantly reduced in hyperthyroid patients. A similar reduction in connectivity occurs in individuals with depressive illness. Those with the greatest loss of connectivity had the most severe symptoms of depression and anxiety.

Loss of connectivity between the emotional memory center and distinct areas of the prefrontal cortex cause problems with social cognition and emotional regulation. This connection is critical for decision-making and emotional processing, and a lack of connection may thus further contribute to emotional instability.

The most striking finding has been that hyperthyroidism is associated with a significant decrease in the size and neuroplasticity of the amygdala. The magnitude of the decrease in size is similar to that seen in manic states. This may be one reason that thyroid administration improves antidepressant efficacy

Peter Whybrow, a close friend and colleague of mine at the NIH who became Chief of Psychiatry at UCLA, showed that in patients with treatment-resistant bipolar disorders on antidepressants, large doses of thyroid hormone reversed the PET scan abnormalities in rapid cyclers, and patients recovered from their rapid cycling. Peter subsequently found that very high doses of thyroid hormone helped resolve bipolar depression on its own without other treatment. Hyperthyroid shrinking of the amygdala may play a part in these findings.

Peter had made significant contributions to our understanding of thyroid hormone function in depression and its use in addressing treatment-resistant depression. While treating a female patient for depression, Peter noted that she had relapsed from successful antidepressant treatment after developing hypothyroidism. She did not initially respond to her thyroid replacement doses but became confused about the dosage of thyroid hormone she'd been taking. She took an excessive amount of her thyroid medication, which completely resolved her depression.

Peter and his colleague, Arthur Prange, began to add a dose of thyroid hormone to partial responders to antidepressants even if they had normal thyroid function. A remarkable number of partial responders to antidepressants achieved full remission.

I hoped this approach could help my patient Betty Smith. Betty came to the NIH in 1986 suffering from melancholic depression.

Her depression had begun two years earlier, after she'd broken up with her fiancé of four months. She had previously been engaged four years earlier, but that relationship came to an end as well. She was now forty.

Twenty-five years earlier, Betty had lost her father, who had been the one consistently supportive person in her life. After his death, she'd developed her first experience of severe melancholic depression. Overall, she felt completely bereft of confidence. This loss of confidence was complicated by the fact that she was unemployed most of the time during her depression.

Betty was also extremely inhibited from expressing her anger or distress during any conflict. Growing up, her sister had been loud and assertive. She'd yelled at Betty a great deal, was often unreasonable, and refused to hear her side of any story. Betty felt intimidated and overwhelmed by her. Her mother almost always sided with her sister and was not nearly as affectionate and supportive as her father had been.

When Betty arrived at the NIH, she was overcome with a preoccupation over the possibility of suicide. Betty seemed sufficiently suicidal when she arrived on our unit that she was placed on one-to-one continuous nursing coverage. I met with Betty in psychotherapy three times a week. I got to know her well and built a solid relationship with her.

She was very quiet, almost mute at times. She found her life unbearable. She participated in several protocols, including multiple neuroimaging studies, molecular genetic testing, around-the-clock hormonal sampling, levels of neurotransmitters and CRH in spinal fluid, and multiple metabolic and immune function studies.

The team decided to use Prozac, and Betty showed a partial response to the midrange dosage of Prozac. She felt worse at the highest dosage. The level was dropped back to the midranges, and Betty entered our protocol with the addition of moderate-dose thyroid hormone.

Given that other treatments of Betty's illness had not been successful, she was loathe to try yet another regimen and have yet another disappointment. Yet she agreed.

After five days of this thyroid hormone dose, Betty responded. And very well.

Betty still felt preoccupied by the unresolved issues in her life, but she was not hopeless or suicidal. She could begin to anticipate doing some of the things that brought her pleasure, such as going to classical music concerts. She began to reconnect with friends. Her sleep and appetite returned to normal.

Betty appreciated our psychotherapy and was eager to continue after she left the hospital. We referred her to one of our former colleagues in private practice, a particularly good psychotherapist who could certainly help Betty decode the principal conflicts of her life to reduce the likelihood of a recurrence of her depression.

Major depression and bipolar disorder are both associated with hormonal changes in the brain and throughout the body. Clearly the use of hormones was hugely effective in Betty's treatment. What other hormones might be used in therapy to induce a positive behavioral response? Exploring this question is one of the most exciting frontiers in biological psychiatry today. Major depression and bipolar disorder are likely to represent the most complex and pervasive polyendocrine disorders in clinical medicine. As we understand more about the role that hormones play in depression, we can develop new hormone-based treatments that could play key roles in treating major depression and bipolar disorder.

CHAPTER 9

Depression's True Toll

Changes in the secretion of hormones during depression, associated changes in the sympathetic nervous system, and inflammation produce a myriad of long-term medical consequences. Solving the puzzle of depression isn't just a matter of fascinating scientific inquiry. The medical community needs to wake up to the true and devastating cost of depression. I don't mean the cost of medical care and treatment, though that too is far from trivial. What I am referring to is the toll on an individual's overall health. People who have major depression or bipolar disorder are known to be more vulnerable to serious illnesses, including premature coronary artery disease, diabetes, stroke, and osteoporosis. We now know that people with major depression lose an average of seven years of life; those with bipolar disorder have a life expectancy reduced by ten years or more. This loss of life is independent of smoking, hypertension, obesity, and suicide.

Women are almost twice as likely to suffer from major depression compared to men. In the Third National Health and Nutrition Examination Survey, which studied more than fifteen thousand individuals between 1988 and 1994, women with depression who attempted suicide had a fifteenfold increased risk of coronary artery disease. Young women who had heart attacks before the age of forty were six times more likely to have suffered prior depression.

When you consider that depressive illness affects 15 to 20 percent of the population and that the World Health Organization ranks depression as the second greatest cause of disability among all diseases, depressive illness represents a public health emergency.

Coronary Artery Disease

Sir William Harvey observed over 350 years ago that negative emotions adversely affect the heart, but scant scientific evidence was available to support this claim until the 1930s. Then two longitudinal studies of psychiatric patients discovered that depression was indeed a risk factor for early death, especially related to coronary disease. Even so, physicians didn't seem to dig into understanding these observations until the late 1980s, when interest in the role of depression in coronary artery disease rose sharply after the publication of articles showing that depression increased the risk of heart disease significantly in individuals with depressive illness independent of hypertension, smoking, obesity, or other risk factors for poor health.

An overview of studies that included 106,628 subjects found that the presence of depressive illness produced an 80 percent increase in the rate of coronary artery disease. Cardiac and all-cause mortality more than doubled for those who had depression compared to those who didn't. Some studies have found that depressed subjects with prominent physiological symptoms such as disturbances in sleep and appetite have a greater risk for coronary disease than those in whom symptoms are prominently mood and cognition related.

Depressed patients have many risk factors that are known to predispose a person to coronary artery disease. Foremost among these is inflammation, a common symptom of depression and a major risk factor for coronary disease. The inflammatory process significantly contributes to the growth of arterial plaque that narrows arteries.

We have shown that depressed patients have multiple indicators that point to increased coagulation and decreased clot clearing, clear risk factors for coronary artery disease and stroke. Other studies have shown that depressed patients have significant increases in platelet adhesion.

We and others have found that individuals with depression also have significantly increased levels of plasma cortisol level around the clock, increasing inflammation, blood pressure and heart rate, and cellular oxygen consumption. Cortisol increases arterial and cardiac responses to norepinephrine and also causes insulin resistance, another risk factor for coronary artery disease found in depressed subjects.

Decreased sleep increases the risk of heart attacks. One of the hallmarks of melancholic depression is insomnia, most often early-morning awakening. Low blood testosterone levels in men is a possible risk factor for coronary disease, and men with depressive illness have decreased testosterone levels. Similarly, low blood vitamin D levels are a risk factor for coronary disease, and vitamin D levels are deficient in depressed individuals.

Given these risk factors, it is not at all surprising that patients with depressive illness have such a marked increase in the rate of coronary artery disease, heart attacks, death from heart attacks, and all-cause mortality. The risk of coronary artery disease and coronary events in patient with depressive illness is equivalent to that caused by untreated hypertension, but few physicians meticulously screen for the presence of hidden heart disease in depressed patients.

Type II Diabetes

In looking at a very broad study sample, depressed people had a 41 percent increase for developing type II diabetes. A more recent study of 6,916 subjects showed an even greater rate, with an increased incidence of 60 percent in patients with depression.

Patients with depression have multiple risk factors for type II diabetes. Again, inflammation is an important factor. Inflammatory-producing compounds such as cytokines significantly reduce the response of the insulin receptor to insulin, resulting in insulin resistance and significant increases in blood glucose concentrations.

Significant increases in total body fat heighten the incidence of type II diabetes. We found that compared to healthy women matched for age and body mass index, depressed women have significant increases in total body fat and significant decreases in lean body mass. Hormonal abnormalities such as high cortisol levels contribute to these changes.

Stroke

The increased incidence of stroke among the individuals in a large study excluding individuals with frank hypertension, diabetes, and those who smoked still found that the risk of stroke was 30 percent higher in people who suffered from depression compared to those who didn't.

Another study accumulated data from 16,178 participants fifty years and older and who had been interviewed every two years between 1998 and 2010. Individuals who had frank hypertension, type II diabetes, and who smoked were again excluded. This study demonstrated that individuals with depressive illness studied at two consecutive interviews were more than twice as likely to have had a first stroke compared to people without depression at either interview. They also found that people with depression at the first interview but not the second still had a 66 percent higher stroke risk than nondepressed individuals.

We first identified increased blood coagulation in patients with depressive illness. The coagulation cascades that increase clotting in depressed patients are clear risk factors for stroke. Many depressed patients have significant elevations in plasma glucose without reaching levels that qualify for type II diabetes and increases in blood pressure without going beyond the normal range. Even such moderate elevations increase the risk for stroke. In addition, we showed that patients with depression have significant elevations in norepinephrine levels at rest and in response to mild stressors. Norepinephrine is a potent stimulus to the constriction of blood flow that would decrease the delivery of oxygen to brain cells. Norepinephrine also significantly raises brain oxygen requirements.

Inflammation is another risk factor for cerebral atherosclerosis as well as for coronary artery atherosclerosis, which significantly increases the risk for stroke.

The incidence of atrial fibrillation, a type of irregular heart rhythm, is doubled in patients with depression and is more difficult to resolve in depressed patients, especially those with treatment-resistant illness. This also contributes to an increased likelihood of stroke. Atrial fibrillation increases the burden of clots in the heart atrium and ventricle, which gets transported to the brain to block cerebral arteries.

Osteoporosis

Osteoporosis is a bone disease associated with loss of bone mass and structure that increases susceptibility to fractures. We first reported in the *New England Journal of Medicine* that even premenopausal women with depression had a significant increase in osteoporosis and loss of bone density.

Bone is constantly formed and broken down in cycles that facilitate effective bone mass and strength. As old bone is being resorbed; new bone is being formed.

We found that our patients had substantial increases in plasma cortisol levels. Cortisol greatly increases bone resorption while decreasing bone production leads to bone loss. Many patients on steroids develop osteoporosis.

We also found decreases in plasma osteocalcin, which ordinarily helps with bone production and decreases bone resorption.

The increased norepinephrine levels that we found in melancholic depression also increases the risk for osteoporosis.

Inflammation significantly contributes to osteoporosis. In classic osteoporosis, the loss of bone is greater at the spine than at the hip. In our depressed patients, the loss of bone is greater at the hip than the spine, a pattern seen when inflammation is a significant driver of the osteoporosis. Thus, inflammation is likely to be a principal driver of the loss of bone mineral density and osteoporosis of depression.

The question then arises whether depression is associated with a greater risk of fracture. A pooled analysis of fourteen scientific papers on the topic found that European patients with depression had a 70 percent increase in the risk of bone fracture. In American studies, the risk of fracture was 37 percent greater in depressed patients than in healthy subjects.

Osteoporosis in Children and Adolescents with Depressive Illness

Children and adolescents with depression have the same magnitude of increased cortisol levels and inflammation seen in adults. Thus, one would expect profound decreases in bone mineral density in children and adolescents. Adolescence is a vulnerable period for bone loss, since as much as 25 percent of adult total bone mineral content is formed in the two-year period surrounding the pubertal growth spurt. To date, there have been no formal studies of the integrity of bone mineral density in children and adolescents who have depressive illness. This is unfortunate, because meaningful medical interventions exist for the reversal of osteoporosis and could be very important to consider for childhood and adolescent depressions.

Depression is not only a mental illness, it is a polyendocrine and widespread inflammatory disease. Multiple systems are disrupted, and one result is that the body overproduces inflammatory-inducing compounds. As a result, the brain is not the only significant organ affected by depression. Most major physiological systems within the body are impacted and can result in multiple systemic diseases: coronary artery disease, stroke, diabetes, and osteoporosis. Of course, genetics, lifestyle choices, and risk factors contribute to whether one depressive patient or another will develop any one of these particular illnesses. Unfortunately, many of these illnesses are present together in the same individual.

It is sobering and imperative to look at the widespread effects of depression on the central nervous system and multiple organ systems all over the body. Depression is not a systemic disease but rather a supersystemic disease that profoundly impacts the mind and the body. It is no wonder that depression is the second greatest cause of disability worldwide. It is incomprehensible that depressive illness is not granted full insurance coverage than other, less serious systemic diseases readily receive.

The more we learn about how many of our systems are involved and implicated in depression, the more daunting it can seem to address the roots of this pernicious disease. But we are daily making new discoveries about the underlying physiology of depression and related cutting-edge treatments. In the meantime, simple changes in daily habits can help us prevent and treat the symptoms of depression. Regularizing sleep patterns, creating a bedtime-and-waking routine, getting consistent exercise (even low-impact activities like a ten-minute daily walk), practicing healthy eating, journaling, and taking time for reflection can all have an impact in staving off or alleviating the symptoms of depression.

CHAPTER 10

When Children Suffer

In some cases, sadly, depression can manifest at a very young age. Two to 3 percent of children from the ages of three to eleven develop a true depression. Depression in children is more severe than normal sadness and can significantly interfere with a child's capacity to function. We now know that three- and four-year-old children are capable of significantly more sophisticated emotional experiences than what had been previously thought and are subject to the feelings we recognize more generally in depression, such as guilt and shame. This is often accompanied by feelings of irritability, more so than that seen in adults, intense loneliness, loss of social interests, increased sensitivity to rejection, and changes in appetite and sleep. Other issues often include difficulty in concentrating, lack of interest or participation in events with friends, fatigue, boredom, and severe pessimism.

Relatively few neuroimaging studies have been performed on children suffering from depression, but studies unsurprisingly reveal findings similar to what we see in adults: a significant decrease in the size of the emotional memory center and a subtle decrement in overall brain size. Children who have a first-degree relative—parent or sibling—with major depressive illness show a controller that is reduced in size, while the size of the amygdala is increased. These changes are also similar to those seen in adults with depression, and they significantly contribute to symptoms.

Children with mild depression are usually treated with psychotherapy alone. If the depressive symptoms do not begin to improve within six to eight weeks, or if symptoms worsen, an antidepressant medication may be recommended. Children with moderate to severe depression generally require psychotherapy and one or more medications. This is called combination therapy. Treatment with combination therapy increases the likelihood of improved symptoms and relationships with family and friends; it can also improve self-confidence and the ability to cope effectively.

Unfortunately, bipolar disorder also occurs in children aged three to eleven. In children, manic states are accompanied by grandiosity, rapid speech, decreased need for sleep, and even more irritability than that seen in manic adults. Sometimes confusing matters, the severe chronic irritability, hyperarousal, and hyperreactivity that characterize pediatric bipolar disorder can also occur in ADHD. One thing that distinguishes bipolar disorder from ADHD is that mania is intermittent in bipolar disorder, alternating with depressive episodes and apparent remission. In ADHD, symptoms are continuous, without interruption.

Bipolar disorder in children can be effectively treated with lithium. Anticonvulsants can also be used, and it's generally best to avoid antidepressants, since they can precipitate mania.

Adolescent Depression and Bipolar Disorder

In 2014, an estimated two million adolescents aged twelve to seventeen in the United States had at least one major depressive episode in the past year with severe impairment. This number represented 8.2 percent of the population aged twelve to seventeen. By the end of adolescence, an astounding 20 percent will have had one serious episode during their adolescence. This serious illness is the second greatest cause of mortality in this age group.

Depression in adolescence also predicts a range of mental health disorders in adult life, including anxiety disorders, substance abuse disorders, or bipolar disorders.

There is a strong two-to-one prevalence in major depression in females compared to males after puberty. This preponderance is not due to differences in help seeking or reporting of symptoms. Although the reasons for this postpubertal difference in the incidence of depression are unknown, adolescent depression is more closely tied to female hormonal changes than to chronological age.

Genetics plays a significant role in susceptibility to adolescent depression. The risk is four times greater in patients with a first-degree relative with depressive illness. Genes are not destiny, though. The gene-environment interplay is incredibly important: A genetic predisposition may increase your sensitivity to adversity or inability to cope with it, but it also can increase the probability that you will be exposed to risky and highly stressful environments in the first place.

Depressed adolescents show changes similar to those seen in adults and include decreased size and activity of the controller, increased size changes and activity of the amygdala, decreased size of the emotional memory center, and increased size but decreased responsiveness of the reward and pleasure center. These changes are reversible after effective treatment with psychotherapy and medication.

The FDA has approved Prozac and Lexapro for the treatment of adolescent depression. Unless the clinical condition is very serious, with incapacitation or risk of self-harm, a trial of psychotherapy is recommended as the first-line treatment. In adults, we know that a combination of psychotherapy and medication is the most effective treatment strategy. Medication alone, with no psychotherapy, is not recommended. Some studies suggest that medication can increase the risk of suicide attempts in adolescents, even in the context of psychotherapy. Even so, the benefits of using drugs in serious cases of depression still far outweigh the risks.

Bipolar disorder occurs in 2 to 3 percent of adolescents, approaching the rate we see in adults, and the symptoms are also similar, including grandiosity, racing speech and thoughts, increased energy, decreased need for sleep, excessive irritability, impulsivity, and hypersexuality. The medications used to treat adolescent bipolar disorder are similar to those used to treat adults and include lithium, anticonvulsants, and selected antipsychotic drugs. Again, psychotherapy should always be an important component of therapy. Suicidality must be watched for carefully in all adolescents with bipolar disease. Given their young age, having bipolar disorder is a serious shock and will change their concept of what they have in store for the rest of their lives.

In what is perhaps the scariest statistic for any parent to consider, every year about eight children in one million die by suicide. More than four thousand adolescents kill themselves each year. These numbers are greater than all the deaths caused by accidents, wars, and homicides for this age group around the world. Warning signs and risk of suicide include anxiety, agitation, sleeping difficulties, complaining of being a bad person or rotten inside, expressing no reason for living, and feelings of being hopeless and trapped. Suicidal adolescents may also give or throw away favorite possessions, have a preoccupation with songs of death, withdraw from friends and regular activities, and neglect their personal appearance. Risk factors include biochemical, psychological, or social experiences such as being bullied, having a family history of major depression or bipolar depression and having a family history of suicide.

As a society, we have come a long way in terms of talking about suicide risk, and we need to continue building our awareness. Every parent or adult who works with young people should have a suicide prevention plan. Keep a list of doctors, professionals, and agencies, and program this information into your cell phone. If you suspect a young person might be suicidal, you should remove any substance or object that could be lethal from their reach, involve your school's support staff, and ask tough questions. If you ask someone about suicidal thoughts, this does not increase the risk of suicide. Children are often relieved to talk about it. Be prepared to act. If you cannot wait, take your child to the nearest hospital or emergency room. If your child resists, don't be afraid to call the police. Take the issue seriously, as their very lives might be at stake. These issues are not all in our minds, and we cannot solve them for others. Professional interventions are sometimes required, and thankfully, skilled clinicians, doctors, and researchers are paving the way toward treating more and more people, young people included, with increasing effectiveness.

CHAPTER 11

Bipolar Disorder

Prior to the recent emergence of spectacular new data regarding the mechanisms underlying depressive illness, we knew very little about what caused the type known as bipolar depression, and even less about bipolar mania. The limits in our understanding translated into limits in treatment. Now we can begin to offer relief to people who suffer from this peculiarly disruptive form of depression.

Thanks to new and significant breakthroughs, we now know that bipolar illness is associated with a surprisingly large number of alterations in the size and activity of key structures scattered throughout the stress system that generate manic behaviors. These include changes in prefrontal and limbic system areas contributing to manic symptomatology that compromise the elaborate apparatus for maintaining goal-appropriate response selections, counter impulsivity, and restrain the obsessive search for pleasure regardless of the cost.

New breakthroughs have also identified an area in the brain that contributes to the switches between depression and mania and back again, pathologic changes in the default mode network and its relationship to other major networks, and entirely new data on critical neurotransmitter changes that occur in mania.

Recent genetic studies have also identified key genetic mutations, including those in CLOCK genes, that contribute to the multiple disturbances in biological rhythms during both bipolar depression and mania. These include the prolonged sleeplessness in manic patients that can go on for several days. Tom Wehr has now presented data on twenty bipolar patients studied for months to years whose mood cycles are coupled to lunar rhythms. In addition, scientists have identified many epigenetic changes that are significantly influenced by lithium and anticonvulsants.

Until recently, the only known neurotransmitter abnormality in bipolar disorder was an increase in dopamine activity during mania, contributing to the preoccupation with pleasurable stimuli and experiences in bipolar individuals. Recently, abnormalities in the glutamate and GABA systems have been identified that provide the context for multiple new classes of antidepressants and antimanic agents.

Bipolar disorder is a specific type of mood disorder that is notoriously difficult to treat. Bipolar disorder affects 2 to 4 percent of the population; in contrast to major depression, which affects more women than men, it affects males and females equally. It most often first arises in sixteen- to twenty-four-year-olds but can first manifest itself at any stage of life. It is highly heritable. If one of two identical twins has the disorder, the likelihood of the other twin's having bipolar disorder is as high as 80 percent. The incidence of the illness in first-degree relatives of bipolar patients is increased tenfold. Even unaffected family members may show subtle signs and symptoms of bipolar illness in the absence of a full-blown diagnosis.

Bipolar illness is a chronic, recurrent illness characterized by three phases: a depressive phase, a manic phase, and apparent recovery. The depressions that bipolar patients experience are more often atypical than melancholic. While bipolar depressions can resemble depressive episodes in major depression, they are associated with marked mood instability over a single day that can be disturbing and disorienting. While it has not been definitively established, the repertoire of genes that are altered in bipolar disorder is likely to be significantly greater than in major depression. This may contribute to the difficulty of treatment.

Antidepressants alone are generally not recommended for treatment in bipolar depression because they can readily precipitate a switch into mania. Not long ago, clinicians found that the anticonvulsant Lamictal was somewhat effective in treating bipolar depressed patients and considered this to be an important breakthrough. Two other drugs now on the market, Latuda and Vrylar, show partial efficacy in treating bipolar depression as well. Despite these discoveries, bipolar depression is still more difficult to treat than depressions associated with major depression.

In contrast to the depression that arises in bipolar disorder, the other side of the coin, mania, consists of excessive emotional reactivity, irritability, impulsivity, the obsessive pursuit of pleasure, and difficulty in expressing appropriate emotional responses. Mania is also often associated with hypersexuality, decreased need for sleep, lack of coherence in expressing a stream of unrelated thoughts, and grandiosity. Many people in manic states also experience heightened energy, creativity, and euphoria. In a small number of individuals, mania can be associated with psychotic thinking and hallucinations, making it sometimes difficult to distinguish from schizophrenia. Mania can also coexist with depression. This is known as a mixed state and can be especially dangerous because the energy of the mania can set into motion the suicidality of the depression.

We now know that symptoms persist even in the bipolar recovery phase, especially the cognitive deficits, which can be pronounced and tend to worsen over time. Many of the other features of bipolar disorder also progress over time, including immune dysfunction, enhanced oxidative stress which destroys cells, the reduction in the availability and actions of brain-derived neuro-trophic factor (BDNF), and the loss of neurogenesis and neuro-plasticity. To get to the roots of understanding bipolar disorder and how we might best treat it, we need to examine how it affects the brain as an organ, the molecules it impacts within the brain, and the genetic mutations associated with it.

Changes in Brain Tissue Sizes and Activity in Bipolar Disorder

Bipolar disorder is associated with loss of tissue in multiple areas in the brain. These neurodegenerative changes lead to altered brain function, and this finding gives credence to the discovery that depressive illnesses are neurodegenerative diseases. Many of these findingsrepresent exciting new breakthroughs.

Depressed bipolar patients have shrinkages in the controller part of the prefrontal cortex, greater than those in patients with major depression. Because the controller normally restrains the amygdala, the amygdala is enlarged and hyperactive in people experiencing of bipolar depression. The decrease in the activity of the pleasure and reward center in bipolar depression is also greater than in major depression, so the anhedonia of bipolar dis-order is generally more severe. There is a significant loss of vol-ume and tissue in the emotional memory center.

In mania, the controller increases in size and activity. Since the controller restrains the amygdala, its increased size results in an inhibition of amygdala effects. This results in a decrease in amygdala-mediated fear that ordinarily contributes to the restraint of inappropriate behavior. The increased size and activity of the controller also leads to an increase in the activity of the pleasure and reward center, contributing to bipolar patients' incessant search for and excessive responses to pleasurable stimuli.

Manic patients' prefrontal cortex structures, which support emotional regulation and inhibitory control, are often smaller and less active in ways not found in those of people with major depression. One important area in the prefrontal cortex is located just behind the eyes. This site is important in making decisions when comparing the relative value of several options, and its decreased activity contributes to reckless decisions that are not in the best interest of the manic person.

Another component of the prefrontal cortex near the controller exerts cognitive control of thought over emotion, and its size and activity are significantly reduced in mania. This area also provides regulatory feedback to the amygdala, and its decrease in size and activity result in decreased amygdala-mediated controls on inappropriate behavior, especially impulsivity. The shrinking of this region is exacerbated by a 30 percent reduction in the cells that make the coating for nerve fibers in this structure. This further compromises its function since nerve conduction in these fibers is impaired: In other words, a message to be more measured in one's actions is just not getting through.

Another area of the prefrontal cortex that shrinks in manic patients is one related to response inhibition and goal-appropriate response selection. The magnitude of the reduced activity of this site directly correlates with the duration of the last manic episode. In rapid-cycling bipolar patients, cellular density in this particular area of the prefrontal cortex is more profoundly diminished than it is in other mood states. It's no wonder then that rapid-cycling bipolar depression is extremely difficult to treat.

Taken together, these deficits contribute to the irritability, recklessness, and excessive indulgence of the drive for pleasure; difficulty in showing appropriate emotional responses; irritability; incoherent flow of speech; and impairments in cognitive and attentional processes that are the hallmarks of a bipolar person. These features impair the functional capacity of bipolar manic persons, often profoundly.

Preliminary data suggest that deficits in the prefrontal cortex represent different clinical states based on their presence in the right or left side. Marked underactivity of the structure just behind the eyeballs in the right prefrontal cortex occurs only during mania. In contrast, underactivity of the structure just behind the eyeballs in the left prefrontal cortex occurs only during depression.

Another area of the brain involved in bipolar disorder is the insula, a structure that has many functions related to networks in the brain. One of these networks is the default mode network, which focuses on matters such as assessment of self-worth. Another is the salience network, whose function is to identify the most relevant among multiple internal and external stimuli. A third is the central executive network, which helps us manipulate information and make decisions. Under ordinary circumstances, these networks work together so that, for the most part, none of them is unduly influential. But during depression, the default mode network, which focuses negatively on issues like self-esteem, dominates significantly over the salience and central executive networks. On the other hand, recent studies convincingly demonstrate that during mania, the salience network is highly predominant and suppresses the others.

During the switch from depression to mania, there is an insula-mediated transition from the default mode network to the salience-mode network. Attention shifts markedly from an exclusive focus on the self to an exclusive focus on the outside world. This is an extremely important event in the natural history of bipolar illness, and determining the mediators that promote this shift is one of the most significant goals of bipolar illness research.

Neurotransmitters Most Implicated in Bipolar Disorder

As noted earlier, glutamate is by far the most plentiful neurotransmitter in the central nervous system, mediating neurotransmission of 50 percent of the neurons in brain. Glutamate plays a major role in almost all the components of the prefrontal cortex that are dysfunctional in bipolar illness. During severe chronic stress or trauma, the glutamate system is activated excessively, causing nerves to fire so rapidly that they deplete their energy supply and die. This leaves the remaining neurons somewhat depleted of glutamate. As I shall note later, rapid-acting antidepressants such as ketamine cause a modest release of glutamate in the controller and the emotional memory center, which sets in motion a cascade that effectively counters the depressed state.

GABA is another neurotransmitter that plays an active role in bipolar illness. GABA is the second most plentiful neurotransmitter in the brain, present in approximately 20 percent of neurons in the central nervous system (CNS). In contrast to glutamate, which is a potent excitatory force in the CNS, GABA is inhibitory. Pharmacological stimuli of the GABA system reduce both anxiety and arousal, and can be sedating. The GABA system is insufficiently active in bipolar disease, increasing arousal and anxiety substantially. In addition, because GABA restrains dopamine neurotransmission, dopamine activity goes up significantly in mania. This dopamine excess contributes to the hyperactivity of the pleasure and reward center, whose activation plays an important role in most of the features of mania.

CLOCK Genes and Biological Rhythms in Bipolar Disorder

Biological rhythms involved in hormonal secretion, stages of sleep, the sleep-wake cycle, and the timing of manic and depressive episodes are disturbed in bipolar illness. The CLOCK genes iare important regulators of biological rhythms, and a mutation in one or more of theCLOCK genes is associated with bipolar illness. This results not only in abnormal circadian rhythms but also an increase in excitatory dopamine release. A test animal with an abnormal variant of the master CLOCK gene is hyperactive, has increased exploratory drive, lowered depression-like behavior, abnormal sleep-wake cycles, increased reward responsiveness, and higher impulsivity. The manic behavior of these animals is reversed by treatment with lithium or restoring a functional clock gene. Another gene associated with bipolar disease, GSK3b, also contributes to circadian abnormalities in bipolar disorder. In addition, a mutated GSK3b gene promotes programmed cell death, decreases neuronal plasticity, and is associated with an increase in the rate of psychosis.

Many patients with mania show a marked decrease in hours of sleep. This may exacerbate manic states. Lack of adequate sleep routinely provokes a switch from depression into mania or a worsening of manic episodes. In experimental animals, it produces several manic-like behaviors, including increased locomotion, aggressive behavior, and hypersexuality, all of which can be normalized by lithium treatment. Sleep deprivation also interferes with GABA neurotransmission.

Inflammation in Bipolar Disorder

Inflammation in the body and brain occurs in subjects with bipolar disorder. Cytokines and other inflammatory markers are elevated in the blood and cerebrospinal fluid in bipolar patients, and there is also inflammation in their central nervous systems. Bipolar patients with substantial inflammation are highly treatment resistant. In postmortem studies we can see that suicide victims with bipolar disorder have significant, apparently recent increases in microglia density in multiple areas of the prefrontal cortex, including the controller. Given that microglia are the principal mediators of inflammatory activation in the brain, these findings suggest suicidality may be a consequence of a surge in the severity of the disease. There is a remarkable overlap between the sites of cellular abnormalities and the brain regions with altered structure and functioning, as assessed by neuroimaging of bipolar illness.

Mitochondrial Dysfunction in Bipolar Disorder

Mitochondrial dysfunction is also found in bipolar disorder. Mitochondria are components in a cell that generate more than 90 percent of the chemical energy needed to power the cell's biochemical reactions. Mitochondria make energy for cells from the chemical energy stored in the food we eat via chemical reactions like oxidation. The by-products of oxidation, in excessive amounts, are toxic to brain cells and can cause their deaths. Of all the organs in the body, the brain appears most vulnerable to mitochondrial defects, suggesting that neurons are particularly sensitive to bioenergetic fluctuations, and, consequently, that mitochondria regulate fundamental aspects of brain function.

Mitochondria also contain their own DNA, which can mutate up to ten times faster than DNA in an ordinary cell. Mitochondrial DNA contains thirty-seven genes, all of which are essential for normal mitochondrial function. Many mitochondrial genes are mutated in patients with bipolar disorder, impacting energy production in the cells of bipolar patients and predisposing these cells to vulnerability and premature death.

BDNF Deficiency in Bipolar Disorder

BDNF is a key molecule involved in bipolar disorder. It is essential for normal neuroplasticity and neurogenesis. It is also involved in neuronal maturation, differentiation and survival, long-term memory formation and storage, and neuroprotection. A mutation in the BDNF gene that reduces BDNF production by 50 percent occurs in patients with bipolar disorder. This mutation increases many features of bipolar illness, particularly the reduced volumes of the controller and the emotional memory center, impaired cognition, and increased suicidal behavior. BDNF deficiency also leads to decreased neurogenesis and neuroplasticity. Stress, in general, and high cortisol levels also contribute to the substantial decrease in BDNF production and release during bipolar illness. Clinical studies have shown that in many patients, treatment with lithium increases BDNF in multiple sites in the brain, instilling hope for treatment.

Neurohormones and Neurotransmitters in Bipolar Disorder

CRH (corticotropin-releasing hormone), as noted, controls cortisol secretion, activates the sympathetic nervous system, and sets into motion behaviors associated with stress such as anxiety and fear-related behaviors that include remaining immobile to avoid detection by a predator. CRH also has a significant effect on stimulating inflammation in the brain and the body.

Changes in genes involved in the regulation of dopamine and serotonin are also involved in bipolar disorder. The abnormalities in these neurotransmitter systems are not likely to play as important a role as the glutamate system. Instead they are involved in fine-tuning, in contrast to the capacity of altered glutamate neurotransmission to directly set into motion the major manifestations of bipolar disorder. Nevertheless, the use of drugs that influence norepinephrine, dopamine, and serotonin can precipitate mania in susceptible depressed individuals, though not necessariy through these neurotransmitters.

Glutamate plays a major role in the pathophysiology of bipolar illness. Its impact in mania seems greater than its considerable impact on depressive pathophysiology.

Genetics of Bipolar Disorder

Although hundreds of studies have examined genetic factors of possible relevance to bipolar disorder, only a few have been validated by replication in additional studies. This is because candidate gene studies have not yet borne fruit, possibly because we have not yet identified enough genuine, relevant candidate biological processes. Most genome-wide association studies have so far not often yielded studies that could be replicated because the numbers of patients needed for an adequate study can approach a million or more. The genome is vast, and looking for non-hypothetical associations of particular genes in bipolar populations is extremely difficult using fewer numbers of subjects.

One of the earliest genes to be implicated in bipolar disorder was the gene that encodes ANK3, a protein involved in the sheathing of nerve tracts, especially in the brain. Knockout, or ablation, of this gene results in cyclic changes in behavior that resemble bipolar disorder and that respond to lithium. Another gene mutation found in bipolar disorder has to do with CACNA1Ct. Knockout of this gene alters a variety of behaviors thought to reflect mood. This gene is involved in calcium mediated neurotransmission, which is widely regarded to be abnormal in bipolar disorder.

Epigenetic changes undoubtedly influence the expression and biological manifestations of bipolar disorder. Both lithium and the anticonvulsant Depakote help address epigenetic changes, as well as traditional antidepressants such as tricyclics, which induce epigenetic changes after about three weeks. Rapid-acting antidepressants such as ketamine also exert epigenetic effects, but within hours rather than weeks, and to a much greater extent than traditional antidepressants.

Psychotherapy is as important in the effective treatment of bipolar disorder as it is in major depression. In addition to medication and psychotherapy, lifestyle rearrangements are critical for people with bipolar disorder. These involve getting adequate and consistent sleep and becoming highly effective at stress management. Those with a bipolar diagnosis should strive to develop a lifestyle that employs an effective balance of scheduling and predictable structure and learn to self-monitor or self-observe so that they can perceive and appropriately adjust to changes in mood and energy. In addition, they should stay away from the destabilizing effects of psychoactive substances such as alcohol, narcotics, and amphetamines.

Despite the enormous challenges presented by bipolar disorder, we are making rapid advances in our understanding of the disease and the new treatments that can help address it. This is especially important, since bipolar disease can be a malignant process that can destroy lives.

I distinctly recall feeling that could be the case with one of my patients, a thirty-year-old woman admitted to the Clinical Center in an acute manic state in September 1974. Anna Jackson had been awake for three consecutive nights, yet she was highly energetic. She was intrusive, irritable, spoke rapidly, and hurled obscene epithets at the staff. She was delusional, insisting the CIA was pursuing her because she had information vital to the security of the country. In keeping with the almost universal increase in libido during mania, Anna also inappropriately flirted with the male staff. Sadly, after the mania passes, most patients like Anna are mortified by their actions, which often contradict their most closely held values.

Because her mania seemed to escalate in the presence of other people, she was taken to a safe, quiet room where she could not harm herself or others. She was attended to on a one-to-one basis with a nurse twenty-four hours a day. She remained on one-to-one observation for the first fourteen days of her hospitalization.

Anna had experienced two episodes of severe mania prior to her admission with us at the NIH. During the first episode, she was sleepless, irritable, grandiose, had a flight of ideas, and talked quickly. Early in the mania, she was impulsive and hypersexual, and slept with a few men whom she barely knew, despite the fact that she would never dream of doing such a thing if she were well or depressed. She told her husband. He was upset but forgiving, attributing it to her illness. This episode lasted almost five months.

Six months later she had a similar episode. In the first week, she was unfaithful to her husband again. She confessed when she was in a very angry state, denouncing him as an unfit husband. She slapped him twice but was otherwise not physical. She was very irritable with her children. Because of her impulsivity and self-destructive behavior, her therapist committed her to the hospital.

Three months after the resolution of her mania, she developed a severe depression for which she was again hospitalized. She felt entirely unmotivated and could not summon energy or enthusiasm for any activity. She felt detached and had few memories except of hard times in the past. The present seemed flat and unappealing. She did not feel close to anyone and was consequently terribly lonely. Physically, she felt exhausted, wanted to sleep all the time, and slept longer hours than when she was well. She was perennially hungry. Moreover, she clearly felt better in the morning than at any other time of day. A month into the depression, she became suicidal. She was hospitalized for a total of six weeks.

I learned a considerable amount about her earlier life from her prior doctor's notes. She was the first of four children. Three brothers followed her. She was a happy, stable child and an outstanding student. She was the kind of person who drew others to her because of her quick wit, infectious laugh, and good nature. Anna enjoyed being with others and often found it hard to be alone for more than a few hours. She could not account for the anxiety she felt when she was alone.

Despite Anna's likable features, her mother criticized her a great deal. Her mother was an intelligent person who had wanted to become a nurse. She abandoned this dream when she had to marry at age eighteen after getting pregnant with Anna. I learned that Anna's mother had suffered two major depressive episodes. The first occurred postpartum after Anna's birth and lasted for three months. She ceased being able to find pleasure in anything, was withdrawn, and assiduously avoided other people, including her child. She was passively suicidal, voicing many times that she hoped she would contract a disease that would take her life. She was extremely fatigued and slept excessively. She consumed food voraciously. She felt somewhat better in the mornings than in the evenings.

Anna's mother's second depression occurred when Anna was seventeen and ready to go off to college. This episode lasted for seven months. Antidepressants were not available for the treatment of either depressive episode. This second depression resembled her first in its pronounced fatigue, withdrawal, and diurnal pattern. As during the first depression, she fundamentally disappeared from her children. The children knew that their mother was very sad and tired, and that they could not depend on her. Anna became de facto mother of her three younger brothers.

In addition to her mother, Anna's maternal grandmother had manic-depressive illness. She had attempted suicide twice but had survived. Anna's mother had described to Anna a tumultuous, unstable household because of her own mother's relatively frequent episodes.

Anna was an exceptional student and leader. She went off to college when she was seventeen. She majored in political science at Radcliffe and wanted to become a community organizer. She met her husband, Jonathan, at Harvard when they were both first-year students, and they married right after receiving their diplomas. They wrote their own wedding vows and pledged themselves to a lifetime of love and service.

Two months after her hospitalization for her most recent depression, Anna's husband sued for divorce and for custody of the children. He felt that she was unable to take proper care of the children when she was depressed, and that her irritability made it dangerous for her to be around the children when she was manic. Anna was devastated and became manic a week later.

Her brother arranged for her to be formally evaluated for admission to the Clinical Center. What I best remember was his heartbreak that such a fine person's life could be totally ruined by an illness that that seemed to turn her into another person. She was a generous, caring person with excellent judgment, he told me. People often called her for advice. She had many truly close friends. When she was well, she was a wonderful mother. "How could this have happened to her?" he asked me. And, "Can you help her?" I replied that I believed we could with a new medication, but that I couldn't be sure. That medication was lithium. As with imipramine, at the time of Anna's admission to our unit, no one in Washington was using lithium.

Anna was still quite manic when we started the lithium. Her irritability, however, was modestly reduced as she got to know me and the rest of the staff. She was thus willing to sign consent forms. She knew she was in trouble and needed treatment badly, and the NIH was one place for which she still held out hope. At this point, she was sleeping only three hours a night, was very talkative, hyperactive, and still flirtatious, but less so than on admission.

Anna's lithium trial was designed as a double-blind, placebo-controlled study. This meant that neither she nor I, nor the nurses who did twice-daily mood ratings, knew whether she started with an active drug or a placebo. The trial was planned for twenty-one days' administration of either placebo or lithium, in random order. If the placebo were given first, it would probably take seven weeks or more to see if she would respond to medication. As with imipramine, the response to lithium took weeks rather than days.

Anna remained continuously manic for over a month. The first sign of a possible response was that her sleep was increasing. The next clinical indication that she was responding was that her delusional symptoms decreased so that by day thirty-eight she was virtually free of them. Gradually, her sleep, hyperactivity, increased talkativeness, and flirtatiousness diminished, and by day forty-six her mania was in a virtually complete remission. She had been on lithium for twenty-five days. Her manias in the past had generally lasted for five months or more. She was thoroughly demoralized after the resolution of the mania, largely because her life had dissolved around her during the course of her illness. She, however, did not have any of the classic depressive symptoms such as disturbances in sleep and a diurnal variation in mood. Perhaps the lithium was having a mood-stabilizing effect, though no drug could fully ease her pain.

When we looked at the results of her bloodwork and studied her cerebrospinal fluid (CSF), which we obtained through a spinal tap, we saw the metabolite levels of norepinephrine and dopamine in Anna's cerebrospinal fluid were elevated, a trend that we had seen in a large group of patients. High norepinephrine activity could contribute to the hyperarousal of mania, and high dopamine to the euphoric, disinhibited component.

Her responses to the intravenous dopamine infusion were exaggerated, consistent with the evidence that her dopamine system was activated. Her thyroid gland reacted normally while she was manic and showed evidence of a slight decrease while on lithium therapy. Years later, my colleagues and I showed in a large series of patients that lithium caused a subtle, significant decrease in thyroid function without causing hypothyroidism except in patients who already had borderline low levels. We were unable to get sleep studies while she was manic, and her sleep EEG recording after recovery from mania was normal. When we looked at her cerebrospinal fluid after lithium-induced recovery from mania, it showed lower levels of the metabolites of norepinephrine and dopamine. The appearance of Anna's chromosome was normal. No extra chromosomes or breaks were evident.

Anna and I were not able to participate in ordinary psychotherapy during her mania because of the degree of her agitation. But I visited with her frequently to remind her that I was her doctor and that we were doing everything we could to help her. My experience in the past was that bearing with a psychotic patient during the worst phase of her illness promoted a powerful alliance after the psychosis passed.

Anna was humiliated by her impulsive sexuality during her manias. Her husband was continuing the process of obtaining a divorce and petitioning for custody of the children. She had dropped out of graduate school because of the frequency and severity of her manic episodes. She had no income except alimony from her husband, though she was eventually awarded one-half possession of the house. She decided not to take possession and deprive the children of the familiar home where they had lived all their lives.

She was close to all her brothers and was fortunate in that her older brother was very successful and had a large home with a guesthouse on the premises. She decided to accept his offer to live in the guesthouse as long as she liked.

I tried my best to help her grieve the loss of her family. I believe my presence was useful, but her loss was so devastating that it was impossible for her to fully resolve her grief in a short period of time, and I suspected that she would never fully resolve it. If she could reconstruct her life with new relationships and meaningful work, the pain might gradually become less searing.

Anna blamed herself for all her problems. She felt that she should have been able to control herself better than she had during her manic episodes. I told her as emphatically as I could that her behavior was due to the biology of her illness. Her manic episode had classic features that corresponded to the episodes described in textbook after textbook. Her response to lithium strongly implicated a biological illness. I could later tell her that her biological findings normalized after recovery, further lending credibility to her having a biological disorder. Though there were not large studies available to verify the long-term effects of lithium, to the best of our knowledge it was proving to be a good mood stabilizer.

Anna worried about the effect of her illness on her children. They missed their mother, but at the time they had no demonstrable behavioral abnormalities and were doing well in school. Although we now know there are genetic components to bipolar disorder, there were no good data at the time regarding the level of increased risk to offspring of a parent with bipolar illness.

After discharge, I felt it was very important that Anna receive outpatient psychotherapy and management of her medications. An experienced therapist could help her manage her grief and the enormous anger she felt toward her husband for leaving her and taking the children. She steadfastly refused, however, to accept help from her brother for psychotherapy. She did not have health insurance to cover a rehospitalization, but I let her know she could come back to the Clinical Center if she relapsed. She responded well to lithium in a little over three weeks. She was discharged on lithium with instructions to take it indefinitely. Given the malignant natural history of her illness, I emphasized that she if she stopped the lithium, she would be vulnerable to potentially fatal severe manic or depressive episodes.

Anna stayed on lithium for six years. I then received a call from her brother saying that Anna had become depressed and had stopped her lithium, hoping it would release a mild, but manageable manic episode. Sadly, she became even more seriously depressed, left home quietly, checked into a hotel, and took her life with an overdose of aspirin. She was thirty-six years old. I and the rest of the NIH staff who had interacted with her were very upset to hear of Anna's death. For me, the loss felt personal. I still think of her often.

As I have seen through the years, bipolar disorder is a particularly destructive form of depression that we still have a long way to go toward solving. Thankfully, there are drugs that hold promise in treating, if not curing, this difficult disease.

CHAPTER 12

The Power and Promise of Lithium

Until recently, the means by which lithium helped to treat bipolar disorder was virtually unknown. This was especially true for mania, in part, because manic patients are so difficult to study. Thanks to recent advances, we now know that lithium downregulates almost all the pathophysiological mechanisms that encode the manic state. For starters, lithium decreases the size of the controller whose size is increased during the manic state. Since the controller restrains the amygdala, the lithium induced decrease in the size of the controller disinhibits, or increases the activity of the amygdala. The anxiety associated with a more active amygdala eventually exerts a brake on the erratic and inappropriate behavior characteristic of the manic state. The controller also enhances the activity of the pleasure and reward center. A lithium-induced decrease in the size and activity of the controller exerts the therapeutic effect of decreasing the manic subject's obsessive pursuit of pleasure.

Lithium also helps restore the volume and activity of multiple. prefrontal cortex structures that support emotional regulation and inhibitory control, and that counter impulsivity. In addition, lithium increases cognitive control over emotion. Thus, lithium promotes the capacity of the manic patient to contain impulsive, self-destructive acts.

Lithium decreases activity of the insula site that promotes the cycling between depression and mania. It also turns on the default mode network that had been inhibited in mania, and this supports introspection, as opposed to behavior in which inordinate risks are taken to secure rewards from the environment. Lithium also diminishes the activity of the salience network, which ordinarily biases attention to the outside world, further reinforcing a look inward

Our understanding of lithium's powerful neuroprotective effects is rapidly developing. Lithium stimulates BDNF secretion and its actions, improving neuroplasticity and neurogenesis and safeguarding neurons in multiple other ways. For instance, lithium increases the integrity of white matter and its viability: White matter is the sheathing of nerve fibers necessary for their optimal function. Lithium decreases programmed cell death by protecting against glutamate's action, which induces cell death by forcing neurons to deplete their energy supplies. Lithium significantly decreases telomere shortening, is anti-inflammatory, and significantly decreases the levels of cytokines in the blood.

Bipolar patients have significant abnormalities in mitochondrial function which impair their capacity to produce enough energy to keep cells alive. Lithium corrects defects in mitochondrial function, increasing neuronal energy production and, thus, safeguarding the neuron. The heart and brain are two organs that require large amounts of energy, making them susceptible to damage if the energy production of mitochondria is impaired— showing the seriousness of depression once again. At the same time, lithium diminishes the production of oxidating molecules that are produced in excess in the context of mitochondrial dysfunction, thus further safeguarding the cell.

In animal studies, lithium has been found to decrease neurodegeneration and enhances memory function. Scientists have thus suggested using lithium in the prevention and/or treatment of Alzheimer's disease and other CNS neurological illnesses associated with neurodegeneration. Lithium's neuroprotective effects may be one of its principal modes of action as a successful antimanic agent and mood stabizer.

Scores of gene-wide association studies have examined the potential effects of lithium on gene function that illuminate its mode of action. Unfortunately, none have been conducted with adequate numbers of subjects to be informative. Such large studies are in progress. Similarly, none of the candidate gene studies has passed the test of replication by multiple groups, so this strategy is awaiting both more relevant targets and larger studies in order to provide useful information.

It is striking that lithium influences so many processes that scientists have identified as dyregulated in bipolar disorder. It seems unlikely that lithium's capacity to influence such an array of processes is random, and more likely that these processes are part of an organized system that exerts important behavioral and biological effects on cognition, mood, and, pathophysiology. As we figure out more about lithium's biological effects, we will likely uncover previously unknown components of the overall complex neurobiology of bipolar disorder.

Unfortunately, only about 40 percent of bipolar patients have a complete response to lithium. This may reflect the fact that different biological forms of bipolar disorder exist or because of a variation in the biological abnormalities we group under the label of bipolar disorder. The presence of enormous stressors or interpersonal conflicts could potentially override the impact of lithium treatment, as could not taking medication regularly as directed, or lifestyle issues like drug abuse.

The Story of the Discovery of Lithium in the Treatment of Bipolar Disorder

Though it is not a miracle cure, the discovery of lithium has the quality of a fairy tale. It features the work of an investigator in a remote location that involves discovery, loss, and rediscovery. Remarkably, it represents another rare instance of a time a clinician hit the bull's eye on the very first try—similar to the discovery of imipramine.

The story begins with the psychiatrist John Cade, living in the small town of Horsham, Australia. (Edward Shorter relates this anecdote beautifully in his book, *The History of Psychiatry*. During World War II, Cade, a psychiatrist, was a prisoner of war for three and a half years. During his imprisonment in Japan, he observed the emergence of mental disorders in his fellow prisoners that he thought had a biologic origin. After the war, he resumed clinical practice and went about trying to study the biology of psychiatric disorders in work with the guinea pig. He postulated that there might be something toxic in manic-depressive patients that would be released in the urine.

He noted that the urine from manic-depressive patients, if injected into the abdominal cavity of the guinea pig, was much more toxic than was urine from individuals who were not ill. He first postulated that the offending agent was urea, but injecting urea alone caused no problems. He next investigated the possible role of uric acid. In order to conduct the experiment, he had to dissolve uric acid in lithium, which makes uric acid and its salts more soluble. He expected the addition of lithium to make the urine more toxic. Instead, the urine containing the compound consisting of uric acid dissolved in a lithium solution was far less toxic than urine alone.

Cade subsequently decided to administer lithium directly to the guinea pigs. The animals were initially sedated and relatively unresponsive for about two hours. Thereafter, they seemed uncharacteristically tame and placid. Amazingly, the animals simply lay there and gazed at him. This was most unusual behavior for wide-awake guinea pigs.

In the fall of 1949, Cade gave lithium alone to ten patients in the manic state. Three were chronically manic and the others had mania of relatively short duration. In all cases, the lithium had a dramatic effect on the mental status of the patients, even in those who had been ill for up to five years. Cade proposed in a paper written in an obscure Australian journal that mania stemmed from "a deficiency of lithium in the body."

Cade wrote these notes about his first patient, "a little wizened man of 51 who had been in a chronic state of manic excitement for five years" who, by the fifth day was in fact more settled, tidier, less disinhibited, and less distractible. "From then on there was steady improvement."

> It was with a sense of most abject disappointment that I readmitted him to the hospital six months later as manic as ever but took some consolation from his brother who informed me that Bill had become lackadaisical about taking his medication and finally ceased taking it about six weeks before. Since then, he has become steadily more irritable and erratic. His lithium carbonate was at once recommended and in two weeks he had again returned to normal. A month later, he was recorded as completely well and ready to go home and work.

The patient had further episodes of mania when he stopped his lithium and subsequent responses to treatment. However, he died some years later of what Cade felt was lithium-induced cardiac toxicity. Many other patients described other toxic effects, including diarrhea, nausea, loss of appetite, abnormal gait, fatigue, cardiac arrhythmias, and depression. These bothered Cade sufficiently that he stopped using lithium entirely.

Mogens Schou, who would also begin working with lithium, was born in Denmark and eventually settled in Norway, where he did his most important work. Schou's father had been a psychiatrist who, ever since the development of electroconvulsive therapy (ECT) in 1939, was convinced that manic-depressive illness was a biological disorder. After his father died, Schou became interested in lithium. "I found it extremely fascinating if lithium salts which are chemically so simple could have a therapeutic effect in psychiatry, especially if they are active against just one disease, which could tell us more about that disease than lots of information concerning the therapeutic effects of complicated compounds like Thorazine, which had no clear preference with regard to the different disorders for which they were used."

Schou conducted a number of large studies with lithium. He felt he had reasonable data to suggest that lithium was not only therapeutic during active disturbances in mood, but was also a mood stabilizer—that is, it prevented the patient during the well phase from lapsing into either manic or depressive states.

Michael Shepherd, from the psychoanalytic stronghold of the Maudsley Hospital in London, took issue with Schou's clinical design and belittled his work. Shepherd was especially upset by the claim that lithium was mood stabilizing, since one didn't know if a remission was secondary to lithium or occurred naturalistically. Schou's work was quite convincing, but Shepherd argued it wasn't scientifically rigorous. Moreover, when Schou told Shepherd that many members of his own family had manic-depressive illness and that for them lithium was a godsend, Shepherd concluded that Schou was a "believer" rather than a scientist.

The debate became extraordinarily bitter. Nathan Kline, an eminent American psychopharmacologist and Lasker Award winner, wrote a defense of Schou's work and urged his colleagues to treat manic-depressive illness with lithium. He was attacked by Shepherd, who wrote that Kline's "editorial will be highly prized by collectors of original enthusiasms tempered by subsequent experience. Only time will tell whether your eulogy will earn you the fate that your analysis deserves—to join Cinderella's godmother in the pages of mythology." To transform "just plain old lithium into the elixir of life, on the evidence available, is an advancement second only to converting a pumpkin into a stagecoach." Kline replied, "Your delightful letter reads as if it were written by one of Cinderella's spiteful sisters. There is even a feeling of faint personal similarity with your warning which reminds me of some of the caveats concerning the introduction of both antipsychotic and antidepressant agents. Of course, it may also be that you are not convinced that any of these drugs have been demonstrated to be of any use."

Although John Cade wrote his paper on lithium in 1949, lithium was not available as a treatment for manic-depressive illness for many years, and only first gained approval by the FDA in 1970. There were four overlapping reasons for the delay. First, lithium had been in many patent medicines and had led to some serious side effects, including death by cardiac arrhythmia. This ultimately was shown to be due to unnecessarily high doses of lithium. A second reason was that Thorazine was available as an antimanic agent. However, Thorazine did not turn out to be mood stabilizing, as lithium did, and left patients with manic-depressive illness feeling far less alive and more apathetic. Third, there was acrimonious debate about whether lithium had been proven to be a mood stabilizer. Ultimately, this was shown to be true beyond a reasonable shadow of a doubt. Fourth, and perhaps most disturbing, lithium was a simple element and was not patentable. Medicine had entered the age where the profit motives of drug companies were their first consideration, and if drug companies did not advertise a drug, it rarely found its way into clinical medicine.

Lithium is routinely measured in the blood of patients who take it to keep the blood levels in a safe, normal range. When lithium levels are too high, patients experience hand tremors, unsteady balance, nausea, and diarrhea. In large overdoses, lithium can cause cardiac arrhythmias. Lithium is routinely prescribed on an outpatient basis, and most patients can take it for years without running into trouble with toxicity. Thanks to its relative safety and effectiveness, lithium has become one of the most common treatments for bipolar disorder.

CHAPTER 13

Shock Therapy

Some types of treatment for depression are thought of in the popular imagination as a last resort. For a long time, this was the case for electroconvulsive therapy (ECT)—which, despite its negative public perception, has been an essential treatment for severe mood disorders for more than eighty years. ECT's relative safety and efficacy have been proven through multiple studies. Untreated severe depressive and psychotic illnesses are associated with high rates of suicide and hospitalization, prolonged depressions, and reductions in quality of life. Studies have consistently shown that ECT results in a diminished risk of suicide, improves clinical outcomes, significantly increases in the quality of life, and decreases rates of rehospitalization. Trials of ECT for major depressive disorder in patients with treatment-resistant depression have shown pooled response rates of 80 percent. Although antidepressants and lithium are powerful tools in our arsenal to combat depression, they do not always work. When almost all else fails, was can usually rely on ECT. Thankfully, we now understand far more how and why it works and how to more safely administer it.

The development of electroconvulsive therapy in 1939 was

preceded by dangerous and invasive procedures that showed some efficacy in relieving depression but were in general too potentially toxic to be adopted as routine interventions. ECT was portrayed quite horrifically in Ken Kesey's 1962 novel *One Flew over the Cuckoo's Nest*, which was drawn from the author's firsthand experience working as an orderly in a mental hospital in California. Most readers will be familiar with another most extreme physical intervention, the lobotomy, which severed the frontal lobe from other parts of the brain. It was popular in the 1930s and '40s despite devastating outcomes for many patients, including death. Other procedures included inducing fever to cure psychosis, sleep therapies with bromine and barbiturates, and insulin-induced coma. All of these had unacceptable side effects and were potentially dangerous.

Ugo Cerletti, an Italian neurologist and head of the Institute for Neuropsychiatry in Rome, began to study the possibility of using electric shock instead of drugs to induce seizures in 1939. Cerletti gave his assistant Lamberto Bini the task of studying electroshock-induced seizures as a potential for treatment of depression, first using animal studies. Bini discovered that electroshock-induced seizures could be given safely to pigs if the electrodes were placed over each temple. Over the next few months, Bini determined the lowest possible voltage to induce a seizure reliably and safely.

Edward Shorter, in his *History of Psychiatry*, gives a vivid report of the first patient to receive electroconvulsive therapy. Cerletti and his colleagues started with eighty volts for a tenth of a second. No response. They stepped it up to ninety. No seizure, but the patient began to sing. Cerletti turned up the voltage to maximum. The patient had a classic epileptic fit and stopped breathing for a few moments. After forty-eight seconds the patient began breathing again. The patient emitted a profound sigh, as did Cerletti. After eleven applications of ECT, the patient recovered, was discharged a month later, and a year later remained in remission from depression.

Lothar Kalinowsky, a psychiatrist at Columbia, took the lead on ECT in America. Psychoanalysts strongly objected to ECT, saying that by zapping people, it appeared that biological psychiatrists thought it better to risk being a contented imbecile than a schizophrenic.

One of the drawbacks of ECT turned out to be that the seizure could at times result in severe back injuries or fractures. This problem was overcome by Walter Freeman, who thought of the idea of temporarily inducing paralysis to protect the patient from potentially violent seizures and their risks. This helped solve ECT-induced back injuries. Early versions of ECT also induced severe memory deficits in some patients.

By 1959, ECT became the treatment of choice for severe psychotic depressions. Unfortunately, the antipsychiatry movement virtually brought ECT to a halt. It was not to emerge again until the 1980s. It is been refined considerably with respect to reducing the strength and duration of current. Electrode placement has also been adapted; instead of placing electrodes on both sides of the head, they are placed only on one side at sites that still induce seizures but cause much less disturbances in memory. ECT is now very safe. Severe complications occur in less than four individuals per hundred thousand. Many of us who specialize in neuropsychiatry still believe ECT is the best treatment for otherwise treatment-resistant severe depressions.

ECT exerts multiple effects on the brain that are likely to be involved in its mechanism of action. ECT stimulates BDNF release and actions. In doing so it creates a pronounced increase in neurogenesis and neuroplasticity and increases neuronal volume and cortical thickness, especially in the emotional memory center and prefrontal cortex. ECT improves deficits in neuronal connectivity in depressed patients, and corrects abnormalities in synaptic function. It normalizes the metabolic activity of the controller and facilitates its effective functioning. ECT also has anticonvulsant properties related, in part, to its stimulation of GABA neurotransmission. While it increases the release of serotonin, this is not thought to be its primary mode of action.

Many centers are actively studying the mechanism by which ECT exerts its therapeutic effects. Because of its high rate of efficacy, investigators hope to uncover fundamental pathophysiological mechanisms underlying depressive illness. Studies are also underway to determine via neuroimaging factors that predict a positive response to ECT.

One patient who benefitted from ECT was James Miller, who came to the NIH Clinical Center in December 1982. He was married, fifty-four years old, and had three grown children. His depression had begun four years earlier after having been passed over for a job promotion, even though he felt he was performing at a higher level than the person who was promoted. He had an atypical depression associated with fatigue, a sense of remoteness from himself, his family, and his friends. In addition, he ate excessively and slept at least twelve to fourteen hours per night.

We started James on an experimental drug, zimelidine, which, like Prozac, was a specific serotonin uptake inhibitor, apparently working by increasing the availability of serotonin for neurotransmission in key sites in the stress system. Prozac would not be available for several more years. All three of the patients to whom we had given zimelidine prior to James responded. James had failed to respond to all the other the antidepressants that he had received, including imipramine, Wellbutrin, and lithium. He also failed to respond to a four-week course of zimelidine. We next tried the MAO inhibitor Parnate, but he failed to respond to this compound as well. I should note that, in general, the response rate to antidepressants in patients with atypical depression is lower than those who suffer from depression with melancholia. Melancholia responds very well to tricyclic antidepressants, while atypical depression is resistant to tricyclic therapy. This might reflect the fact that stress system activity is diminished in atypical depression, while we showed that tricyclics turn off the stress system.

During his extensive workup, James showed EEG evidence of hypersomnia, but with decreased deep, deep sleep. His thyroid function was normal. We administered multiple tests of adrenal cortisol secretion, which, looked at together, showed evidence of reduced cortisol secretion rather than the high cortisol secretion seen in melancholia. His lumbar puncture showed evidence of significantly low norepinephrine and CRH levels. Thus, it was as if his stress system was locked in the off position.

By 1982, the NIMH Intramural Program had shifted so that patients stayed for much shorter trials and were discharged into the care of ex–NIMH Intramural physicians practicing in the community. If the patients lived out of town, we invested considerable effort in finding them an effective local psychiatrist. I met with James three times a week for an hour and got to know him and his experience with depression well. I learned that he was born into a high-achieving family where failure was not an option, and thus he had great difficulty coming to terms with any disappointments, which he felt were signs of personal failure. Though he was often criticized by his very demanding father, he never assertively defended himself or expressed any anger at his mistreatment. In general, his assertiveness was quite inhibited and made it hard for him to communicate even his successes, lest others be angry with him. His diffidence probably contributed to his not being promoted.

In light of all of his treatment failures, we elected to proceed with ECT and James concurred. He underwent electroconvulsive therapy on Monday, Wednesday, and Friday for three consecutive weeks. After two weeks, his mood began to lighten, and he began sleeping nine hours per night instead of twelve. He progressively improved over the last three treatments, and in the following week, he progressively improved so that after his ninth treatment, he was completely remitted. He had no pain following each treatment, did not dread the treatments, and showed mild memory impairments that resolved within eight weeks of the termination of his treatment. He remained in complete remission two years after discharge from the hospital. We attributed this partly to the fact that he formed attachments well and had begun working on a regular basis with a competent psychiatrist to whom he was referred. He continued to see this therapist for at least two years after he left the NIH.

Deep Brain Stimulation

An additional invasive procedure that delivers electrical impulses to the brain to treat patients who are extraordinarily treatment resistant is deep brain electrical stimulation.

In cases of severe, profoundly treatment-resistant depression, clinicians have utilized deep brain stimulation as a last resort.

The first study implanted electrodes directly into the controller. Pulsing reversed a twenty-year-long depression in a patient who had not responded to seventeen prior interventions.

The second study implanted electrodes into the pleasure and reward center. Pulsing reversed a profound, prolonged depression that had not responded to fifteen prior interventions.

A great deal of work is ongoing to refine electrode implant therapy for severe refractory depressions to simplify the procedure and insure its safety. There have been no substantive side effects in these preliminary studies.

Repetitive Transcranial Stimulation rTMS

Repetitive transcranial magnetic stimulation (rTMS) is a relatively new tool that stimulates the brain directly in the hopes of alleviating depressive symptoms. It consists of repeated magnetic pulses, applied via electrodes placed in critical positions on the skull, to stimulate areas such as the controller or the pleasure and reward center. As each magnetic pulse passes through the skull and into the brain, this induces brief changes in the activity of brain cells underlying the magnetic treatment coil. rTMS is a much more benign intervention than ECT. It is painless and requires no sedation; patients can drive themselves home minutes after finishing an rTMS treatment. It does not affect memory.

Clinicians first utilized rTMS in the treatment of depression because electroconvulsive treatment had provided ample evidence that regional electromagnetic stimulation of the brain could in fact treat depression. New data emerged showing that key cortical regions and those below the cortex in the emotional brain were involved in depression, some of which could be directly stimulated by rTMS.

Investigators made initial educated guesses about many issues, including coil location, intensity, frequency, total number of pulses per day, dosing schedule, and number of pulses in the treatment course. It took more than a decade to refine these choices, and work still continues to improve rTMS.

During the first rTMS session, clinicians make several measurements to ensure that the coil is placed over the correct portion of the prefrontal cortex. The physician then administers several brief pulses to determine the patient's motor threshold. This threshold varies from one patient to another and is determined by the amount of energy necessary to stimulate neurons that cause a thumb twitch.

Treatment sessions vary in length depending on the coil utilized and the number of pulses chosen. A single session lasts for thirty to forty minutes. Patients receive rTMS five days per week, and a typical course is four to six weeks, depending on the patient's response to treatment.

Preliminary data indicate that coil locations are important in treating specific symptoms. Anxious patients tend to do better in a coil location that is different from the coil location for those patients with anhedonic and dysphoric symptoms. If this finding is definitively validated, it would be an exciting advance.

Recent preliminary data also indicate that a mutant BDNF

gene predicts a better response to rTMS. Clinicians are attempting to find other features that might indicate the benefits of specific elements of rTMS treatment.

In the largest study to date, 257 treatment-resistant depressed patients successfully completed an rTMS course and agreed to be followed up for fifty-two weeks. Forty-five percent responded positively. The placebo response was less than 5 percent.

Consider the case of Marilyn Jacobs, who had been depressed for most of her life. She was first diagnosed at age twenty-one, but she recalled that her depression started much earlier. At forty-eight, she developed the most severe depression of her life. Prior to this time, she had seen psychologists and taken antidepressants, which produced only modest decreases in her depression. In 2009, desperate for new options, she flew to Los Angeles for a new therapy, rTMS. After three weeks of treatment, she began to emerge from her depression. The FDA approved rTMS as a treatment for depressed individuals who had failed to respond to pharmacologic interventions. It may well have saved Marilyn's life.

A Quantum Leap in the Application of rTMS

We are still refining the use of rTMS. In 2021, a group at Stanford made a significant alteration in the rTMS treatment schedule, testing a much more frequent stimulation protocol for a five-day period, in contrast to single-session treatments over a period of four to six weeks in standard rTMS treatment.

In the first placebo-controlled double-blind trial, 80 percent of treatment-resistant patients achieved remission in the four weeks following the five-day course of treatment! The remission rate in the placebo group was less than 15 percent. This paradigm could thus be utilized in emergency or inpatient units where rapid-acting interventions are needed. In addition, it could potentially emerge as a major modality for the treatment of depressive illness. In a remarkably short time after the first clinical studies, the FDA gave fast-track approval for this rTMS procedure.

The Stanford protocol utilizes pulses applied in bursts of three, delivered at a frequency of two seconds. Scientists developed these parameters based on the frequency of theta rhythms emanating from the site in the emotional memory center most associated with depressive pathophysiology.

Over each day of the five-day course, a total dose of eighteen thousand pulses equaled that of the entire six-week course of standard rTMS. Despite the higher doses, no serious side effects occurred in any of the trials. The most common side effect was a rate of headache equal to what occurred in standard rTMS.

rTMS aims to hit the precise spot in the prefrontal cortex that has the greatest effect on the controller. This spot differs from person to person. To identify this spot, each patient receives an MRI brain scan when the individual is not focusing on any particular mental task, the default mode state. This enables greater specificity of the pulses tied to the person's actual functional anatomy. The targeting of the controller also leads to restoration of its usual functions in a way that is normally associated with remission from depression. Another site that we have targeted with great results is the dorsolateral prefrontal cortex, whose activity is markedly reduced in depression. This site participates in mood regulation, in part by exerting cognitive control over emotion. In experimental animals, rTMS has been shown to activate both the production of BDNF and to increase activity of its receptor.

Larger double-blind, placebo-controlled trials for this new version of rTMS are in the works. In addition, clinicians are sampling a variety of protocols to optimize the clinical effects obtained with rTMS treatment. If the findings hold up in these ongoing trials, psychiatry will have a powerful new tool to combat the epidemic of depressive illness we are now facing.

Seizures and Stimulation

While the grand mal seizure induced by electroconvulsive seizures is the best-known seizure subtype, seizures of the limbic system can also occur. Limbic seizures don't involve uncontrolled muscular contraction, but instead have behavioral manifestations. Limbic seizures occur in some patients with temporal lobe epilepsy and have symptoms that overlap somewhat with bipolar phenomena.

Bob Post, a colleague of mine at the NIH, found that he could produce limbic seizures by injecting cocaine into the amygdala of experimental animals. Interestingly, he found that daily repeated cocaine administration at the same dosage made the amygdala more sensitive to cocaine rather than tolerant of it. After a few days of stimulation by the same dose of cocaine, the limbic seizures became more severe and longer lasting. After a number of weeks of regular cocaine administration at the same dose, the seizures became autonomous and occurred regularly without needing to be induced through cocaine administration—and did not settle down until anticonvulsants were given. This phenomenon became known as kindled limbic seizures.

Bob saw a connection between autonomously occurring seizures after regular cocaine administration and the experience of some patients with cyclic bipolar disorder. Early in the course of untreated bipolar disorder, severe stressors are needed to trigger an episode of depression or mania. Over time, some bipolar individuals began having more severe episodes of depression and mania that occurred more frequently than in the initial phase of the illness—and for many, even milder stressors were able to precipitate the more frequent episodes of depression and mania. Finally, if the illness went untreated for years, individuals started having switches into depression or mania autonomously without any apparent precipitant whatsoever. By this point, most patients were resistant to lithium and virtually any other interventions available to treat bipolar illness, and many were untreatable.

Ken Kendler, an eminent psychiatric geneticist, ultimately discovered that this kindling phenomenon became apparent after the first seven to nine episodes.

Bob postulated that these patients had something akin to kindled limbic seizures and decided to give anticonvulsants to these patients, with excellent results. Jim Ballenger, my roommate at the Duke University School of Medicine, played an important role in these studies. Bob and Jim utilized the anticonvulsant Tegretol, a drug very effective in treating temporal lobe epilepsy. Over the years, other anticonvulsants such as Lamictal have also been effective in treating bipolar patients, even in the extremely difficult situation of longstanding bipolar disorder.

One of Bob's principal goals now is to try to initiate treatment in children who begin suffering from bipolar disorder with anticonvulsants as early as the age of three. These unfortunate youngsters with such an early course of illness are known to have more malignant forms of bipolar disorder that may be due to kindling that starts not long after birth. Bob believes we can save these kids a lot of trouble over their lifetime if treatment is started early. Treating such a pernicious form of bipolar disorder is like treating cancer. It's a lot harder to treat cancer after it has metastasized.

The use of anticonvulsants in addressing bipolar disorder and other forms of depression is a recent and exciting new treatment tool to consider as we look to the future. The search for more effective anticonvulsants to treat cyclic bipolar disorder continues, and even more can be expected from this class of drugs as seizures are better understood and improved medicines become available to treat them.

CHAPTER 14

Psychedelics and Connection

Psychedelics have been used by humans for millennia to create changes in consciousness and induce experiences that remove us from our everyday reality. How they do this, and what happens in our brains when we are tripping is something that we've only recently begun to understand in a scientific manner.

As in so many instances, the science was actually set into motion not by a decision to undertake rigorous study but by a serendipitous accident. In 1943, Dr. Albert Hofmann decided to synthesize as many compounds as he could from the ergot alkaloid, a fungus. Ergot has been the source of a variety of drugs useful in medicine, from asthma to labor induction. Sandoz, the company for whom Hofmann worked, thought that ergot alkaloids could be the source of many more useful medicines. Hofmann went on to synthesize fifty-one new ergot derivatives. One accidently got on his hands, and he ingested it. Afterward, as quoted by Michael Pollan in his book *How to Change Your Mind,* he went home and "in a dreamlike state with eyes closed, I perceived an uninterrupted stream of fantastic pictures, and extraordinary shapes with an intense, kaleidoscopic play of colors." Later, when he walked out into his garden after a soaking rain, "everything glistened and sparkled in a fresh light."

Aldous Huxley, in his book *The Doors of Perception*, wrote that after a psychedelic session, the most mundane objects glowed with the light of divinity. Even the folds of gray flannel trousers were charged with "is-ness." When he gazed upon a bouquet of flowers, he felt that they were "shining with their own inner light, and all but quivering under the pressure of the significance with which they were charged." He also felt as if the boundaries between himself and other people disappeared, and he felt a kinship with all living things.

In the '50s and '60s, psychiatrists administered LSD and psilocybin while monitoring patients for two hours or more and found that it markedly helped in the treatment of depression. Psilocybin, in use for thousands of years by indigenous populations in Central and South America, has been shown in multiple papers to exert antidepressant effects. It has fewer negative or harmful effects than LSD and was used by psychiatrists to treat depression in the '50s and '60s with good results. Prior to their 1971 prohibition, psilocybin and LSD were administered to approximately forty thousand patients, including those with terminal cancer, alcoholics, and those suffering from depression and obsessive-compulsive disorder. The results of the early clinical studies were promising.

These early studies went underground, however, when psychedelic drugs gained a subversive reputation. Journalists reported bad trips, psychotic breaks, flashbacks, and terrifying dreams lasting for days after taking LSD. Timothy Leary sealed their doom with the battle cry "Tune in, turn on, and drop out." Accompanying this exhortation, the government mounted a campaign that put out seemingly endless warnings, such as "This is your brain on drugs," with the images of eggs sizzling in a frying pan.

In 1990, two scientists, Roland Griffiths at the Johns Hopkins hospital, and Robin Carhart-Harris at the Imperial College, London, were able to get permission for the experimental use of psychedelics for the treatment of depression. This work culminated in a recent original article in the *New England Journal of Medicine* reporting that psilocybin has robust antidepressant effects that exceed those of standard SSRIs.

One premise behind the therapeutic mechanism of psychedelic drugs centers on the concept that psychedelic agents suppress or dissolve the ego to let deeply buried capacities to think, feel, and experience kinship with the world emerge. This may very well be so, but there are also fundamental biological effects occurring that correct many of the stress system abnormalities that accompany depressive illness.

Pollan, in conversations with experts about the mechanisms of action of psychedelic drugs, shares with them a perhaps overly pessimistic view of the ego and its selfish role in suppressing the kind of oceanic feeling of connectedness and increased sensory perception of which individuals are capable after years of disciplined training or in the context of psilocybin treatment. Pollan notes that the ego is often an inner neurotic who insists on running the show; who is wily and doesn't relinquish power without a struggle. Deeming itself indispensable, it will battle ceaselessly against its diminishment. Pollan notes that the ego is good at performing the activities that natural selection values: getting ahead, getting liked and loved, getting fed, and having sex. Keeping us on task, the ego ferociously suppresses anything that might distract us from the work at hand, whether that means regulating our access to unconscious knowledge about our oneness with others and our special relationship to the world.

Pollan goes on to write that the ego fails to see that there is a whole world of souls and spirits, and many subjective experiences other than our own. It seems plausible that psychedelic-induced deeper insight into the world simply happens in the space that opens up in the mind when all egotism vanishes. Wonders and terrors we ordinarily defend against flow into our awareness; the far ends of the sensory spectrum, which are normally invisible to us, emerge in all their glory. In contrast, depression is a state in which the ego is in self-assessment overdrive, fueled by an activated amygdala to promote feelings of worthlessness, compelled by the great activation of the default mode network. As I stated earlier in the book, depression is a deeply constricted state, filtering out powerful feelings like sadness. As noted, sadness is often associated with cherished, loving memories of, for instance, a lost loved one, and, at times, a bittersweet feeling encompassing both the bounties of life and the harsh reality that all relationships must come to an end. However, many severely depressed patients often cannot feel this kind of sadness or even cry. Rather, depressed patients lose contact with their true selves and are restricted to a deadening litany of self-excoriation and hopelessness, so that they are narrowly self-focused rather than being in touch with others and the world.

During depression, the default mode network is highly activated. This results in turning the individual inward while judging the self exceedingly harshly. The depressed person is out of touch with many ordinary feelings and profoundly alienated from others. All of this keeps him isolated from deeper layers of consciousness and connectedness.

According to psychopharmacologist David Nutt, people get locked into disorders like depression because they develop a system of thinking that is entirely constricted. Psychiatry has a term for such thinking: rumination. The idea behind psychedelic therapy is that the drug places individuals in a receptive state where they are open to fresh ideas about how to think about the past and future, which the therapist can reinforce. In depression, patients continually ruminate about their failings, reiterate thoughts of guilt, and engage in self-critical inner narratives. Psychedelics likely work by interrupting these habits of thought and behavior, allowing the systems that control them to recalibrate.

Turning off the default mode network pries open one's sense of community with others and connectedness to the world. If the ego is (temporarily) fully removed from the equation, psychedelic agents provide access to a level of consciousness which exists in us all, but which is rarely accessible.

Currently, psilocybin therapy for psychiatric disorders is given within a structured psychotherapeutic setting with considerable therapist input. There is always a preparatory session before drug administration. There is always one therapist, and in some studies two therapists, present during the psychedelic session, which lasts up to six hours. The next day, and beyond, there are further integration sessions with the same therapists to help patients talk through and thereby ground their experiences. It will be important to see if psychedelics exert their effects if given intravenously to depressed individuals who are asleep or under light anesthesia. Alternatively, analogs of current psychedelics that do not promote the psychedelic experience may be developed that nevertheless have full antidepressant efficacy. Psilocybin is especially safe and effective. Multiple medical schools and research institutes are studying the impact of psilocybin in the treatment of depression, obsessive-compulsive disorder, generalized anxiety disorder, and anorexia nervosa. The results may provide a revolutionary new way of treating psychiatric illness.

In partial contrast to the idea that the ego works hard to prevent expanding consciousness, Roy Shafer has written a rather splendid note on how a highly developed ego can reject the heroic idea that "everything turns out for the best." In his book *A New Language for Psychoanalysis*, he wrote a chapter entitled "The Psychoanalytic Vision of Reality." In it, he states that the tragic view is more accurate. By tragic, he does not mean gloomy or hopeless, but rather that:

> The tragic view is expressed in the keen responsiveness to the great dilemmas, paradoxes, ambiguities, and uncertainties pervading human action and subjective experience. It manifests itself in alertness to the inescapable dangers, terrors, mysteries, and absur-

dities of existence. It requires one to recognize the elements of defeat in victory and of victory in defeat. The pain in pleasure and the pleasure in pain; the guilt in apparently justified action; the loss of opportunity entailed by every choice and by growth in any direction; the inevitable clashes between passion and duty; the reversal of fortune that hovers over those who are proud or happy or worthy owing that its being in the nature of people to be inclined to reverse their own fortunes as well as to be vulnerable to accident and unforeseen consequences of their acts and the acts of others. The person with the tragic sense of life knows the renunciations that are intermingled with the conditions of gratification; the necessity to act in ignorance and bear the fear and guilt of action; the burden of unanswerable questions and incomprehensible afflictions; the probability of suffering while learning or changing; and the frequency with which it is true that only in the greatest adversity do people realize themselves most fully.

In my estimation, this psychoanalytic construct represents the pinnacle of ego development in the service of acknowledging the truth about the human condition and how to attempt to adapt to it. It is missing, however, a few key elements of which I have become aware in writing this chapter. It does not include reference to heightened states of consciousness that can be obtained by discipline or through the use of psychedelics, including an expansive feeling of connection with all living things. It also ignores the sources of human happiness, the capacity and necessity of being able to love, or constructs such as courage, gratitude, generosity, and sacrifice. These, too, are in large measure ego functions that enhance the quality of life for the individual in an otherwise difficult world full of challenges and setbacks.

Psychedelic drugs are promising agents that when used effectively in the presence of a skilled psychotherapist can have a greater impact on depression and related disorders than standard antidepressants, in part due to their profound biological effects.

One biological effect that unites all psychedelic compounds is that they active the serotonin 2a receptor. If the serotonin 2a receptor is blocked, none of the psychedelic compounds exert psychedelic effects. The first data regarding the biological effects of psychedelics that relate to their antidepressant efficacy show that they turn off an activated default mode network that is an invariably activated in depression. As noted, activation of this network in depressed patients promotes a looking inward and ruminations about one's deficiencies. The salience network, which focuses on the outside world, and the executive mode, which deals with problem solving, are isolated from each other and from the default mode network and are also often low-functioning in depressed patients. Notably, these networks all contain the most concentrated expression of serotonin 2a receptors in the brain.

The brain exists of countless modules whose interconnectedness and integration vary considerably during changing conditions. When these networks become disconnected from each other, as we see more often in depressed patients than in controls, a lack of communication between the default, salience, and executive modes causes a multitude of issues. A recent elegant paper in the prestigious journal *Nature Medicine* reveals that a double-blind, placebo-controlled trial of psilocybin was associated with a pronounced decrease in modularity and a profound increase in global integration of multiple loci in the brain. In a side-by-side comparison with an SSRI, whose antidepressant effects were of much slower onset and not as robust, there was no increase in global integration of the brain. This finding points to the unique capacity of psychedelics to exert rapid antidepressant responses that last for many days after a single administration and that are more robust than those seen with traditional antidepressants. The global integration fostered by psychedelics may contribute to their capacity to induce a state of mind that is more holistic than what is characteristic of normal consciousness. This in turn seems to facilitate the experience of seeing connections among all living things.

Psychedelics also have robust effects in activating the BDNF system. This activation is associated with increased connections among neurons, increased neurogenesis, and restoration of the emotional memory center's volume. Psychedelics also seem unique in their capacity to activate glutamate AMPA receptors, which I will later show are key to the therapeutic efficacy of ketamine. They also promote the extinction of conditioned fear responses that bombard the emotional memory center with negatively charged emotional memories.

Psychedelics also effect the thickness of the posterior cingulate cortex part of the brain, which is related with personality traits, including religiousness, transpersonal feelings, and spirituality.

Psychedelics activate anti-inflammatory programs in part via activating the serotonin 2a receptor. This is not surprising, since almost all immune cells contain serotonin receptors, including the serotonin 2a receptor. Psilocybin and LSD are two of the psychedelics that possess potent anti-inflammatory effects.

There are several reasons why the emergence of psychedelic compounds for the treatment of depression and related illness is extremely timely, regardless of the mode of action. First, these disorders represent a massive, unmet, health burden at a time where several major drug companies have pulled out of psychiatric research. There is growing evidence of psychedelics' safety and efficiency. They have limited abuse potential and are not addictive. They have rapid and often enduring treatment efficacy. Finally, they represent an ideal bridge between psychotherapy and psychopharmacology.

A recent paper published in the prestigious journal *Nature*, reported on a drug that binds to serotonin 2a receptors in mice without causing the usual behavioral features that mice show when given psychedelics. This agent exerted prolonged antidepressant responses after a single dose. We now need to see the same result in human trials, but it is a promising lead.

Psychedelics or drugs that activate the serotonin 2a receptor without psychedelic effects are poised to play a unique role in the next generation of antidepressant agents.

Psychedelics have been a part of many cultural traditions and healing rituals for millennia, and finally modern science is beginning to catch on to why.

CHAPTER 15

A Newer Understanding of Older Antidepressants

The hypothesis that imbalances in norepinephrine and serotonin are the most important biological causes for depression has dominated psychiatry for more than fifty years. This model has informed almost all of the research attempting to develop new treatments in the recent past. Now that we are beginning to learn more about the underlying causes of depressive illness, we have identified a multiplicity of new targets for the next generation of antidepressants. Thus, the primary importance of norepinephrine and serotonin is being called into question.

We now know that drugs like the SSRIs that work on the serotonin system are still effective even when the serotonin system is blocked, removed, or otherwise not engaged. Interestingly, even when key elements of the serotonin system are removed, the biochemical, behavioral, and electrophysiological effects produced by SSRIs are still found in mice that are given the drugs, indicating that serotonin is not essential to the mechanism of action of SSRIs. This suggests we need a new model explaining the mechanisms of antidepressant effects of these drugs.

There is enormous evidence showing that BDNF plays critical roles in multiple nervous system processes, including the ability to mount a normal stress response. A recent paper showed conclusively that traditional antidepressants like imipramine and the SSRIs do not work in experimental animals in whom the genes for either BDNF or its receptor are inactivated. Thus, by process of elimination we have determined that BDNF is essential to the therapeutic effects of traditional antidepressants.

To more directly examine the role of BDNF in how antidepressants take effect in the brain, an infusion of BDNF directly into the brain stem was found to produce an antidepressant response. Additional studies showed a single BDNF infusion into the emotional memory center was sufficient to promote antidepressant responses in three days.

This single infusion of BDNF continued to produce an antidepressant response for up to twelve days after the infusion into the emotional memory center. This is well past the interval for the actual degradation of the protein, indicating that BDNF is likely to be setting into motion sustained effects that relate to brain plasticity.

Experimental deactivation of the BDNF gene or its receptor abolishes the antidepressant effects of not only the SSRIs but the tricyclic antidepressants as well. In addition, studies indicate that other antidepressants such as Wellbutrin, Effexor, and Cymbalta also binds to the BDNF receptor.

Although traditional antidepressants activate the BDNF system, they do so in a weak fashion. This probably accounts for why they must be given for two to three weeks or more until their concentrations reach a critical point where they can activate the BDNF system; it also accounts for the fact that at least 40 percent of patients do not respond to the traditional antidepressant regimens.

BDNF and its receptor are also crucial for the therapeutic effects of ketamine. Experimental deactivation of the genes for BDNF or its receptor extinguished the antidepressant efficacy of ketamine. Ketamine is much more potent an activator of the BDNF system than traditional antidepressants.

Overall, BDNF signaling in the emotional memory center seems to represent a crucial component of antidepressant responses to conventional antidepressants. This, of course, does not mean other sites in the brain are not involved; multiple neural circuits are essential for antidepressant efficacy. Nevertheless, the impact of BDNF on the emotional memory center in the mediation of antidepressant responses offers an important clue regarding the neural circuitry involved in the depressive process.

While BDNF is the crucial link promoting the antidepressant effects of traditional agents as well as ketamine, serotonin or norepinephrine do in fact also play a role, though one we haven't completely yet determined. Serotonin may activate the BDNF system indirectly and diminish the activity of the amygdala while increasing the activity of the controller. On the other hand, we know that dopamine is crucial for the anticipation and experience of pleasure, and its actions are clearly reduced in experimental models of depression. Unfortunately, Wellbutrin is only a very weak stimulus to dopamine activity, and it is unclear to what extent this effect plays in its antidepressant efficacy. Scientists are actively looking for other compounds that vigorously and safely augment the dopamine system to counter the anhedonia of depression. So far, this has not proved to be an easy task.

Dr. Ron Duman made many contributions to our understanding of the basic mechanisms underlying depressive illness and the mechanisms of action of antidepressants. He and Eric Nestler launched the Laboratory of Molecular Psychiatry at Yale. It was one of the world's first research laboratories focused on the molecular and cellular biology of depression and other psychiatric disorders.

The Duman lab was the first to demonstrate that chronic stress inhibited BDNF expression in the emotional memory center of experimental animals. He also first demonstrated that antidepressants increase BDNF function in the emotional memory center to an extent that initiated and sustained antidepressant effects, and made many contributions to our understanding of how ketamine works.

Ron also first discovered that multiple classes of antidepressants stimulate neurogenesis in the hippocampus and has spurred the search for generating neurogenesis stimulators in the treatment of depressive illness.

He was among a select group of neuroscientists who moved away from a focus on neurotransmitters and their receptors in the causation of depression to focus on the diversity of cell types in the brain, the intricate web of interactive coordinating molecules, and the molecular and cellular underpinnings in specific brain circuits that contribute to depression. He applied the most sophisticated neuroscientific and molecular methodologies in order to produce a body of work that will stand the test of time.

Ron grew up in a lively and loving household of seven children, in close proximity to a large, close-knit network of immediate relatives in the small town of Ebensburg, Pennsylvania. He was the House Jameson Professor of Psychiatry and Neuroscience at the Yale University School of Medicine, and has earned many honors, including election to the National Academy of Medicine.

Sadly, Ron died suddenly and unexpectedly of a heart attack in 2021 at the age of sixty-six during a hike with his family in the Adirondacks. Many tributes attested to his devotion to his family and his enormous contributions to the training of many now well-established scientific investigators, as well as to his kind and generous nature, his integrity, and his gentle sense of humor.

The work on unraveling depression continues, but Ron certainly put us miles further down the path.

CHAPTER 16

The Promise and Peril of Ketamine

The recent discovery that ketamine could exert significant antidepressant effects within minutes is one of the most important events in depression research in the last fifty years.

Scientists have known for years that ketamine works through the glutamate system. Since the 1950s, ketamine has been used as a safe anesthetic. Ketamine's extraordinary antidepressant effects led to an intense focus on glutamate in depression research laboratories around the world. In contrast to compounds like norepinephrine, dopamine, and serotonin, which are present in about 3 percent of brain nerve cells, glutamate is present in 50 percent of nerve cells. It is the main neurotransmitter in the brain that has excitatory effects on nerve cells. Compared to neurotransmitters like norepinephrine, which plays a modulatory roll in structures like the controller and the emotional memory center, glutamate plays a much greater regulatory role. It is not entirely surprising that ketamine, acting through glutamate, exceeds standard antidepressants by acting much faster, inducing greater rates of remission, and preventing relapse to a much greater extent.

During sustained periods of severe stress large amounts of

glutamate are released. This can cause nerve cells to fire so rapidly that the cell's energy supplies are depleted and the cell dies. Afterward, there is a modest decrease in glutamate stores remaining, resulting in a depressed state. It is in this context that ketamine administration results in a modest release of glutamate that activates the glutamate AMPA receptor. This activation in turn almost immediately promotes the release of BDNF in the controller and emotional memory center. The cumulative effect within hours is noticeable in increased connections among nerve cells, increased neuroplasticity in areas of the prefrontal cortex and limbic system, increased neurogenesis in the emotional memory center, and markedly improved synaptic function. Ketamine also has anti-inflammatory properties that likely contribute to its effectiveness in treating depressive illness.

Scientists and clinicians have found that the greater the decrease in the initial size of the controller and emotional memory center, the stronger the response to ketamine. Decreased deep sleep is a common component of melancholic depression, and those with the greatest reductions in deep sleep have the best responses to ketamine. Ketamine also rapidly improved cognitive function.

Abnormalities with circadian CLOCK genes also predict a response to ketamine. Circadian disturbances in depression affect neurotransmitters and hormones, resulting in marked alterations in the rest-activity cycle, and short- and long-term cycling between depression and mania. A prospective trial dosing ketamine at different points of the circadian cycle is currently underway to shed more light on how ketamine affects our body's daily clock both biologically and clinically.

Ketamine may serve as a prototype for entirely new classes of antidepressants that can selectively target elements it affects while producing few side effects. Data indicate that the combination of psychotherapy with ketamine administration results in a greater rate of recovery and fewer recurrences than either alone.

The discovery of ketamine is important not only because it

indicates that rapid-acting depressants exist, but because it can be used as an important therapeutic tool in its own right. However, a minority of patients have dissociative reactions, meaning patients don't know who or where they are. These symptoms clear in a few hours, but they are disturbing and require a physician's attendance for the first few hours after ketamine administration. Other compounds are being developed that have ketamine's efficacy without these troubling reactions.

The question then arises regarding the extent to which ketamine could change what it means to have depression. A compound that acts almost immediately to produce long-term positive results and that has obvious effects on a patient's neurobiology could significantly decrease the stigmatization of depression. Finally, perhaps people will understand that depression is a disease based on physiology, much like heart disease. This could go a long way in removing some of the stigma associated with mental illness—and should also lead toward parity in insurance coverage.

Robert's Story

When Robert Wilson first came to the NIH, he had been depressed for most of his life. His father had left home when he was four, precipitating his first depression. An uncle had molested him on numerous occasions before the age of ten.

In the middle of his freshman year of college, Robert had attempted suicide. The impetus had been the breakup of his relationship with his girlfriend and academic difficulties because he was unable to study.

Robert was thirty-four now. His current depression was characterized by feelings of worthlessness, anxiety, loss of appetite, early-morning awakening, and an incapacity to feel any form of pleasure. It was a severe, classic melancholic depression. However, we could not identify a clear precipitant to his current depression. He told me, "Dr. Gold, you know how much adversity I endured.

I would get depression after depression, but each time I would tough it out and do what had to be done. Much of the time I put on an act so no one would suspect that I was depressed. I can't do that anymore. But I won't let my family down the way my dad did with us. I promise this to myself and to you."

By the time Robert had come to the NIH Clinical Center, he had already tried imipramine, Prozac, Wellbutrin, Effexor, Cymbalta, and Lexapro, an SSRI that was new at the time. None of these had proved effective. However, there was a new drug for which we were currently conducting trials. That drug was ketamine.

Robert's participation in the ketamine trials included multiple PET scans with multiple capacities. We use them to help assess anatomic changes in areas of the stress system and the rest of the brain, changes in the metabolic activity of these centers, the connectedness among these structures, the magnitude of brain inflammation, and the activity of multiple neurotransmitters and hormones. Neuroimaging has revolutionized our understanding of biological factors involved in depression and the mechanism of action of effective antidepressant medications.

Along with PET scans, Robert's entire DNA sequences were obtained and analyzed. He had overnight standard EEG sleep studies, as well as a specialized sleep study called a magnetoencephalogram, which picks up a wave frequency specific to depression that is corrected by ketamine. Regular blood draws helped us track inflammation and stress hormones, metabolic and coagulating parameters, and to examine the circadian patterns of his hormonal secretion.

Robert showed evidence of a significant decrease in the sizes of the controller and the emotional memory center. His amygdala was enlarged. He had evidence of brain inflammation, especially in the stress system. His magnetoencephalogram was highly abnormal. His stress hormones, especially cortisol and norepinephrine, were highly elevated, and he had increased blood glucose concentrations, increased inflammation in his body and brain, and an activated coagulation system.

Completing this workup was the main goal of Robert's first two weeks at the hospital. On his fifteenth day in the hospital, the trials began in earnest. Robert received a small intravenous infusion of a microdose of ketamine.

Six hours after the infusion, Robert felt calmer and moderately less burdened by his severe depression. In another two hours, he felt completely well. When Robert registered this dramatic change, he began to cry. "I never believed I could ever feel this way again," he said.

We were all astonished. Rather than the two- to three-week latency for standard antidepressants, ketamine acted in a matter of hours.

Yet, we didn't know what the long-term effects would be. That is, at that time, we didn't know whether his remission would last.

Robert's depression returned ten days after the single infusion. Although Robert felt, of course, discouraged, his initial response to the infusion proved critical in helping him understand he could feel well again. It gave him hope. When Robert had tried an SSRI in the past, he had no response. When we tried the SSRI Lexapro now, he responded. There are some data that a ketamine-induced remission reduces the threshold for responses to subsequent antidepressant trials.

Other early trials of ketamine, however, demonstrated clear risks. At another center, for example, a patient who responded acutely to a single dose of ketamine became despondent after he lost the response. He committed suicide. As with any drug, we had to be careful in its administration.

Ketamine's half-life is only 2.5 hours. This means that after 150 minutes only half of the amount of dose of the drug administered is still present in blood plasma, yet despite the fact that ketamine clears the body quickly, a single dose produces an antidepressant response that often lasts almost two weeks. Clearly ketamine sets into motion downstream changes that last far longer than its half-life. Long-term studies with ketamine reveal that it is effective when given every two weeks for periods now of up to a year. Some have sustained long-term antidepressant responses long after ketamine had been discontinued.

Of significant importance is the fact that ketamine gave us an important clue about the possible critical effects the neurotransmitter glutamate plays in depression, as well as the roles of BDNF, the BDNF receptor, and the AMPA receptor. Many new drugs are emerging from this promising area of research.

Ketamine is a powerful tool in our arsenal of the treatment of depression, but it is not without significant risk. It is also dangerous when used as a recreational drug, known by the street name Special K. Since it is an anesthetic, it can produce a feeling of pleasant detachment, but it can also make the user unaware of injuries, even serious ones. Overdoses can lead to rapid heartbeat, high blood pressure, seizures, and death.

CHAPTER 17

Breaking Through Depression

It is an exciting time to be working in the field of neuropsychiatry. We have entered a new era in terms of promising treatments for depression, after a half century of little progress. Well over thirty new compounds and procedures have recently emerged on the basis of recent research into the neurobiology of depression and will be presented in this chapter. They represent an entire departure from the last generation of antidepressants and procedures. Most are rapid-acting (within hours), long-lasting, and induce higher rates of remission than their predecessors. It is difficult for me to express how excited and pleased I am by these breakthroughs after so many years of not getting to the core pathophysiological features of depressive illness.

Ketamine, a glutamate NMDA receptor antagonist, is the first of these new-generation agents. NMDA receptors are one of the principal glutamate receptors found throughout the central nervous system. They influence many key processes ranging from learning and memory to mood, cognition, and respiration.

Microdoses of ketamine can be used as an antidepressant. These low doses do not damage neurons. As noted earlier, the binding of these low doses of ketamine to the NMDA receptor activates the gentle release of glutamate in both the controller and the emotional memory center. This in turn leads to activation of the AMPA glutamate receptors, which then go on to activate the BDNF system and, perhaps, other effects that contribute to ketamine's antidepressant efficacy that we don't yet fully understand.

The first ketamine-like drug approved for depression was Esketamine, a drug that acts exactly like ketamine and has a virtually identical chemical formula. If ketamine is given as an oral medication, it is degraded in the gastrointestinal tract and thus will not exert therapeutic effects. For it to enter the brain it must be administered intravenously or taken as a nasal spray, a route which gives it access to the central nervous system. The first clinical studies with esketamine were highly successful, with a 72 percent response rate within hours that could last two weeks after a single administration. The placebo response rate was less than 5 percent. Studies show that its intermittent administration can produce sustained antidepressant responses for at least a year. These trials are now ongoing. Esketamine mimics ketamine's effects on the glutamate AMPA receptor with subsequent activation of the BDNF system. Esketamine was approved for use in treating depression in 2019.

Scientists have developed several more NMDA antagonists that have gone through promising clinical trials. The first of these, AXS-05, is a combination of dextromethorphan, long-known to be an NMDA antagonist, and Wellbutrin. AXS-05 received breakthrough designation from the FDA for use in major depressive disorder and Alzheimer's disease. AXS-05 is also effective in helping with smoking cessation. AXS-05 also depends upon post-NMDA blockade effects involving the AMPA receptor and BDNF.

Nitrous oxide is also an NMDA receptor antagonist. One hour of inhalation of 50 percent nitrous oxide (identical to that given in the dentist's office) provoked a significant response in alleviating symptoms of depression within two hours; that dose was still effective at two weeks. A single inhalation of nitrous oxide produced no serious adverse events, but more than that can cause headache and nausea in some people. Recent data reveal that a dose of just 25 percent nitrous oxide is just as effective for treatment-resistant depression. Studies to determine its safety for long-term usage are underway. If the data hold up that a single inhalation is good for at least two weeks, long-term administration should not be a problem. Interestingly, part of nitrous oxide's effectiveness comes from the fact that it also releases dopamine.

Esmethadone (REL-1017) is a variant of methadone. Esmethadone exerts mild to moderate NMDA-blocking properties. Improvements in depression were seen after four days of usage and lasted for the whole duration of the fourteen-day trial. Full remission rates ran over 50 percent while the placebo response was only 5 percent. Mild side effects include headache and nausea. Patients who took Esmethadone in a trial experienced no dissociative or psychotic events, as well as no opioid effects or withdrawal symptoms.

New Antidepressants That Do Not Have to Block NMDA Receptors

Rapid antidepressant action does not necessarily require blockade of NMDA receptors. There are other means by which rapid antidepressants can be effective. Norketamine is a breakdown product of ketamine formed when ketamine is metabolized by enzymes. On its own, Norketamine has potent antidepressant effects analogous to ketamine. It does not, however, act as an NMDA antagonist; rather, it rapidly creates an antidepressant effect by causing the acute release of glutamate to activate AMPA receptors and the BDNF system.

Cannabidiol is a non–psychologically active component of cannabis. In studies in experimental animals, cannabidiol given as a single dose induced rapid and sustained antidepressant-like effects associated with increases in BDNF levels in the prefrontal cortex and the emotional memory center. This activation of BDNF release does not involve the NMDA receptor, and is accompanied by rapid, significant increases in neuroplasticity and neurogenesis. Studies are now underway to determine optimal dosages and safety of cannabidiol for its efficacy, as well as cannabis itself.

Compounds That Directly Act on the Glutamate System

In addition to NMDA and AMPA receptors, there is another class of glutamate receptors called mGlu receptors, consisting of nine different subtypes. When the type 2 mGlu glutamate receptor is blocked, it leads the brain to rapidly release glutamate into the prefrontal cortex and emotional memory center. This action almost immediately results in increased neuroplasticity in the prefrontal cortex and increased neurogenesis in the emotional memory center.

In addition to antagonists to the type 2 mGlu receptor, preliminary data show that antagonists to the type 3, type 5, and type 9 may also have therapeutic effects. This is an enormous area of new research, and these new agents may eclipse several of the other new medication classes in terms of antidepressant efficacy.

The Search for Agents to Directly Stimulate the Glutamate AMPA Receptor

Investigators all over the world are searching for compounds that can effectively and safely activate the glutamate AMPA receptor directly, which leads to activation of the BDNF system. This goal has so far been elusive because available AMPA receptor agents have so far proven to be toxic.

GABA Agonists in the Treatment of Depression

Next to glutamate, GABA is the second most plentiful neurotransmitter in the brain, present in 20 percent of all neurons. In contrast to glutamate, GABA is an inhibitory neurotransmitter, shutting off neurons rather than exciting them. Several GABA agonists are employed as antianxiety agents or sedatives.

Multiple lines of evidence indicate that GABA neurotransmission is diminished in depressive illness. GABA concentrations are reduced in the brains of patients with depression, and its levels are reduced in the blood and cerebrospinal fluid.

A recent major advance is the finding that allopregnanolone (brand name Brexanolone) is the first truly effective treatment for postpartum depression, a notoriously difficult-to-treat and sometimes life-destroying illness. Brexanolone is a member of the neurosteroid family and is a stimulator of GABA activity. Neurosteroids have identical structures to some of the adrenal, ovarian, and andrgenic steroids but are produced entirely in the brain. Brexanolone also has progesterone-like effects, which is logical in the light of data that progesterone withdrawal after delivery is thought to significantly contribute to the severity of this depressive subtype.

Zuranolone is highly similar to Brexanolone and is also a GABA agonist effective in treating postpartum depressions and major depression, and it can be administered orally. It too represents a breakthrough.

Psychedelics in the Rapid Treatment of Depression

Another major recent advance is our growing understanding of how psychedelic compounds behave as effective, rapid-acting antidepressants. As noted earlier, their novel effects may make them a preeminent class of antidepressant agents.

By far the standard for psychedelic antidepressants, psilocybin, aka "magic mushrooms," received fast-track status from the FDA, meaning approval for its use should be forthcoming soon. A lead article in the *New England Journal of Medicine* reported that its efficacy was equal to or superior to that of the SSRIs, with data that suggest psychedelics may revolutionize the treatment of depression. Psilocybin is a very rapid-acting antidepressant.

The naturally occurring ayahuasca, derived from two plants found in the Amazon basin, combines the psychedelic DMT which, like other psychedelics, activates serotonin 2A receptors. A single dose of twenty-one milligrams demonstrated significant improvement in depressed subjects by day seven.

LSD has long been known to relieve depressive symptoms but has also been perceived as dangerous (which in high doses it certainly is—an LSD overdose can induce aggression, homicidal or suicidal thoughts, and cause seizures, irregular heartbeat, and brain hemorrhage). A recent study in healthy volunteers involved administration of LSD in microdoses, similar to those used for the administration of psilocybin. None of the untoward effects seen with standard doses of LSD occurred. Animal studies with these microdoses show highly effective antidepressant effects. LSD is now involved in studies to examine its antidepressant effects in treatment-resistant patients. Results are pending. (See more on psychedelics in chapter 14).

Anti-Inflammatory Agents as Effective Antidepressants

Given the substantial role of inflammation in patients with depressive illness, trials of anti-inflammatory compounds in the treatment of depression are underway. Celecoxib, a potent non-steroidal anti-inflammatory (NSAID), significantly improves antidepressant responses to standard antidepressants. Other potent NSAIDS worked as well.

Antagonists to cytokines, the compounds white blood cells produce to stimulate the immune response, and other immune suppressants also demonstrate antidepressant efficacy. Antagonists to TNF-a, interleukin 6, interleukin 12, and interleukin 23 have preliminarily demonstrated antidepressant efficacy in their own right and also in amplifying the effects of other classes of antidepressants.

Omega-3 fatty acids have multiple metabolic and anti-inflammatory effects and have also demonstrated antidepressant effects in multiple trials alone and in combination with other antidepressants.

There is a myriad of anti-inflammatory compounds available, and many of these will enter clinical trials to determine which are most effective in alleviating the symptoms of depression. Researchers are working continually to develop new, more effective anti-inflammatory agents that act quickly and have minimal side effects,

New Treatments for Bipolar Depression

Caplyta is a drug that acts as an antagonist to serotonin 2a and dopamine D2 receptors. This drug does not cause psychedelic phenomena, adverse metabolic effects, or weight gain, compared to other members of its class, and could be a replacement for Seroquel, a highly effective treatment for bipolar disorder with pronounced metabolic and appetite-stimulating properties.

A New, Improved Treatment for the Agitation of Mania

Precedex is a sedating agent that does not interfere with alertness and resolves bipolar agitation in more than 90 percent of patients within twenty minutes.

Botox

A brief article published in the prestigious journal *Science* reported that asking depressed patients to hold a smile interrupted their depression for as long as they could sustain the smile. Following up on this, investigators injected Botox to more permanently affix a smile, and found that 55 percent of patients responded compared to 5 percent who responded to a placebo. The therapeutic effect of Botox administration depended entirely on its capacity to promote a sustained smile.

New Drugs Affecting Norepinephrine and Serotonin

Fetzima is a serotonin-norepinephrine reuptake blocker. Unlike other serotonin-norepinephrine uptake blockers like Effexor and Cymbalta, which are predominantly serotonin uptake block-ers (90%/10%), Fetzima is 50/50, much like imipramine. Thus, Fetzima could be a good treatment for melancholia without the dangerous cardiac side effects. Tricyclics are among the most effective treatments for melancholic depression.

Drugs Affecting the Opioid System

Our bodies make a variety of neurotransmitters and hormones that bind to receptors throughout the brain that can also bind with morphine and related opioid compounds. These compounds are called endogenous opioids and include beta endorphin. Another is a kappa opioid that binds to a specific kappa opioid receptor. There is an extensive set of preclinical studies suggesting that kappa opioid antagonists are likely to have therapeutic effects in those with mood and anxiety spectrum disorders.

A number of studies indicate that the kappa opiate system is critical for mediating the adverse effects of stress. An important aspect of stress-related pharmacology is the dynorphins, a group of opioid peptides that exert their effects primarily through bind-ing to kappa opioid receptors.

The depression-like behaviors caused by chronic stress, uncon-trollable stress, and social defeat stress are mediated, in part, by kappa opiate receptors. Mice treated with kappa opioid antago-nists show a reduction of stress-induced, depression-like behavior.

In one recent study, six patients who had failed to respond to antidepressant medications and ECT were found to improve with buprenorphine, a kappa receptor antagonist. Findings of a double-blind, placebo-controlled pilot study in thirty-two patients with treatment-resistant depression treated with buprenorphine indicate this kappa antagonist had a positive therapeutic effect. Clinical trials of kappa antagonists to treat depression are proceeding at multiple sites.

The Genius Behind Many Recent Breakthroughs in the Neurobiology of Depression

Many of the recent breakthroughs in our understanding of neurobiological treatments for depression had their origins in the studies done by Solomon Snyder, one of the most influential neuroscientists in the world and one of the field's most highly cited authors. He has made extraordinary contributions to neuroscience, which include his discovery that the body has its own opiate receptors located throughout the brain. The best-known endorphin (endogenous opiate) receptor binds morphine. There are several more opioid compounds that bind to several additional opiate receptors. Many scientists believe that the body's own opiates are what produce the elevated mood that athletes feel after vigorous exercise. Opioids are also involved in the mood elevation associated with alcohol ingestions, and recent studies reveal that the antagonist to the morphine opioid receptor, naloxone, significantly helps individuals addicted to alcohol to stop drinking. Trials are still ongoing to determine the extent to which the body's own opioids can be harnessed to effectively treat subgroups of individuals with depressive illness. The activation of the kappa opiate receptor often leads to depression.

Sol also established the gas nitric oxide as a key player in neurotransmission, in inflammation, and in mediating penile erection. This latter function led to the development of drugs like Viagra. Repeated nitric oxide exposure exerts antidepressant effects when targeting the prefrontal cortex. In addition to blocking NMDA receptors, nitrous oxide activates the nitric oxide system, which may contribute to its antidepressant efficacy.

Sol has cloned multiple neurotransmitter and nerve growth factor receptors and worked out the mechanisms of many psychoactive compounds. His work has highly influenced research into both schizophrenia and depression. The Johns Hopkins Department of Neuroscience is now called the Solomon Snyder Department of Neuroscience. He is a recipient of the Lasker Award for basic science.

He initially went to college in order to become a psychiatrist but had little interest in science. He liked thinking about how the brain works, and he cared about people's feelings. His ideas about science changed after spending several summers at the NIH. He soon discovered that lab research was very different from science in textbooks and college courses. It was creative, very artistic, and lots of fun. Working at the NIH also inculcated a fascination with the power of biochemical tools to address all sorts of questions.

The seminal experience in all of his training was working in Julius Axelrod's lab. He had met Julie during his summers at NIH and he went to Julie's lab to inquire if he might train with him during the course of an NIH fellowship. Julie noted, "Sol, most applicants for research associate positions in my lab are valedictorians from Harvard and Yale. You only went to Georgetown University, so normally I wouldn't have a job for you. However, the fellow who matched with me decided not to come, so I have an opening. I liked what you were doing in the lab in medical school, so I suppose it's OK for you to work with me."

Sol didn't mind the lukewarm welcome. He just needed a job. His years with Julie were the most important in his professional life. Julie was a mentor par excellence and a remarkable inspiration to him and all the others who worked with him. Julie was so productive that it was thought that he had fifty postdocs working for him. In fact, when he was there, there were only five. All the fellows in the lab at that time would become world-famous scientists. Julie was remarkably open to new ideas, though usually the most creative ideas were Julie's. For example, something Julie said in passing one day made Sol think about looking for the body's own opiate receptors and the compounds that bound to them. Other offhand suggestions led to his identification of multiple serotonin, acetylcholine, and histamine receptors. Sol also isolated multiple nerve growth factors that play significant roles in the loss of tissue in key sites of the stress system that contribute to the clinical and biochemical manifestations of depression.

Sol, like Axelrod, trained many students who went on to develop distinguished careers in neuroscience, He felt that he based his mentoring on what he had learned from Julie. Being a mentor for students is the same as being a parent for your children. It is also akin to certain forms of psychotherapy, such as the unconditional positive regard that Carl Rogers emphasized. Sol tries to encourage people through positive reinforcement. When something goes bad, he never says, "You stupid idiot." He just says nothing or tries to learn from the failure. When things go well, he provides unstinting praise. He constantly asks students what they think should be done and always encourages their ideas.

In beginning with a student in the lab, because of their relative inexperience, Julie suggests what the first project should be. The first project is well structured with a high probability of success, a strategy that builds self-confidence. Gradually, the student weans away from the dependence on the mentor. This process varies greatly with different students. The goal, which Julie hopes to attain after a year or so, is for the student to come up with 90 percent of the ideas. In terms of managing research in the lab, he believes in management by walking around. He simply hangs around with the students and engages them in scientific discussions. I modeled my mentoring after Julie and enormously enjoyed my post-docs.

Countering the Action of CRH

CRH (corticotropin-releasing hormone) sets into motion many of the behavioral and physiological manifestations of melancholic depression, such as anxiety and fear-related behaviors, activation of the repertoire of stress hormones, inflammation, and inhibition of appetite, sleep, and sexual behavior. We figured that a CRH antagonist is a good candidate to treat melancholia. To accomplish this task, we had to utilize a small molecule that was not degraded by the GI tract, then crossed the blood-brain barrier and antagonized the CRH receptor by binding in a small pocket at a critical point at the receptor site. Others have tried CRH antagonists, but they made the error of including patients with atypical depression, in whom we demonstrated that the stress system and CRH activity are diminished. Thus, a CRH antagonist would be likely to worsen atypical depression and wash out any findings. Also, they did not use appropriate doses. We have worked out the precise dosage that has maximal behavioral and physiological effects. This project will commence in the near future.

Developing an Oral Pill That Is a Direct Stimulus for the BDNF System

I have saved perhaps the best potential pharmacologic intervention for last. Throughout the book I have emphasized the key role of BDNF in the pathophysiology of depression and in the mechanisms of action of almost all antidepressant drugs. BDNF cannot be given orally because it is broken down in the gastrointestinal tract. It cannot be given intravenously because it cannot pass the blood-brain barrier to get access to the brain.

Our antalarmin project is a successful example of getting around the problem of impediments to oral absorption and passage of a compound across the blood-brain barrier. The same strategies for developing such a small molecule that can activate the BDNF receptor is one means of directly activating this critical system. One of the holy grails of psychiatric research in depressive illness is the development of such a compound for treating depression that can be taken orally. This compound must be orally absorbed intact, cross the blood-brain barrier, and bind to the BDNF receptor very tightly. This is an entirely feasible project.

Admittedly, it is easier to design such a compound as an antagonist because it doesn't have to fit perfectly into the pocket to exert its blockade of the receptor. Medicinal chemists know that to activate a receptor, you need a more perfect fit. It will be harder to develop a small molecule that will activate the BDNF receptor because of this fact.

We also need to further elucidate the mechanism of BDNF synthesis and degradation. If we know what turned off the BDNF system, we could develop a blocker to this molecule. Similarly, identifying compounds that activate BDNF secretion would be another way to harness this compound as an effective antidepressant. While ketamine and all other antidepressants seem to be capable of activating the BDNF receptor indirectly, other compounds could be found that do so much more effectively and, hopefully, for longer periods of time.

As noted, the CLOCK gene is mutated in patients with bipolar disorder. Pharmacologists have designed a host of small molecules that are orally absorbed, cross the blood-brain barrier, and modify the functional activity of the CLOCK gene. Studies are just getting underway to study their efficacy in bipolar disorder.

Many of these breakthroughs related to our understanding of how the brain functions can be traced back to discoveries made by Eric Nestler who is, in my opinion, the most outstanding neuroscientist in psychiatry today. He has made exceptional contributions to molecular psychiatric research. More than any other investigator, he has worked out molecular mechanisms underlying reward, addiction, depression, and resiliency. His work has led to the development of multiple medications to treat addiction, depression, and increase resilience.

He is the son of first-generation immigrant parents who encouraged him at a very early age to consider medicine. He chose medicine out of his own interests rather than because of the wishes of his parents, and he has loved both his medical and scientific education and his forty years as a researcher.

He received his undergraduate, medical school, and PhD training all at Yale. As a postdoctoral fellow, he worked in the laboratory of Nobel laureate Paul Greengard. He found Dr. Greengard to be an exceptional teacher and mentor and considered himself to be a part of the Greengard family. Along with Ron Duman, he founded the first molecular laboratory of psychiatry and is the leading investigator in the world applying the techniques and principles of molecular science to the study of psychiatry. Eric has more than 650 publications, has been President of the Society of Neuroscience, and is a member of the National Academy of Medicine and of the American Academy of Arts and Sciences. He has won numerous national and international prizes for research and is one of the most cited scientists in the world.

Along with Ron Duman, he developed the exceedingly important hypothesis that the neurodegeneration of depressive illness reflected the loss of BDNF, which he had shown to have become deficient in the face of stress. His laboratory is hard at work developing a BDNF stimulator that can be taken orally for the treatment of depression. He is also spearheading another study aimed at developing rapid-acting, effective antidepressants. The first addresses the kappa opioid system, discussed in an earlier section. He is also working on strategies to influence calcium channel dynamics as a way of treating depression.

In addition to his outstanding work in addiction and depression research, he has spearheaded molecular studies underlying resilience and vulnerability to stress that have helped to define the field.

He is a pioneer in the field of the epigenetics of depression and has made the most important contributions to this area of research. He continues to actively investigate this phenomenon to lead the field in related discoveries that could bring help to millions who suffer from depression.

CHAPTER 18

Building Resiliency

One of the goals of contemporary depression research is to learn how to predict and prevent an imminent depressive episode. We've made strides in identifying those at risk and using treatments that can prevent the onset of a full-blown depressive episode. The rapidly evolving field of resiliency research is helping us to accomplish this task.

One of the fundamental questions asked by researchers in the field of resilience is "Why is it that some people seem to thrive even after extreme trauma, while others are brought low and may never bounce back?" I remember one of the most charming, positive people I ever met was a man who, as a teenager, was crammed on a freight car with a hundred others, with no food or water, on the way to a German death camp. It was in the waning days of World War II, when the Allies had finally realized the genocide that was occurring. As the train made its way, it was repeatedly strafed by Allied planes, adding to the death and misery in the cars. Who could survive that psychologically? And yet, this man—in his seventies when I met him—was not depressed or bitter. He was generous and open and had lived a productive life after the war. What allowed him to do that?

This question is of vital importance because, while we might wish that we could provide every human being with a positive, low-stress life, this is not currently possible. People will experience loss, want, and barbarity. Think of abused children, living in poverty in unsafe neighborhoods, for example. We cannot reliably stop the abuse, relieve the poverty, or ensure the safety of their neighborhood. We have neither the skill nor the will as yet. So, an important question is: How can we determine experiences, identify genes, or develop drugs that will help individuals thrive in spite of their negative experiences?

Biological studies of resiliency have exploded in recent years, with contributions from psychiatry, psychology, medicine, neurobiology, and molecular biology. Here are some of the things we're learning: A host of neuroimaging studies has given us many examples of the impact of alterations producing vulnerability to stress in specific areas of the brain that influence cognitive flexibility and cognitive control, as well as factors and brain regions influencing emotional regulation. I will also discuss differences in the neuroanatomy and functional activity of sites in the brain regulating reward responsivity, which directly promotes resilience, and areas of the brain that regulate our ability to extinguish traumatic memories so that individuals would not be haunted by frightening recall in disorders such as depression. Exciting new studies have identified specific genes that confer vulnerability to stressful stimuli that would be likely to result in a depressive episode. Gene therapy would lead to correction of these abnormalities and confer resistance to the development of depressive illness. I will close by detailing multiple pharmacologic studies that have identified agents with the capacity to help a highly vulnerable individual transition into one who is resilient in the face of severe physical and emotional stressors. The development of drugs to promote resilience will surely become one of the most important areas of clinical neuroscience, to be superseded only by gene therapy when it becomes available.

Environmental and Interpersonal Factors That Promote Either Resiliency or Vulnerability

Resiliency is the capacity of adapting well in the face of trauma, tragedy, threats, or significant sources of stress without developing a clinical depression.

In contrast to traditional perspectives of resilience as a stable, trait-like characteristic, resilience is now recognized as a multi-dimensional, dynamic capacity influenced by lifelong interactions between internal and environmental factors. It is an active rather than a passive process. For instance, in response to severe stress, resilient individuals show an increase in the expression of more than three hundred key genes in contrast to vulnerable individuals, who show increases of well under one hundred. Thus, resilience is a complex construct that can be conceptualized as a dynamic process that relates to developmental and environmental factors.

During development, a range of factors help prevent a vulnerability to depression. These include a close relationship with a caring adult who can serve as an object of positive identification, and who accepts the child for who he or she is rather than making unrealistic or perfectionistic demands. Such a caring figure also promotes social competence, provides effective guidance for self-regulation, and protects a child's sense of safety when facing adversity. These are important components of the establishment of a successful, healthy attachments. Research suggests that increased emotional awareness and coping self-efficacy may be two mechanisms by which secure attachment decreases stress reactivity.

Individuals who have an ample capacity to give and to accept help, who have developed effective means of self-care, who have a sense of purpose or meaning, and who can form substantive, enduring attachments to others have considerable resiliency in the face of intense stress or trauma. The capacity to express gratitude, kindness, and compassion also promotes resilience throughout life. Resiliency can be augmented in vulnerable individuals in a variety of ways, including psychotherapies that promote a sense of self-esteem and meaning, and pharmacotherapy that counters biologically mediated vulnerabilities.

There is a "mirror neuron system" in humans and animals that promotes an individual's capacity to understand the emotions and intentions of others. A robust capacity of the mirror neuron system for empathy and effective perception of others' intentions promotes resilience, and a decreased capacity in these functions promotes vulnerability.

Positive emotion, optimism, loving caretakers, highly reliable and competent role models, flexibility, the capacity to reframe adversity, and strong social support increase resiliency. Altruism, commitment to a valid cause, a capacity to extract meaning from adverse situations, and a tolerance to emotional pain and sadness promote resilience as well.

Individual coping strategies are particularly relevant to resilience and can be classified into two categories. The first category is active coping responses that are associated with actual or perceived control over the stressful situation. Such coping is considered to lead to changes promoting a resilient response. The second category, passive coping, includes mechanisms such as avoidance or helplessness and is associated with an increase in vulnerability.

Perfectionism decreases the propensity for resilience. This is especially so for those who feel that in order to maintain a sense of self-esteem, they must be as free of losses and disappointments as possible. Both of these are seen as imperfections that could be avoided by truly competent individuals. The inability to experience loss or disappointment without shame markedly decreases the capacity to grieve and hence the capacity to come to terms with the inevitable components of everyday living. Those who are inhibited from expressing assertiveness for fear of hurting others, or because they

fear retaliation or abandonment, are highly vulnerable and susceptible to feelings of helplessness, inefficacy, and ultimately, depression.

Repeated childhood trauma and exposure to uncontrollable
stressors diminish resiliency considerably. Later-adopted children
from institutions have larger amygdalae. In experimental animals, stress-induced adrenal-steroid secretion converts an imma-
ture amygdala into a mature one capable of consolidating and
storing negatively charged emotional memories. In humans, resilient patients who were free from depression had smaller amygdalae, while vulnerable individuals who developed depression had
larger amygdalae. In a study of children who had experienced
institutional care prior to adoption, it was found that children
who showed reduced amygdala responses to images of their parents, compared to strangers, had significantly larger reductions
in self-reported anxiety and depression three years later. Among
adults, lower amygdala reactivity to fearful faces, measured soon
after a significant trauma, was associated with lower self-reported
depressive and PTSD symptoms one year later.

In contrast, mild to moderate stress early in life can have an
inoculating effect. Such experience leads to increased neuroplasticity and neurogenesis and increases in the size of the controller.
An enriched, nurturing environment early in life with exposure
to manageable novelty increases resilience later in life. Regular
exercise and meditation increase plasticity in the central nervous
system and effectively promote resilience as well.

The Neurobiology of Resiliency

Studies in experimental animals validate the concept that we can
divide individuals into highly vulnerable or resilient groups. For
example, when a group of mice are exposed to stress created by
chronic social defeat stress, all of them showed activation of the
stress system and stress-induced compulsive water intake. However, approximately 35 percent of the stressed mice, considered

"resilient," do not exhibit behaviors that the other "vulnerable" mice do, including social avoidance, increased body temperature in response to social interactions, anhedonia-like symptoms (reduced interest in sucrose, high-fat food, or sex) or a metabolic syndrome characterized by overeating, obesity, and central hormonal disturbances. Clearly resilient animals are not totally devoid of symptoms, but they exhibit obvious resistance to many other traits exhibited by the vulnerable animals when both types are exposed to chronic social stress.

The animals classified as extremely disrupted exhibited anxiety-like behaviors and increased startle responses to loud noises, as well as large reductions in the levels of neuropeptide Y (NPY), a resilience-promoting brain hormone.

Most studies of resilience have focused on the absence of behavioral or molecular abnormality in a subset of stressed animals. Only more recently have we made attempts to study the more active mechanisms of resilience—protective changes that occur in resilient individuals.

Neuroanatomy and Resilience

Those with large controllers and the corresponding capacity to restrain the amygdala or to prime the reward system have increased resilience and a decreased incidence of depression. Conversely, a decrease in the size of the controller and its capacity to restrain the amygdala or to promote the activity of the reward system can lead to increased vulnerability and an increase in the incidence of depression. We found that children of depressed mothers studied between the ages of six and ten had smaller controllers even before showing any signs of depression. This finding shows that neuroanatomic anomalies associated with depression may precede the actual onset of the illness and predispose to its development.

A large emotional memory center promotes resilience and decreases the predisposition for depression, while a small emotional memory center increases vulnerability to stress and the propensity for depression. Smaller emotional memory center volumes were found in women with depression who experienced chronic maltreatment in their childhoods. In addition, a decrease in emotional memory center volume in depression has been found to be associated with the duration of depressive episodes. Thankfully, effective psychopharmacological treatment of symptoms has been associated with increases in emotional memory center volume.

Individuals who were resilient and free of depression had more responsive reward systems to pleasurable stimuli, had normal reward systems, could take pleasure in themselves, and hence had greater self-esteem. They were more optimistic and more confident in their responses to stress. Vulnerable individuals who had developed depression had decreased reward system responses to pleasurable stimuli and significantly diminished self-esteem. They were easily daunted by stressful stimuli.

Brain Circuits That Help Us Rethink

One of the ways resilience manifests is in our ability to step back from a situation that makes us uncomfortable or incites a stress response and to reevaluate it. This is called cognitive reappraisal, an effective emotion-regulating strategy. In an fMRI study of healthy women, a higher rate of reappraisal corresponded to lower amygdala reactivity to images of fearful and angry faces, as well as higher activation levels of the prefrontal cortex area that mediates cognitive control over emotion.

Similarly, in a study involving neuroimaging in 1,800 teenagers, resilient youth had a larger area of the prefrontal cortex that exerts cognitive control over emotion as well as smaller amygdalae.

Deficits in cognitive function, including working memory, attention, and cognitive flexibility, have been observed in adults with a history of childhood maltreatment and individuals with susceptibility to depression and posttraumatic stress disorder.

The association between childhood trauma and executive function difficulties is clear, and we now have a better idea of how to address it.

Erasing Fearful Memories

The ability to put aside fearful memories is essential for adaptive functioning when we move out of a dangerous to a safe environment. The controller has been identified as a core brain structure for adaptively extinguishing negatively charged emotional memories that are no longer of use in both human and animal studies. We see greater activity in the controller and the emotional memory center of resilient individuals.

Genetic Factors

Multiple small genetic mutations can make us more vulnerable to stress or depression. The mutations can lead to increased fear to increased behavioral and physiological responses to stress; low optimism, low perceived social support, and emotional volatility; and to higher susceptibility to depression. Mutations in genes that lead to decreased neurogenesis and impair activity of the BDNF gene, and a mutation that hinders repair and recovery from injuries that arise in the stress response, also play a role. Mutations can also raise our risk of impulsivity and suicidal behaviors, decrease activity in anxiety-reducing genes, and prompt stronger amygdala activity after exposure to threatening faces. All of these factors point to the potential for excessive stress responses and vulnerability to depression.

Glutamate System

The glutamate system is significantly involved in cortex over-reaction to stress and plays a major role in the pathogenesis of depression. Recent postmortem studies in patients with depressive disorders who committed suicide showed significant increases in glutamate levels in the frontal cortex and in the area of the prefrontal cortex that exerts cognitive control over emotion. A mutation in a gene that removes glutamate from the synapse results in its decreased removal, raising glutamate levels; this rise in glutamate levels is associated with significant vulnerability.

The GABA System

GABA is an inhibitory neurotransmitter system whose activation leads to reduced anxiety. As we saw previously, GABA agonists are widely used as antianxiety agents. GABA levels are reduced in the brains of patients with major depression. They are also decreased in their plasma and CSF and are normalized following chronic treatment with antidepressants. The gene for a key enzyme promoting GABA synthesis is impaired in vulnerable individuals.

Dopamine

In a study of 30,000 PTSD cases and 170,000 controls, the Parkinson's disease gene involved in dopamine regulation, PARK2, was significantly associated with overreaction to stress in women. The results of the study were subsequently evaluated in a sample of eighty-one families with strong histories of depression. This mutation in the dopamine receptor among women with depression was approximately three times more prevalent in women with a history of depression and elevated the risk of developing another major depressive disorder by 450 percent.

The CRH Receptor 1 Gene

A mutation in the CRH receptor gene impairs sensitivity to social cues and the capacity to sense what others might be feeling.

Another mutation in the CRH receptor promotes increased hormonal and autonomic responses to stress. Both of these lead to increased vulnerability to stress.

The Calcium Voltage-Gated Channel Subunit ALPHA1 (CACNAIC) Gene

Calcium channel receptors play important roles in neurotransmission and are thought to be abnormal in depressive illness. A mutation in this gene in men is associated with higher emotional reactivity to stress, lower perceived social support, and decreased optimism. In women, this mutation results in lower emotional responses to stress, a higher perceived sense of support, and increased optimism. We do not know why men and women react so differently to the same mutation.

Two Genes Involved in Neurogenesis

The TCF4 gene and the BDNF gene are involved in successful neurogenesis. Mutations in these genes impair our capacity to mount a normal stress response, which is key to promoting resilience in the face of significant stress.

The APOE4 Gene

The APOE4 gene is best known for at least doubling the risk of Alzheimer's disease in those who carry it. There is a significant association between exaggerated stress responses and vulnerability with the APOE4 gene variant found in 30 percent of the population. This is associated with a greater than 25 percent increase in the incidence of depression. This gene may hinder repair and recovery that is necessary after injury related to extensive stress exposure. Given that patients with PTSD and depression are at greater risk for dementia, the APOE4 gene may be a shared pathway for the development of both conditions. People with the APOE4 gene also have a significantly higher incidence of late-life depression and cognitive dysfunction.

The Serotonin Transporter Gene

The serotonin transporter removes serotonin from the synapse and decreases overall serotonin neurotransmission. A mutation in the serotonin transporter gene increases vulnerability to stress and depression in individuals already at risk.

The MONOAMINE OXIDASE (MAO) Gene

A mutation in the MAO gene decreases resilience and increases the incidence of depression and suicide. This gene is involved in metabolizing and reducing the amounts of dopamine, serotonin, and norepinephrine, and its function is increased in vulnerable and depressed individuals. Low dopamine function is associated with anhedonia and depression, and low serotonin function may be associated with depression, impulsivity, and suicide. On the other hand, norepinephrine is augmented in melancholic depression and may be diminished in atypical depression.

The COMT Gene

The COMT gene leads to the degradation of norepinephrine. Its activity is reduced in vulnerable individuals at high risk for melancholic depression when norepinephrine neurotransmission increases. We found excessive norepinephrine secretion to be a major biological sign of melancholic depression. Children with this mutation often present with the early onset of depressive illness.

Neuropeptide Y

Studies largely in rodents demonstrate a role for NPY in promoting a positive coping with stress. NPY possesses potent antianxiety effects, and its release is induced by stress. NPY is abundantly expressed in regions of the limbic system that are implicated in arousal and in the assignment of emotional value to stimuli and memories. Mutations in the NPY gene that lower its production decrease resilience and predispose people to depression.

The FKBP5 Gene

Childhood abuse and depression make people more sensitive to a defect in the FKBP5 gene, which increases susceptibility to depression by significantly reducing the biological effects of cortisol. Subjects who carry this defect have great vulnerability in response to severe stressors and often develop stress-induced depressions. Significant childhood abuse along with this mutation more than quadrupled the rate of major depression.

Pharmacological Means of Enhancing Resilience

We now know enough about the neurobiology and genetics of resilience to design trials of multiple agents that might promote resilience and decrease vulnerability. We'll look at six agents that have shown promising features for considering them as therapeutic interventions in the promotion of resilience.

Acetyl L-carnitine possesses several characteristics that make it attractive in trials aimed at improving resiliency. L-acetyl carnitine influences glutamate release in the prefrontal cortex and the amygdala. It possesses potent anti-inflammatory effects and decreases the levels of cytokines in the blood and the brain. In addition, l-acetyl carnitine plays a profound role in supporting neuronal energy production, which is genetically compromised in bipolar patients. Taken together, these findings show the power of L-acetyl carnitine to both increase resiliency to stress and to exert antidepressant effects in animal models of depression.

A standard means of assessing resiliency to stress in experimental animals is the social defeat stress paradigm. This procedure involves exposing naïve mice to highly aggressive mice. A vulnerable group is identified by showing signs of social withdrawal and severe anxiety. A resilient group is identified which shows much less social withdrawal and anxiety. An overall group of mice exposed to the social defeat paradigm given l-acetyl carnitine consistently showed much less withdrawal and anxiety. Thus, the drug converted vulnerable mice to resilient ones.

Recent data have shown that plasma levels of l-acetyl carnitine are highly reduced in depressed patients, independent of antidepressant status. The reductions were most pronounced in those who experienced early neglect or trauma and early onsets of depressive illness. Studies are currently in progress to examine its role in producing resilience to experimentally applied anxiety-producing paradigms in healthy subjects and in treating a subtype of depression associated with early neglect, trauma, and early onset of depressive illness.

Ketamine

Ketamine has the ability to rapidly induce neuroplasticity and neurogenesis. New research aims to take advantage of this to enhance psychotherapy by opening new pathways for considering one's life and relationships with others. This rethinking is a key component of resiliency. Further evidence from studies in experimental animals revealed that ketamine reduced learned fear after stressful stimuli and prevents significant rises in cortisol, severe anxiety, and pronounced isolation after social defeat stress when administered preventatively.

Neuropeptide Y

Neuropeptide Y (NPY) a neuropeptide involved in reducing anxiety-related behavior. Its levels are correlated with better behavioral performance and increased resilience in Special Forces soldiers. Higher NPY levels during stress were associated with lower self-reported dissociation and less overall distress, suggesting that NPY might be associated with resilience during uncontrollable stress. Studies are underway giving a potent stimulus to NPY secretion or by administering NPY intranasally.

Methylenedioxymethamphetamine (MDMA)

MDMA was first permitted for use in therapy for PTSD in 2017. Patients with PTSD with a mean duration of twenty years responded positively to MDMA, and the responses were long-lasting—several years after original dosing. The positive and long-term effects were replicated in several other studies that related the efficacy of this compound. In the most conservative results, 54 percent responded with complete remission compared to 20 percent responses to a placebo. MDMA was also capable of converting vulnerable individuals to resilient ones.

MDMA also seems to optimize important elements of responses to psychotherapy for several reasons. First, it promotes a therapeutic alliance and trust between the patient and the therapist. Second, it promotes a desire for connectedness. Third, it promotes self-compassion. All of these factors may allow the patient to engage and process a difficult past without feeling overwhelmed.

Many other psychedelic agents have been proven to have potent antidepressant qualities. Among their many actions, psychedelic agents suppress the default mode network that is highly activated in depressed and vulnerable individuals.

Norepinephrine Receptor Blockers

The administration of a blocker to the beta norepinephrine receptor has preliminarily demonstrated the capacity to prevent adverse consequences of a traumatic event when given within twelve hours of the event.

Effects of Inflammation Blockers

When mice were exposed to social defeat stress, resilient mice had lower blood levels of the immune stimulus IL-6 and cortisol than vulnerable mice. Taking vulnerable mice and giving them an IL-6 blocker converted them to resilient animals. Thus, the burden of inflammation contributes significantly to traits that specify vulnerability,

As we can see, now that we better understand what makes a person predisposed to be vulnerable or resilient, it should be less difficult to identify a vulnerable individual and intervene early to prevent the onset of an actual, full-blown depression. It is conceivable, moreover, that psychotherapy alone could prevent the transition from a vulnerable state to frank depression. By avoiding a full-blown depression, one might prevent the cycle where one depression increases the susceptibility to another, until after nine or so episodes patients can fall into depression spontaneously without a discernible trigger.

Antidepressants reverse many of the structural and neurobiological changes associated with depression. There is substantial overlap between mediators that are regulated in resilience and those that are regulated by chronic antidepressant treatment, raising the possibility that one way in which existing antidepressants work is by inducing in depressed individuals some of the same adaptations that occur naturally in inherently resilient individuals. These insights thus suggest a new path forward for the development of new treatments of stress-related disorders. In addition to looking for ways to prevent or reverse the deleterious effects of stress, or depression, it should be possible to induce natural mechanisms of resilience, distinct from the actions of existing antidepressants.

New and Evolving Procedures for the Treatment of Depression

As we better understand the neuroanatomical, cellular, biological, and molecular landscape of the stress system, we will enhance our knowledge to better treat depression.

The next few years will see an avalanche of new treatments for depression that far supersede the traditional antidepressants in speed, in efficacy, and in the coverage of all subtypes of depressive illness. Clinicians will have to familiarize themselves with a host of new agents and take the time to carefully master mechanisms of action, interactions, and their optimal application. Giving a patient one of the new drugs and following them every few weeks should not be an option. Patients need to be seen frequently to evaluate their progress and tolerance of side effects. Moreover, it will be more important than ever to follow patients psychotherapeutically and to carefully evaluate behavior and cognition during the administration of such agents.

An entirely new era has emerged in our understanding and treatment of depressive illness that has identified key targets for the rapid and effective treatment of depression. We have just scratched the surface and have many new directions to follow. More effective neuroprotective agents could serve as extremely effective antidepressants, and active searches for these compounds are proceeding all over the world. New compounds that induce neuroplasticity and neurogenesis more rapidly and thoroughly are likely to emerge based on research efforts that are now in progress.

ACKNOWLEDGMENTS

2 pages [Text TK]

Acknowledgments

BIBLIOGRAPHY

Chapter 1. William's Anguish

1. Jouanna J. *Greek Medicine from Hippocrates to Galen.* Edited by Philip van der Eijk. Brill Publishers. Leiden, the Netherlands. 2012:335–360.
2. Garofalo I. Galen's commentary of Hippocrates' De humoribus. *Stud Anc Med.* 2005;31:445–56.
3. Kraepelin E. *One Hundred Years of Psychiatry.* Literal Licensing. New York. 1921.
4. Kraepelin E. *Manic-Depressive Insanity and Paranoia.* Wentworth Press. New York. 1903.
5. Semrad EV. *Semrad: The Heart of a Therapist.* Edited by Susan Rako and Harvey Mazer. Jason Aronson. New York. 2003.
6. Gold PW, Goodwin FK, Chrousos GP. Clinical and biochemical manifestations of depression. Relation to the neurobiology of stress (2). *N Engl J Med.* 1988;319:413–20.
7. Gold PW, Goodwin FK, Chrousos GP. Clinical and biochemical manifestations of depression. Relation to the neurobiology of stress (1). *N Engl J Med.* 1988;319:348–53.
8. Gold PW. The organization of the stress system and its dysregulation in depressive illness. *Mol Psychiatry.* 2015;20:32-47.
9. Gold PW, Gabry KE, Yasuda MR, Chrousos GP. Divergent endocrine abnormalities in melancholic and atypical depression: clinical and pathophysiologic implications. Endocrinol *Metab Clin North Am.* 2002;31:37–62.
10. van Velzen LS, Dauvermann MR, Colic L, et al. Structural brain alterations associated with suicidal thoughts and behaviors in young people:

results from 21 international studies from the ENIGMA Suicidal Thoughts and Behaviours consortium. *Mol Psychiatry.* 2022; in press.

11. Aqil M, Roseman L. More than meets the eye: the role of sensory dimensions in psychedelic brain dynamics, experience, and therapeutics. *Neuropharmacology.* 2022; 2022;223:109300.

12. Gold PW, Chrousos GP. Melancholic and atypical subtypes of depression represent distinct pathophysiological entities: CRH, neural circuits, and the diathesis for anxiety and depression. *Mol Psychiatry.* 2013;18:632–34.

13. Casarotto PC, Girych M, Fred SM., et al. Antidepressant drugs act by directly binding to TRKB neurtrophin receptors. *Cell.* 2021;184:1299–313.

14. Björkholm C, Monteggia LM. BDNF—a key transducer of antidepressant effects. *Neuropharmacology.* 2016;102:72–79.

15. Gold PW, Wong ML, Goldstein DS, et al. Cardiac implications of increased arterial entry and reversible 24-h central and peripheral norepinephrine levels in melancholia. *Proc Natl Acad Sci USA.* 2005;102:8303–8.

Chapter 2. When Psychiatry Met Biology

1. Kuhn R. The treatment of depressive states with G 22355 (imipramine hydrochloride). *Am J Psychiatry.* 1958;115:459–64.

2. Kraepelin E. *One Hundred Years of Psychiatry.* Literal Licensing. New York. 1921.

3. Gold PW, Goodwin FK, Chrousos GP. Clinical and biochemical manifestations of depression. Relation to the neurobiology of stress (1). *N Engl J Med.* 1988;319:348–53.

4. Gold PW, Goodwin FK, Chrousos GP. Clinical and biochemical manifestations of depression. Relation to the neurobiology of stress (2). *N Engl J Med.* 1988;319:413–20.

5. Gold PW. The organization of the stress system and its dysregulation in depressive illness. *Mol Psychiatry.* 2015;20:32–47.

6. Gold PW, Chrousos GP. Melancholic and atypical subtypes of depression represent distinct pathophysiological entities: CRH, neural circuits, and the diathesis for anxiety and depression. *Mol Psychiatry.* 2013;18:632–34.

7. Casarotto PC, Girych M, Fred SM., et al. Antidepressant drugs act by directly binding to TRKB [BDNF] neurtrophin receptors. *Cell.* 2021;184:1299–313.

8. Björkholm C, Monteggia LM. BDNF—a key transducer of antidepressant effects. *Neuropharmacology.* 2016;102:72–79.

9. Axelrod J. Studies on sympathomimetic amines I. The biotransformation

and physological disposition of l-ephedrine and l-norephedrine. *J Pharmacol Exp Ther.* 1953;109:62–73.

10. Axelrod J, Whitby LG, Hertting G. Effect of psychotropic drugs on the uptake of H3-norepinephrine by tissues. *Science.* 1961;133:383–84.

11. Axelrod J. Noradreneline: fate and control of its biosynthesis. Nobel lecture. *Science.* 1971:173: 598–606.

12. Hertting G, Axelrod J. Fate of tritiated noradrenaline at the sympathetic nerve-endings. *Nature.* 1961;192:172–73.

13. Gold PW, Loriaux DL, Roy A, et al. Responses to corticotropin-releasing hormone in the hypercortisolism of depression and Cushing's disease. Pathophysiologic and diagnostic implications. *N Engl J Med.* 1986;314:1329–35.

14. Neurobiology of depression. *N Engl J Med.* 1989;320:869–70.

15. Gold PW, Wong ML, Goldstein DS, et al. Cardiac implications of increased arterial entry and reversible 24-h central and peripheral norepinephrine levels in melancholia. *Proc Natl Acad Sci USA.* 2005;102:8303–8.

16. Roy, A, et al.Corticotropin-releasing hormone in the hypercortisolism of depression and Cushing's disease. *N Eng J Med.* 1987;316:217–19.

17. Schildkraut JJ. The catecholamine hypothesis of affective disorders: a review of supporting evidence. 1965. *J Neuropsychiatry Clin Neurosci.* 1995;7:524–33; discussion 533–34.

18. Thase ME, Kupfer DJ, Fasiczka AJ, et al. Identifying an abnormal electroencephalographic sleep profile to characterize major depressive disorder. *Biol Psychiatry.* 1997;41:964–73.

Chapter 3. Stressed and Depressed

1. Lee BH, Kim YK. The roles of BDNF in the pathophysiology of major depression and in antidepressant treatment. *Psychiatry Investig.* 2010;7:231–35.

2. Roozendaal B, Okuda S, de Quervain DJ-F, McGaugh JL. Glucocorticoids interact with emotion-induced noradrenergic activation in influencing different memory functions. *Neurosci.* 2006;138:901–10.

3. Jankord R, Herman JP. Limbic regulation of hypothalamo-pituitary-adrenocortical function during acute and chronic stress. *Ann N Y Acad Sci.* 2008;1148:64–73.

4. McCall JG, Al-Hasani R, Siuda ER, et al. CRH engagement of the locus coeruleus noradrenergic system mediates stress-induced anxiety. *Neuron.* 2015;87:605–20.

5. Ferry B, Roozendaal B, McGaugh JL. Role of norepinephrine in

mediating stress hormone regulation of long-term memory storage: a critical involvement of the amygdala. *Biol Psychiatry.* 1999;46:1140–52.

7. Sheline YI, Barch DM; Price JL, et al. The default mode network and self-referential processes in depression. *Proc Natl Acad Sci USA.* 2009;106:1942–47.

8. Benarroch EE. The locus ceruleus norepinephrine system: functional organization and potential clinical signficance. *Neurology.* 2009;73:1699–704.

9. Gold PW. The organization of the stress system and its dysregulation in depressive illness. *Mol Psychiatry.* 2015;20:32–47.

10. Gold PW, Goodwin FK, Chrousos GP. Clinical and biochemical manifestations of depression. Relation to the neurobiology of stress (2). *N Engl J Med.* 1988;319:413–20.

11. Wong ML, Kling MA, Munson PJ, et al. Pronounced and sustained central hypernoradrenergic function in major depression with melancholic features: relation to hypercortisolism and corticotropin-releasing hormone. *Proc Natl Acad Sci USA.* 2000;97:325–30.

12. Gold PW, Wong ML, Goldstein DS, et al. Cardiac implications of increased arterial entry and reversible 24-h central and peripheral norepinephrine levels in melancholia. *Proc Natl Acad Sci USA.* 2005;102:8303–8.

13. Gold PW, Chrousos GP. The endocrinology of melancholic and atypical depression: relation to neurocircuitry and somatic consequences. *Proc Assoc Am Physicians.* 1999;111:22–34.

14. Lyra E Silva NM, Lam MP, Soares CN, et al. Insulin resistance as a shared pathogenic mechanism between depression and type 2 diabetes. *Front Psychiatry.* 2019;10:57.

15. Gold PW, Wong ML, Chrousos GP, Licinio J. Stress system abnormalities in melancholic and atypical depression: molecular, pathophysiological, and therapeutic implications. *Mol Psychiatry.* 1996;1:257–64.

16. Roozendaal B, Brunson KL, Holloway BL, et al. Involvement of stress-released corticotropin-releasing hormone in the basolateral amygdala in regulating memory consolidation. *Proc Natl Acad Sci USA.* 2002;99:13908–13.

17. Drevets WC, Price JL, Simpson JR Jr, et al. Subgenual prefrontal cortex abnormalities in mood disorders. *Nature* 1997;386:824–27.

18. Drevets WC, Savitz J, Trimble M. The subgenual anterior cingulate cortex in mood disorders. *CNS Spectr.* 2008;13:663–81.

19. Anacker C, Luna VM, Stevens GS, et al. Hippocampal neurogenesis confers stress resilience by inhibiting the ventral dentate gyrus. *Nature.* 2018;559:98–102.

20. Disner SG, Beevers CG, Haigh EAP, Beck AT. Neural mechanisms of the cognitive model of depression. *Nat Rev Neurosci.* 2011;12:467–77.

Bibliography

21. Arnsten AFT. Stress signalling pathways that impair prefrontal cortex structure and function. *Nat Rev Neurosci*. 2009;10:410–22.

22. McEwen BS, Nasca C, Gray JD. Stress effects on neuronal structure: hippocampus, amygdala, and prefrontal cortex. *Neuropsychopharmacology*. 2016;41:3–23.

23. Frodl T, Meisenzahl E, Zetzsche T, et al. Enlargement of the amygdala in patients with a first episode of major depression. *Biol Psychiatry*. 2002;51:708–14.

24. Gold PW, Chrousos G, Kellner C, et al. Psychiatric implications of basic and clinical studies with corticotropin-releasing factor. *Am J Psychiatry*. 1984;141:619–27.

25. Gold PW, Loriaux L, Roy A Corticotropin-releasing hormone in the hypercortisolism of depression and Cushing's disease. *N Eng J Med*. 1987;316:217–19.

26. Neurobiology of depression. *N Engl J Med*. 1989;320:869–70.

27. Gold PW, Loriaux DL, Roy A, et al. Responses to corticotropin-releasing hormone in the hypercortisolism of depression and Cushing's disease. Pathophysiologic and diagnostic implications. *N Eng J Med*. 1986;314:1329–35.

28. Akiyama T, Koeda M, Okubo Y, Kimura M. Hypofunction of left dorsolateral prefrontal cortex in depression during verbal fluency task: a multi-channel near-infrared spectroscopy study. *J Affect Disord*. 2018;231: 83–90.

29. Popoli M, Yan Z, McEwen BS, Sanacora G. The stressed synapse: the impact of stress and glucocorticoids on glutamate transmission. *Nat Rev Neurosci*. 2011;13:22–37.

Chapter 4. The Brave New World of Psychiatric Drugs

1. López-Muñoz F, Alamo C. Monoaminergic neurotransmission: the history of the discovery of antidepressants from 1950s until today. *Curr Pharm Des*. 2009;15:1563–86.

2. Brunello N, Mendlewicz J, Kasper S, et al. The role of noradrenaline and selective noradrenaline reuptake inhibition in depression. *Eur Neuropsychopharmacol*. 2002;12:461–75.

3. Asberg M, Martensson B. Serotonin selective antidepressant drugs: past, present, future. *Clin Neuropharmacol*. 1993;16 Suppl. 3:S32–44.

4. Brown WA, Rosdolsky M. The clinical discovery of imipramine. *Am J Psychiatry*. 2015;172:426–29.

5. Kuhn R. The treatment of depressive states with G 22355 (imipramine hydrochloride). *Am J Psychiatry*. 1958;115:459–64.

6. Wong DT, Perry KW, Bymaster FP. Case history: the discovery of fluoxetine hydrochloride (Prozac). *Nat Rev Drug Discov.* 2005;4:764–74.

7. Patel K, Allen S, Haque MN, et al. Bupropion [Wellbutron]: a systematic review and meta-analysis of effectiveness as an antidepressant. *Ther Adv Psychopharmacol.* 2016;6:99–144.

8. Alam A, Voronovich Z, Carley JA. A review of therapeutic uses of mirtazapine [Remeron] in psychiatric and medical conditions. *Prim Care Companion CNS Disord.* 2013;15:PCC.13r01525.

9. Rodriques-Amorim D, Olivares JM, Spuch C, Rivera-Baltanás T. A systematic review of efficacy, safety, and tolerability of duloxetine [Cymbalta]. *Front Psychiatry.* 2020;11:554899.

10. Quitkin F, Rifkin A, Klein DF. Monoamine oxidase inhibitors [MAOI]. A review of antidepressant effectiveness. *Arch Gen Psychiatry.* 1979;36:749–60.

11. Suchting R, Tirumalajaru V, Gareeb R, et al. Revisiting monoamine oxidase inhibitors for the treatment of depressive disorders: a systematic review and network meta-analysis. *J Affect Disord.* 2021;282:1153–60.

12. Cruz MP. Vilazodone HCl (Viibryd): a serotonin partial agonist and reuptake inhibitor for the treatment of major depressive disorder. *P&T.* 2012;37:28–31.

Chapter 5. The Art of Therapy

1. Semrad EV. *Semrad: The Heart of a Therapist.* Edited by Susan Rako and Harvey Mazer. Jason Aronson. New York. 2003.

Chapter 6. Genetics, Destiny, and Depression

1. Nasca C, Zelli D, Bigio B, et al. Stress dynamically regulates behavior and glutamatergic gene expression in hippocampus by opening a window of epigenetic plasticity. *Proc Natl Acad Sci USA.* 2015;112:14960–65.

2. Mossakowska-Wójcik J, Orzechowska A, Talarowska M, et al. The importance of TCF4 gene in the etiology of recurrent depressive disorders. *Prog Neuropsychopharmacol Biol Psychiatry.* 2018;80(Pt C):304–8.

3. James LM, Engdahl BE, Georgopoulos, AP. Apolipoprotein E: the resilience gene. *Exp Brain Res.* 2017;6:1853–59.

4. Liu X, Hou Z, Yin Y, et al. CACNA1C gene rs11832738 polymorphism influences depression severity by modulating spontaneous activity in the right middle frontal gyrus in patients with major depressive disorder. Front Psychiatry. 2020;11:73–94.

Bibliography

5. Kang JI Kim SJ, Song YY, et al. Genetic influence of COMT and BDNF gene polymorphisms on resilience in healthy college students. *Neuropsychobiology*. 2013;68:174–80.

6. Haeffel GJ, Getchell M, Koposov RA, et al. Association between polymorphisms in the dopamine transporter gene and depression: evidence for a gene-environment interaction in a sample of juvenile detainees. *Psychol Sci*. 2008;19:62–69.

7. Coleman JRI, Gaspar HA, Bryois J, et al. The genetics of the mood disorder spectrum: genome-wide association analyses of more than 185,000 cases and 439,000 controls. *Biol Psychiatry*. 2020;88:169–84.

8. Caspi A, Sugden K, Moffitt TE, et al. Influence of life stress on depression: moderation by a polymorphism in the 5-HTT gene. *Science*. 2003;301:386–89.

9. Bigos KL, Mattay VS, Callicott JH, et al. Genetic variation in CACNA1C affects brain circuitries related to mental illness. *Arch Gen Psychiatry*. 2010;67:939–45.

10. Arrúe A, González-Torres MA, Basterreche N, et al. GAD1 gene polymorphisms are associated with bipolar I disorder and with blood homovanillic acid levels but not with plasmic GABA levels. *Neurochem Int*. 2019;124:152–61.

11. McGrath LM, Cornelis MC, Lee PH, et al. Genetic predictors of risk and resilience in psychiatric disorders: a cross-disorder genome-wide association study of functional impairment in major depressive disorder, bipolar disorder, and schizophrenia. *Am J Med Genet B Neuropsychiatr Genet*. 2013;162B:779–88.

12. Li Y, Cao Z, Wu S, et al. Association between the CLOCK gene polymorphism and depressive symptom mediated by sleep quality among non-clinical Chinese Han population. *J Affect Disord*. 2022;298(Pt A):217–23.

13. Ferrer A, Costas J, Gratacos M, et al. Clock gene polygenic risk score and seasonality in major depressive disorder and bipolar disorder. *Genes Brain Behav*. 2020;19:e12683.

14. Sheikh HI, Kryski R, Smith HJ, et al. Catachol-O-methyltransferase gene val158met polymorphism and depressive symptoms during early childhood. *Am J Med Genet B Neuropsychiatr Genet*. 2013;162B:245–52.

15. Fries GR, Saldana VA, Finnstein J, Rein T. Molecular pathways of major depressive disorder converge on the synapse. *Mol Psychiatry*. 2022;6:1–14.

16. Gandal MJ, Haney JR, Parikshak NN, et al. Shared molecular neuropathology across major psychiatric disorders parallels polygenic overlap. *Science*. 2018;359:693–97.

17. Krishnan V, Han MH, Graham DL, et al. Molecular adaptations

underlying susceptibility and resistance to social defeat in brain reward regions. *Cell.* 2007;131:391–404.

18. Grimm S, Wirth K, Fan Y, et al. The interaction of corticotropin-releasing hormone receptor gene and early life stress on emotional empathy. *Behav Brain Res.* 2017;329:180–85.

19. Pu M, Zhang Z, Xu Z, et al. Influence of genetic polymorphisms in the glutamatergic and GABAergic systems and their interactions with environmental stressors on antidepressant response. *Pharmacogenomics.* 2013;14:277–88.

20. Feder A, Nestler EJ, Charney DS. Psychobiology and molecular genetics of resilience. *Nat Rev Neurosci.* 2009;10:446–57.

21. Levey DF, Stein MB, Wendt FR, et al. Bi-ancestral depression GWAS in the million veteram program and meta-analysis in >1.2 million individuals highlight new therapeutic directions. *Nat Neurosci.* 2021;24:954–63.

22. Hernández-Díaz Y, González-Castro TB, Tovilla-Zárate CA, et al. Association between FKBP5 polymorphisms and depressive disorders or suicidal behavior: a systematic review and meta-analysis study. *Psychiatry Res.* 2019;271:658–68.

23. Laje G, Lally N, Mathews D, et al. Brain-derived neurotrophic factor Val66Met polymorphism and antidepressant efficacy of ketamine in depressed patients. *Biol Psychiatry.* 2012;72:e27–28.

24. Ogilvie AD, Battersby S, Bubb VJ, et al. Polymorphism in serotonin transporter gene associated with susceptibility to major depression. *Lancet.* 1996;347:731–33.

25. Network and Pathway Analysis Subgroup of the Psychiatric Genomics Consortium. Psychiatric genome-wide association study analyses implicate neuronal, immune and histone pathways. *Nat Neurosci.* 2015;18:199–209.

26. Gandal MJ, Haney JR, Parikshak NN, et al. Shared molecular neuropathology across major psychiatric disorders parallels polygenic overlap. *Science.* 2018;359:693–97.

27. Nestler EJ, Waxman SG. Resilience to stress and resilience to pain: lessons from molecular neurobiology and genetics. *Trends Mol Med.* 2020;26:924–35.

28. Peyrot WJ, Price AL. Identifying loci with different allele frequencies among cases of eight psychiatric disorders using CC-GWAS. *Nat Genet.* 2021;53:445–54.

29. Stahl EA, Breen G, Forstner AJ, et al. Genome-wide association study identifies 30 loci associated with bipolar disorder. *Nat Genet.* 2019;51:793–803.

Bibliography

Chapter 7. Darkness Visible

1. Wehr TA, Wirz-Justice A, Goodwin FK, et al. Phase advance of the circadian sleep-wake cycle as an antidepressant. *Science.* 1979;206:710–13.
2. Wehr TA, Helfrich-Förster C. Longitudinal observations call into question the scientific consensus that humans are unaffected by lunar cycles. *Bioessays.* 2021;43:e2100054.
3. Wehr TA. Bipolar mood cycles and lunar tidal cycles. *Mol Psychiatry.* 2018;23:923–31.
4. Wehr TA. Bipolar mood cycles associated with lunar entrainment of a circadian rhythm. *Transl Psychiatry.* 2018;8:151.
5. Joseph-Vanderpool JR, Rosenthal NE, Chrousos GP, et al. Abnormal pituitary-adrenal responses to corticotropin-releasing hormone in patients with seasonal affective disorder: clinical and pathophysiological implications. *J Clin Endocrinol Metab.* 1991;72:1382–87.
6. Helfrich-Förster C, Monecke S, Spiousas I, et al. Women temporarily synchronize their menstrual cycles with the luminance and gravimetric cycles of the moon. *Sci Adv.* 2021;7:eabe1358.
7. Avery DH, Wehr TA. Synchrony of sleep-wake cycles with lunar tidal cycles in a rapid-cycling bipolar patient. *Bipolar Disord.* 2018;20:399–402.
8. Avery DH, Alexander EM, Wehr TA. Synchrony between bipolar mood cycles and lunar tidal cycles ended after initiation of light treatment and treatment of hypothyroidism. *J Psychiatr Pract.* 2019;25:475–80.
9. Ferrer A, Costas J, Gratacos M, et al. Clock gene polygenic risk score and seasonality in major depressive disorder and bipolar disorder. *Genes Brain Behav.* 2020;19:e12683.
10. Ketchesin KD, Becker-Krail D, McClung CA. Mood-related central and peripheral clocks. *Eur J Neurosci.* 2020;51:326–45.
11. Li Y, Cao Z, Wu S, et al. Association between the CLOCK gene polymorphism and depressive symptom mediated by sleep quality among non-clinical Chinese Han population. *J Affect Disord.* 2022;298(Pt A):217–23.
12. Sato S, Bunney B, Mendoza-Viveros L, et al. Rapid-acting antidepressants and the circadian clock. *Neuropsychopharmacology.* 2022;47:805–16.
13. von Schantz M, Leocadio-Miguel MA, McCarthy MJ, et al. Genomic perspectives on the circadian clock hypothesis of psychiatric disorders. *Adv Genet.* 2021;107:153–91.
14. Xing C, Zhou Y, Xu H, et al. Sleep disturbance induces depressive

behaviors and neuroinflammation by altering the circadian oscillations of clock genes in rats. *Neurosci Res.* 2021;171:124–32.

15. Ehlers CL, Frank E, Kupfer DJ. Social zeitgebers and biological rhythms. A unified approach to understanding the etiology of depression. *Arch Gen Psychiatry.* 1988;45:948–52.

16. Geoffroy PA, Palagini L. Biological rhythms and chronotherapeutics in depression. *Prog Neuropsychipharmacol Biol Psychiatry.* 2021;106:110158.

17. Campbell PD, Miller AM, Woesner ME. Bright light therapy: seasonal affective disorder and beyond. *Einstein J Biol Med.* 2017;32:E13–E25.

18. Dauphinais DR, Rosenthal JZ, Terman M, et al. Controlled trial of safety and efficacy of bright light therapy vs. negative air ions in patients with bipolar depression. *Psychiatry Res.* 2012;196:57–61.

19. Virk G, Reeves G, Rosenthal NE, et al. Short exposure to light treatment improves depression scores in patients with seasonal affective disorder: a brief report. *Int J Disabil Hum Dev.* 2009;8:283–86.

20. Rosenthal NE. Issues for *DSM-V*: seasonal affective disorder and seasonality. *Am J Psychiatry.* 2009;166:852–53.

Chapter 8. Hormones and Depression

1. Knoll MJ, Twisk JWR, Beekman ATF, et al. Depression as a risk factor for the onset of type 2 diabetes mellitus. A meta-analysis. *Diabetologia.* 2006;49:837–45.

2. Gold PW. The organization of the stress system and its dysregulation in depressive illness. *Mol Psychiatry.* 2015;20:32–47.

3. Gold PW, Wong ML, Chrousos GP, Licinio J. Stress system abnormalities in melancholic and atypical depression: molecular, pathophysiological, and therapeutic implications. *Mol Psychiatry.* 1996;1:257–64.

4. Miller AH, Maletic V, Raison CL. Inflammation and its discontents: the role of cytokines in the pathophysiology of major depression. *Biol Psychiatry.* 2009;65:732–41.

5. Carrillo-de Sauvage MA, Maatouk L, Arnoux I, et al. Potent and multiple regulatory actions of microglial glucocorticoid receptors during CNS inflammation. *Cell Death Differ.* 2013;20:1546–57.

6. Brady LS, Whitfield HJ Jr, Fox RJ, et al. Long-term antidepressant administration alters corticotropin-releasing hormone, tyrosine hydroxylase, and mineralocorticoid receptor gene expression in rat brain. Therapeutic implications. *J Clin Invest.* 1991;87:831–37.

7. Gold PW, Licinio J, Pavlatou MG. Pathological parainflammation and

endoplasmic reticulum stress in depression: potential translational targets through the CNS insulin, klotho, and PPAR-γ systems. *Mol Psychiatry*. 2013;18:154–65.

8. Chiu SL, Chen CM, Cline HT. Insulin receptor signaling regulates synapse number, dendritic plasticity, and circuit function in vivo. *Neuron*. 2008;58:708–19.

9. Liu F, Day M, Muñiz LC, et al. Activation of estrogen receptor-beta regulates hippocampal synaptic plasticity and improves memory. *Nat Neurosci*. 2008;11:334–43.

10. Brann DW, Dhandapani K, Wakade C, et al. Neurotrophic and neuroprotective actions of estrogen: basic mechanisms and clinical implications. *Steroids*. 2007;72:381–405.

11. Rune GM, Frotscher M. Neurosteroid synthesis in the hippocampus: role in synaptic plasticity. *Neuroscience*. 2005;136:833–42.

12. Walther A, Breidenstein J, Miller R. Association of testosterone treatment with alleviation of depressive symptoms in men: a systematic review and meta-analysis. *JAMA Psychiatry*. 2019;76:31–40.

13. Votinov M, Wagels L, Hoffstaedter F, et al. Effects of exogenous testosterone application on network connectivity within emotion regulation systems. *Sci Rep*. 2020;10:2352.

14. Volman I, Toni I, Verhagen L, Roelofs K. Endogenous testosterone modulates prefrontal-amygdala connectivity during social emotional behavior. *Cereb Cortex*. 2011;21:2282–90.

15. Frye CA, Rhodes ME, Rosellini R, Svare B. The nucleus accumbens as a site of action for rewarding properties of testosterone and its 5alpha-reduced metabolites. *Pharmacol Biochem Behav*. 2002;74:119–27.

16. Bauer M, Whybrow PC. Thyroid hormone, neural tissue and mood modulation. *World J Biol Psychiatry*. 2001;2:59–69.

17. Kapoor R, Fanibunda SE, Desouza LA, et al. Perspectives on thyroid hormone action in adult neurogenesis. *J Neurochem*. 2015;133:599–616.

18. Bauer M, London ED, Silverman DH, et al. Thyroid, brain and mood modulation in affective disorder: insights from molecular research and functional brain imaging. *Pharmacopsychiatry*. 2003;36 Suppl 3:S215–21.

19. Cooke GE, Mullally S, Correia N, et al. Hippocampal volume is decreased in adults with hypothyroidism. *Thyroid*. 2014;24:433–40.

20. Gold PW, Chrousos GP. Melancholic and atypical subtypes of depression represent distinct pathophysiological entities: CRH, neural circuits, and the diathesis for anxiety and depression. *Mol Psychiatry*. 2013;18:632–34.

21. Joseph-Vanderpool JR, Rosenthal NE, Chrousos GP, et al. Abnormal

pituitary-adrenal responses to corticotropin-releasing hormone in patients with seasonal affective disorder: clinical and pathophysiological implications. *J Clin Endocrinol Metab*. 1991;72:1382–87.

22. Magiakou MA, Mastorakos G, Rabin D, et al. Hypothalamic corticotropin-releasing hormone suppression during the postpartum period: implications for the increase in psychiatric manifestations at this time. *J Clin Endocrinol Metab*. 1996;81:1912–17.

23. Gold PW, Chrousos GP. The endocrinology of melancholic and atypical depression: relation to neurocircuitry and somatic consequences. *Proc Assoc Am Physicians*. 1999;111:22–34.

24. Gold PW, Wong ML, Chrousos GP, Licinio J. Stress system abnormalities in melancholic and atypical depression: molecular, pathophysiological, and therapeutic implications. *Mol Psychiatry*. 1996;1:257–64.

25. Roozendaal B, Barsegyan A, Lee S. Adrenal stress hormones, amygdala activation, and memory for emotionally arousing experiences. *Prog Brain Res*. 2008;167:79–97.

26. Roozendaal B, Brunson KL, Holloway BL, et al. Involvement of stress-released corticotropin-releasing hormone in the basolateral amygdala in regulating memory consolidation. *Proc Natl Acad Sci USA*. 2002;99:13908–13.

27. Odaka H, Adachi N, Numakawa T. Impact of glucocorticoid on neurogenesis. *Neural Regen Res*. 2017;12:1028–35.

28. Gold PW, Chrousos G, Kellner C, et al. Psychiatric implications of basic and clinical studies with corticotropin-releasing factor. *Am J Psychiatry*. 1984;141:619–27.

29. Gold PW, Goodwin FK, Chrousos GP. Clinical and biochemical manifestations of depression. Relation to the neurobiology of stress (2). *N Engl J Med*. 1988;319:413–20.

30. Gold PW, Wong ML, Goldstein DS, et al. Cardiac implications of increased arterial entry and reversible 24-h central and peripheral norepinephrine levels in melancholia. *Proc Natl Acad Sci USA*. 2005;102:8303–8.

31. Wong ML, Kling MA, Munson PJ, et al. Pronounced and sustained central hypernoradrenergic function in major depression with melancholic features: relation to hypercortisolism and corticotropin-releasing hormone. *Proc Natl Acad Sci USA*. 2000;97:325–30.

Chapter 9. Depression's True Toll

1. Barefoot JC, Schroll M. Symptoms of depression, acute myocardial infarction, and total mortality in a community sample. *Circulation*. 1996;93:1976–80.

Bibliography

2. Gold PW, Wong ML, Goldstein DS, et al. Cardiac implications of increased arterial entry and reversible 24-h central and peripheral norepinephrine levels in melancholia. *Proc Natl Acad Sci USA.* 2005;102:8303–8.

3. Goldfarb M, De Hert M, Detraux J, et al. Severe mental illness and cardiovascular disease: JACC state-of-the-art review. *J Am Coll Cardiol.* 2022;80:918–33.

4. Warriach ZI, Patel S, Khan F, Ferrer GF. Association of depression with cardiovascular diseases. *Cureus.* 2022;14:e26296.

5. Lotufo PA. Mental disorders and heart disease: from William Harvey to today. *San Paulo Med J.* 2017;135:321–22.

6. Knoll MJ, Twisk JWR, Beekman ATF, et al. Depression as a risk factor for the onset of type 2 diabetes mellitus. A meta-analysis. *Diabetologia.* 2006;49:837–45.

7. Dong JY, Zhang YH, Tong J, Qin LQ. Depression and risk of stroke: a meta-analysis of prospective studies. *Stroke.* 2012;43:32–37.

8. Michelson D, Stratakis C, Hill L, et al. Bone mineral density in women with depression. *N Eng J Med.* 1996;335:1176–81.

9. Whooley MA, de Jonge P, Vittinghoff E, et al. Depressive symptoms, health behaviors, and risk of cardiovascular events in patients with coronary heart disease. *JAMA.* 2008;300:2379–88.

10. Gold PW. The organization of the stress system and its dysregulation in depressive illness. *Mol Psychiatry.* 2015;20:32–47.

11. Gold PW, Chrousos GP. The endocrinology of melancholic and atypical depression: relation to neurocircuitry and somatic consequences. *Proc Assoc Am Physicians.* 1999;111:22–34.

12. Lyra E Silva NM, Lam MP, Soares CN, et al. Insulin resistance as a shared pathogenic mechanism between and depression type 2 diabetes. *Front Psychiatry.* 2019;10:57.

13. Eskandari F, Mistry S, Martinez PE, et al. Younger, premenopausal women with major depressive disorder have more abdominal fat and increased serum levels of prothrombotic factors: implications for greater cardiovascular risk. *Metabolism.* 2005;54:918–24.

14. Gold PW. Endocrine factors in key structural and intracellular changes in depression. *Trends Endocrinol Metab.* 2021;32:212–23.

Chapter 10. When Children Suffer

1. Ruch DA, Heck KM, Sheftall AH, et al. Characteristics and precipitating circumstances of suicide among children aged 5 to 11 years in the United States, 2013–2017. *JAMA Netw Open.* 2021;4:e2115683.

2. Cavelti M, Kaess M. Adolescent suicide: an individual disaster, but a systemic failure. *Eur Child Adolesc Psychiatry.* 2021;30:987–90.

3. Daly M. Prevalence of depression among adolescents in the U.S. from 2009 to 2019: Analysis of trends by sex, race/ethnicity, and income. *J Adolesc Health.* 2022;70:496–99.

4. Bitsko RH, Claussen AH, Lichtstein J, et al. Mental health surveillance among children—United States, 2013–2019. *MMWR Suppl.* 2022;71:1–42.

5. Wickersham A, Sugg HVR, Epstein S, et al. Systematic review and meta-analysis: the association between child and adolescent depression and later educational attainment. *J Am Acad Child Adolesc Psychiatry.* 2021;60:105–18.

6. Costello EJ, Erkanli A, Angold A. Is there an epidemic of child or adolescent depression? *J Child Psychol Psychiatry.* 2006;47:1263–71.

7. Bernaras E, Jaureguizar J, Garaigordobil M. Child and adolescent depression: a review of theories, evaluation instruments prevention programs, and treatments. *Front Psychol.* 2019;10:543.

8. Davey CG, Yücel M, Allen NB. The emergence of depression in adolescence: development of the prefrontal cortex and the representation of reward. *Neurosci Biobehav Rev.* 2018;32:1–19.

9. Oliver A, Pile V, Elm D, Lau JYF. The cognitive neuropsychology of depression in adolescents. *Curr Behav Neurosci Rep* 2019;6:227–235.

10. Shen X, MacSweeney M, Chan SWY, et al. Brain structural associations with depression in a large early adolescent sample (the ABCD study®). *EClinicalMedicine.* 2021;42:101204.

11. Bos MGN, Peters S, van de Kamp FC, et al. Emerging depression in adolescence coincides with accelerated frontal cortical thinning. *J Child Psychol Psychiatry.* 2018;59:994–1002.

12. Gaffrey MS, Barch DM, Singer J, et al. Disrupted amygdala reactivity in depressed 4-to 6-year-old children. *J Am Acad Child Adolesc Psychiatry.* 2013;52:737–46.

13. Redlich R, Opel N, Bürger C, et al. The limbic system in youth depression: brain structural and functional alterations in adolescent in-patients with severe depression. *Neuropsychopharmacology.* 2018;43:546–54.

14. Barch DM, Tillman R, Kelly D, et al. Hippocampal volume and depression among young children. *Psychiatry Res Neuroimaging.* 2019;288:21–28.

15. Baloch HA, Hatch JP, Olvera RL, et al. Morphology of the subgenual prefrontal cortex in pediatric bipolar disorder. *J Psychiatr Res.* 2010;44:1106–10.

16. Gaffrey MS, Luby JL, Repovš G, et al. Subgenual cingulate connectivity in children with a history of preschool-depression. *Neuroreport.* 2010;21:1182–88.

17. Toenders YJ, van Velzen LS, Heideman IZ, et al. Neuroimaging predictors of onset and course of depression in childhood and adolescence: a systematic review of longitudinal studies. *Devel Cogn Neurosci.* 2019;39:100700.

18. Xie C, Jia T, Rolls ET, et al. Reward versus nonreward sensitivity of the medial versus lateral orbitofrontal cortex relates to the severity of depressive symptoms. *Biol Psychiatry Cogn Neurosci Neuroimaging.* 2021;6:259–69.

19. van Velzen LS, Dauvermann MR, Colic L, et al. Structural brain alterations associated with suicidal thoughts and behaviors in young people. results from 21 international studies from the ENIGMA Suicidal Thoughts and Behaviours consortium. *Mol Psychiatry.* 2022; in press.

Chapter 11. Bipolar Disorder

1. van Velzen LS, Dauvermann MR, Colic L, et al. Structural brain alterations associated with suicidal thoughts and behaviors in young people: results from 21 international studies from the ENIGMA Suicidal Thoughts and Behaviours consortium. *Mol Psychiatry.* 2022; in press.

2. Gold PW, Chrousos GP. Melancholic and atypical subtypes of depression represent distinct pathophysiological entities: CRH, neural circuits, and the diathesis for anxiety and depression. *Mol Psychiatry.* 2013;18:632–34.

3. Wehr TA, Wirz-Justice A, Goodwin FK, et al. Phase advance of the circadian sleep-wake cycle as an antidepressant. *Science.* 1979;206:710–13.

4. Wehr TA. Bipolar mood cycles and lunar tidal cycles. *Mol Psychiatry.* 2018;23:923–31.

5. Wehr TA. Bipolar mood cycles associated with lunar entrainment of a circadian rhythm. *Transl Psychiatry.* 2018;8:151.

6. Wehr TA, Helfrich-Förster C. Longitudinal observations call into question the scientific consensus that humans are unaffected by lunar cycles. *Bioessays.* 2021;43:e2100054.

7. Avery DH, Alexander EM, Wehr TA. Synchrony between bipolar mood cycles and lunar tidal cycles ended after initiation of light treatment and treatment of hypothyroidism. *J Psychiatr Pract.* 2019;25:475–80.

8. Avery DH, Wehr TA. Synchrony of sleep-wake cycles with lunar tidal cycles in a rapid-cycling bipolar patient. *Bipolar Disord.* 2018;20:399–402.

9. Helfrich-Förster C, Monecke S, Spiousas I, et al. Women temporarily synchronize their menstrual cycles with the luminance and gravimetric cycles of the moon. *Sci Adv.* 2021;7:eabe1358.

10. Frey BN, Stanley JA, Nery FG, et al. Abnormal cellular energy and phospholipid metabolism in the left dorsolateral prefrontal cortex of

medication-free individuals with bipolar disorder: an in vivo 1H MRS study. *Bipolar Disord.* 2007;9 Suppl 1:119–27.

11. Green EK, Rees E, Walters JTR, et al. Copy number variation in bipolar disorder. *Mol Psychiatry.* 2016;21:89–93.

12. Martino M, Magioncalda P, Huang Z, et al. Contrasting variability patterns in the default mode and sensorimotor networks balance in bipolar depression and mania. *Proc Natl Acad Sci USA.* 2016;113:4824–29.

13. Lopez-Larson MP, Shah LM, Weeks HR, et al. Abnormal functional connectivity between default and salience networks in pediatric bipolar disorder. *Biol Psychiatry Cogn Neurosci Neuroimaging.* 2017;2:85–93.

14. Pacifico R, Davis RL. Transcriptome sequencing implicates dorsal striatum-specific gene network, immune response and energy metabolism pathways in bipolar disorder. *Mol Psychiatry.* 2017;22:441–49.

15. Levey DF, Stein MB, Wendt FR, et al. Bi-ancestral depression GWAS in the million veteram program and meta-analysis in >1.2 million individuals highlight new therapeutic directions. *Nat Neurosci.* 2021;24:954–63.

16. Nielsen RE, Kugathasan P, Straszek S, et al. Why are somatic diseases in bipolar disorder insufficiently treated? *Int J Bipolar Disord.* 2019;7:12.

17. Blacker CJ, Millischer V, Webb LM, et al. EAAT2 as a research target in bipolar disorder and unipolar depression: a systematic review. *Mol Neuropsychiatry.* 2020;5 (Suppl 1):44–59.

18. Lippard ETC, Jensen KP, Wang F, et al. Effects of ANK3 variation on gray and white matter in bipolar disorder. *Mol Psychiatry.* 2017;22:1345–51.

19. Hibar DP, Westlye LT, van Erp TGM, et al. Subcortical volumetric abnormalities in bipolar disorder. *Mol Psychiatry.* 2016;21:1710–16.

20. Ferrer A, Costas J, Gratacos M, et al. Clock gene polygenic risk score and seasonality in major depressive disorder and bipolar disorder. *Genes Brain Behav.* 2020;19:e12683

21. Arrúe A, González-Torres MA, Basterreche N, et al. GAD1 gene polymorphisms are associated with bipolar I disorder and with blood homovanillic acid levels but not with plasmic GABA levels. *Neurochem Int.* 2019;124:152–61.

22. Blumberg HP, Leung HC, Skudlarski P, et al. A functional magnetic resonance imaging study of bipolar disorder: state- and trait-related dysfunction in ventral prefrontal cortices. *Arch Gen Psychiatry.* 2003;60:601–9.

23. Pacifico R, Davis RL. Transcriptome sequencing implicates dorsal striatum-specific gene network, immune response and energy metabolism pathways in bipolar disorder. *Mol Psychiatry.* 2017;22:441–49.

24. Chiou YJ, Huang TL. Brain-derived neurotrophic factor (BDNF) and bipolar disorder. *Psychiatry Res.* 2019;274:395–99.

25. McGrath LM, Cornelis MC, Lee PH, et al. Genetic predictors of risk and resilience in psychiatric disorders: a cross-disorder genome-wide association study of functional impairment in major depressive disorder, bipolar disorder, and schizophrenia. *Am J Med Genet B Neuropsychiatr Genet.* 2013;162B:779–88

26. Durdurak BB, Altaweel N, Upthegrove R, Marwaha S. Understanding the development of bipolar disorder and borderline personality disorder in young people: a meta-review of systematic reviews. *Psychol Med.* 2022 Sep 30:1–14.

27. Whittaker JR, Foley SF, Ackling E, Murphy K, Caseras X. The functional connectivity between the nucleus accumbens and the ventromedial pre-frontal cortex as an endophenotype for bipolar disorder. *Biol Psychiatry.* 2018;84(11):803–809.

28. Cui D, Guo Y, Cao W, et al. Correlation between decreased amygdala subnuclei volumes and impaired cognitive functions in pediatric bipolar disorder. *Front Psychiatry.* 2020;11:612.

Chapter 12. The Power and Promise of Lithium

1. Lambert PD, McGirr KM, Ely TD, et al. Chronic lithium treatment decreases neuronal activity in the nucleus accumbens and cingulate cortex of the rat. *Neuropsychopharmacology.* 1999;21:229–37.

2. Dell'Osso L, Del Grande C, Gesi C, et al. A new look at an old drug: neuroprotective effects and therapeutic potentials of lithium salts. *Neuropsychiatr Dis Treat.* 2016;12:1687–703.

3. De-Paula VJ, Gattaz WF, Forlenza OV. Long-term lithium treatment increases intracellular and extracellular brain-derived neurotrophic factor (BDNF) in cortical and hippocampal neurons at subtherapeutic concentrations. *Bipolar Disord.* 2016;18:692–95.

4. Song J, Sjölander A, Joas E, et al. Suicidal behavior during lithium and valproate treatment: a within-individual 8-year prospective study of 50,000 patients with bipolar disorder. *Am J Psychiatry.* 2017;174:795–802.

5. Puglisi-Allegra S, Ruggieri S, Fornai F. Translational evidence for lithium-induced brain plasticity and neuroprotection in the treatment of neuropsychiatric disorders. *Translat Psychiatry.* 2021;11:366.

6. Usher J, Menzel P, Schneider-Axmann T, et al. Increased right amygdala volume in lithium treated patients with bipolar I disorder. *Acta Psychiatr Scand.* 2010;121:119–24.

7. Zhou Q, Wang K, Qiu J, et al. Comparative transcriptome analysis and

CRISPR/Cas9 gene editing reveal that E4BP4 mediates lithium upregulation of *Per2* expression. *Open Biol.* 2021;11:210140.

8. Kline NS. Lithium comes into its own. *Am J Psychiatry.* 1968;125:558–60.

9. Blackwell B, Shepherd M. Prophylactic lithium: another therapeutic myth? An examination of the evidence to date. *Lancet.* 1968;1:968–71.

Chapter 13. Shock Therapy

1. Espinoza RT, Kellner CH. Electroconvulsive therapy. *N Engl J Med.* 2022;386:667–72.

2. Trifu S, Sevcenco A, Stănescu A, et al. Efficacy of electroconvulsive therapy as a potential first-choice treatment in treatment-resistant depression (review). *Exp Ther Med.* 2021;22:1281.

3. Chakrabarti S, Grover S, Rajagopal R. Electroconvulsive therapy: a review of knowledge, experience and attitudes of patients concerning the treatment. *World J Biol Psychiatry.* 2010;11:525–37.

4. Ousdal OT, Brancati GE, Kessler U, et al. The neurobiological effects of electroconvulsive therapy studied through magnetic resonance: what have we learned, and where do we go? *Biol Psychiatry.* 2022;91:540–49.

5. Cerletti U. and Bini L. Elettroshock. Archivio Generale di *Neurologica.* 1938. 19:266–268.

6. Cerletti U. Old and new information about electroshock. *Am J Psychiatry.* 1921;107:87–94.

7. Kalinowsky LB. Convulsive shock treatment. In American Handbook of Psychiatry, Vol. 2. Edited by Silvano Arieti. Basic Books. New York. 1959. 1499–1520.

8. Boyer B. Fantasies concerning convulsive therapy. *Psychoanal Rev.* 1952; 39:252–70.

9. Herbert W. Berkeley ECT, shock psychiatric profession. *Science News.* 1982;122:309.

10. Shorter E. *A History of Psychiatry.* New York. John Wiley and Sons. 1997. 218–25.

11. Voigt J, Carpenter L, Leuchter A. A systematic literature review of the clinical efficacy of repetitive transcranial magnetic stimulation (rTMS) in non-treatment resistant patients with major depressive disorder. *BMC Psychiatry.* 2019;19:13.

12. Gogulski J, Ross JM, Talbot A, et al. Personalized rTMS for depression: a review. *Biol Psychiatry.* 2022; in press.

13. Cole EJ, Stimpson KH, Bentzley BS, et al. Stanford accelerated intelligent

neuromodulation therapy for treatment-resistant depression. *Am J. Psychiatry.* 2020;177:716–26.

14. George MS, Caulfield KA, Wiley M. Shaping plasticity with non-invasive brain stimulation in the treatment of psychiatric disorders: present and future. *Handb Clin Neurol.* 2022;184:497–507.

15. Wassermann EM, Lisanby SH. Therapeutic application of repetitive transcranial magnetic stmulation: a review. *Clin Neurophysiol.* 2001;112:1367–77.

16. Caulfield KA, Fleischmann HH, Cox CE, et al. Neuronavigation maximizes accuracy and precision in TMS positioning: evidence from 11,230 distance, angle, and electric field modeling measurements. *Brain Stimul.* 2022;15:1192–1205.

17. Hamblin MR. Shining light on the head: photobiomodulation for brain disorders. *BBA Clin.* 2016;6:113–24.

18. Mayberg HS, Lozano AM, Voon V, et al. Deep brain stimulation for treatment-resistant depression. *Neuron.* 2005;45:651–60.

19. Sackheim HA. Modern electroconvulsive therapy: vastly improved yet greatly underused. *JAMA Psychiatry.* 2017. 74:779–780

Chapter 14. Psychedelics and Connection

1. Davis AK, Barrett FS, May DG, et al. Effects of psilocybin-assisted therapy on major depressive disorder: a randomized clinical trial. *JAMA Psychiatry.* 2021;78:481–89.

2. Daws RE, Timmermann C, Giribaldi B, et al. Increased global integration in the brain after psilocybin therapy for depression. *Nat Med.* 2022;28:844–51.

3. Gukasyan N, Davis AK, Barrett FS, et al. Efficacy and safety of psilocybin-assisted treatment for major depressive disorder: prospective 12-month follow-up. *J Psychopharmacol.* 2022;36:151–58,

4. Carhart-Harris R, Giribaldi B, Watts R, et al. Trial of psilocybin versus escitalopram for depression. *N Eng J Med.* 2021;384:1402–11.

5. Goodwin GM, Aaronson ST, Alvarez O, et al. Single-dose psilocybin for a treatment-resistant episode of major depression. *N Eng J Med.* 2022;387:1637–48.

6. Aqil M, Roseman L. More than meets the eye: the role of sensory dimensions in psychedelic brain dynamics, experience, and therapeutics. *Neuropharmacology.* 2022:223:109300.

7. VanderZwaag J, Halvorson T, Dolhan K, et al. The missing piece? A case for microglia's prominent role in the therapeutic action of anesthetics, ketamine, and psychedelics. *Neurochem Res.* 2002; in press.

8. Wong A, Raz A. Microdosing with classical psychedelics: research trajectories and practical considerations. *Transcult Psychiatry.* 2022;59:675–90.

9. Sottile RJ, Vida T. A proposed mechanism for the MDMA-mediated extinction of traumatic memories in PTSD patients treated with MDMA-assisted therapy. *Front Psychiatry.* 2022;13:991753.

10. Obstacles and opportunities: how psychedelic medicine can rise to its challenges. *Nature.* 2022; in press.

11. Beaussant Y, Nigam K. Expending perspectives on the potential for psychedelic-assisted therapies to improve the experience of aging. *Am J Geriatr Psychiatry.* 2023;31:54–57.

12. Glazer J, Murray CH, Nusslock R, et al. Low doses of lysergic acid diethylamide (LSD) increase reward-related brain activity. *Neuropsychopharmacology.* 2022; in press.

13. Stoliker D, Novelli L, Vollenweider FX, et al. Effective connectivity of functionally anticorrelated networks under lysergic acid diethylamide. *Biol Psychiatry.* 2022; in press.

14. Kwan AC, Olson DE, Preller KH, Roth BL. The neural basis of psychedelic action. *Nat Neurosci.* 2022;25:1407–19.

Chapter 15. A Newer Understanding of Older Antidepressants

1. Casarotto PC, Girych M, Fred SM, et al. Antidepressant drugs act by directly binding to TRKB neurotrophin receptors. *Cell.* 2021;184:1299–313.

2. Björkholm C, Monteggia LM. BDNF—a key transducer of antidepressant effects. *Neuropharmacology.* 2016;102:72–79.

3. Cooke JD, Grover LM, Spangler PR, et al. Venlafaxine treatment stimulates expression of brain-derived neurotrophic factor protein in frontal cortex and inhibits long-term potentiation in hippocampus. *Neuroscience.* 2009;162:1411–19.

4. Chen CH, Lee CS, Lee MTM, et al. Variant GADL1 and response to lithium therapy in bipolar I disorder. *N Eng J Med.* 2014;370:119–28.

5. Palmos AB, Duarte RRR, Smeeth DM, et al. Lithium treatment and human hippocampal neurogenesis. *Transl Psychiatry.* 2021;11:555.

6. Gupta R, Gupta K, Tripathi AK, et al. Effect of mirtazapine [Remeron] treatment on serum levels of brain-derived neurotrophic factor and tumor necrosis factor-α in patients of major depressive disorder with severe depression. *Pharmacology.* 2016;97:184–8.

7. Hartig J, Nemes B. BDNF-related mutations in major depressive disorder: a systematic review. *Acta Neuropsychiatr.* 2022; in press.

8. Lee BH, Kim YK. The roles of BDNF in the pathophysiology of major depression and in antidepressant treatment. *Psychiatry Investig.* 2010;7:231–35.

9. Woelfer M, Li M, Colic L, et al. Ketamine-induced changes in plasma brain-derived neurotrophic factor (BDNF) levels are associated with the resting-state functional connectivity of the prefrontal cortex. *World J Biol Psychiatry.* 2020;21:696–710.

10. Kang JI, Kim SJ, Song YY, et al. Genetic influence of COMT and BDNF gene polymorphisms on resilience in healthy college students. *Neuropsychobiology.* 2013;68:174–80.

11. de la Tremblaye PB, Benoit SM, Schock S, Plamondon H. CRHR1 exacerbates the glial inflammatory response and alters BDNF/TrkB/pCREB signaling in a rat model of global cerebral ischemia: implications for neuroprotection and cognitive recovery. *Prog Neuropsychopharmacol Biol Psychiatry.* 2017;79 (Pt B):234–48.

12. Abdallah CG, Sanacora G, Duman RS, Krystal JH. Ketamine and rapid-acting antidepressants: a window into a new neurobiology for mood disorder therapeutics. *Annu Rev Med.* 2015;66:509–23.

13. Autry AE, Monteggia LM. Brain-derived neurotrophic factor and neuropsychiatric disorders. *Pharmacol Rev.* 2012;64:238–58.

14. Duman RS, Monteggia LM. A neurotrophic model for stress-related mood disorders. Biol Psychiatry. 2006;59:1116–27.

Chapter 16. The Promise and Peril of Ketamine

1. Zarate CA Jr, Singh JB, Carlson PJ, et al. A randomized trial of an N-methyl-D-aspartate antagonist in treatment-resistant major depression. *Arch Gen Psychiatry.* 2006;63:856–64.

2. Duman RS. Ketamine and rapid-acting antidepressants: a new era in the battle against depression and suicide. *F1000Res.* 2018;7:F1000 Faculty Rev-659.

3. Krystal JH, Abdallah CG, Sanacora G, et al. Ketamine: a paradigm shift for depression research and treatment. *Neuron.* 2019;101:774–78.

4. Brachman RA, McGowan JC, Perusini JN, et al. Ketamine as a prophylactic against stress-induced depressive-like behavior. *Biol Psychiatry.* 2016;79:776–86.

5. Carrillo P, Petit A-C, Gaillard R, Vinckier F. The next psychoactive drugs: From imipramine to ketamine. *Bull Acad Natl Med.* 2020;204:1034–42.

6. Laje G, Lally N, Mathews D, et al. Brain-derived neurotrophic factor Val66Met polymorphism and antidepressant efficacy of ketamine in depressed patients. *Biol Psychiatry.* 2012;72:e27–28.

7. Price RB. From mice to men: can ketamine enhance resilience to stress? *Biol Psychiatry.* 2016;79:e57–59.

8. Woelfer M, Li M, Colic L, et al. Ketamine-induced changes in plasma brain-derived neurotrophic factor (BDNF) levels are associated with the resting-state functional connectivity of the prefrontal cortex. *World J Biol Psychiatry.* 2020;21:696–710.

10. Gerhard DM, Pothula S, Liu R-J, et al. GABA interneurons are the cellular trigger for ketamine's rapid antidepressant actions. *J Clin Invest.* 2020;130:1336–49.

11. Price RB. From mice to men: can ketamine enhance resilience to stress? *Biol Psychiatry.* 2016;79:e57–59.

12. Duman RS, Li N, Liu R-J, et al. Signaling pathways underlying the rapid antidepressant actions of ketamine. *Neuropharmacology.* 2012;62:35–41.

13. Krystal JH, Abdallah CG, Sanacora G, et al. Ketamine: a paradigm shift for depression research and treatment. *Neuron.* 2019;101:774–78.

14. Swainson J, Thomas RK, Archer S, et al. Esketamine for treatment resistant depression. *Expert Rev Neurother.* 2019;19:899–911.

15. Yokoyama R, Higuchi M, Tanabe W, et al. (S)-norketamine and (2S,6S)-hydroxynorketamine exert potent antidepressant-like effects in a chronic corticosterone-induced mouse model of depression. *Pharmacol Biochem Behav.* 2020;191:172876.

Chapter 17. Breaking Through Depression

1. Davis AK, Barrett FS, May DG, et al. Effects of psilocybin-assisted therapy on major depressive disorder: a randomized clinical trial. *JAMA Psychiatry.* 2021;78:481–89.

2. Daws RE, Timmermann C, Giribaldi B, et al. Increased global integration in the brain after psilocybin therapy for depression. *Nat Med.* 2022;28:844–51.

3. Gukasyan N, Davis AK, Barrett FS, et al. Efficacy and safety of psilocybin-assisted treatment for major depressive disorder: prospective 12-month follow-up. *J Psychopharmacol.* 2022;36:151–58.

4. Carhart-Harris R, Giribaldi B, Watts R, et al. Trial of psilocybin versus escitalopram for depression. *N Eng J Med.* 2021;384:1402–11.

5. Goodwin GM, Aaronson ST, Alvarez O, et al. Single-dose psilocybin for a treatment-resistant episode of major depression. *N Eng J Med.* 2022;387:1637–48.

6. Aqil M, Roseman L. More than meets the eye: the role of sensory

dimensions in psychedelic brain dynamics, experience, and therapeutics. *Neuropharmacology*. 2022; 2022;223:109300.

7. VanderZwaag J, Halvorson T, Dolhan K, et al. The missing piece? A case for microglia's prominent role in the therapeutic action of anesthetics, ketamine, and psychedelics. *Neurochem Res*. 2022; in press.

8. Wong A, Raz A. Microdosing with classical psychedelics: research trajectories and practical considerations. *Transcult Psychiatry*. 2022;59:675–90.

9. Inserra A, Giorgini G, Lacroix S, et al. Effects of repeated lysergic acid diethylamide (LSD) on the mouse brain endocannabinoidome and gut microbiome. *Br J Pharmacol*. 2022; in press.

10. Jones GM. Race and ethnicity moderate the associations between lifetime psychedelic use (MDMA/ecstasy and psilocybin) and major depressive episodes. *J Psychopharmacol*. 2022; in press.

11. Sottile RJ, Vida T. A proposed mechanism for the MDMA-mediated extinction of traumatic memories in PTSD patients treated with MDMA-assisted therapy. Front Psychiatry. 2022;13:991753.

12. Obstacles and opportunities: how psychedelic medicine can rise to its challenges. *Nature*. 2022; in press.

13. Beaussant Y, Nigam K. Expending perspectives on the potential for psychedelic-assisted therapies to improve the experience of aging. *Am J Geriatr Psychiatry*. 2023;31:54–57.

14. Glazer J, Murray CH, Nusslock R, et al. Low doses of lysergic acid diethylamide (LSD) increase reward-related brain activity. *Neuropsychopharmacology*. 2022; in press.

15. Kwan AC, Olson DE, Preller KH, Roth BL. The neural basis of psychedelic action. *Nat Neurosci*. 2022;25:1407–19.

16. Gattuso JJ, Perkins D, Ruffell S, et al. Default mode network modulation by psychedelics: a systematic review. *Int J Neuropsychopharmacol*. 2022; in press.

17. Stoliker D, Novelli L, Vollenweider FX, et al. Effective connectivity of functionally anticorrelated networks under lysergic acid diethylamide. *Biol Psychiatry*. 2022; in press.

Chapter 18. Building Resiliency

1. Nestler EJ, Waxman SG. Resilience to stress and resilience to pain: lessons from molecular neurobiology and genetics. *Trends Mol Med*. 2020;26:924–35.

2. Krishnan V, Han MH, Graham DL, et al. Molecular adaptations

underlying susceptibility and resistance to social defeat in brain reward regions. *Cell* 2007;131:391–404.

3. Han MH, Nestler EJ. Neural substrates of depression and resilience. *Neurotherapeutics.* 2017;14:677–86.

4. Feder A, Fred-Torres S, Southwick SM, Charney DS. The biology of human resilience: opportunities for enhancing resilience across the life span. *Biol Psychiatry.* 2019;86:443–53.

5. Feder A, Nestler EJ, Charney DS. Psychobiology and molecular genetics of resilience. *Nat Rev Neurosci.* 2009;10:446–57.

6. Russo SJ, Murrough JW, Han MH, et al. Neurobiology of resilience. *Nat Neurosci.* 2012;15:1475–84.

7. Southwick SM, Charney DS. The science of resilience: implications for the prevention and treatment of depression. *Science.* 2012;338:79–82.

8. Rutter M. Resilience as a dynamic concept. *Dev Psychopathol.* 2012;24:335–44.

9. Rutter M. Resilience in the face of adversity. Protective factors and resistance to psychiatric disorder. *Br J Psychiatry.* 1985;147:598–611.

10. Kilner JM, Lemon RN. What we know currently about mirror neurons. *Curr Biol.* 2013;23:R1057–62.

11. Campbell-Sills L, Cohan SL, Stein MB. Relation of resilience to personality, coping, and psychiatric symptoms in young adults. *Behav Res Ther.* 2006;44:589–99.

12. Kautz M, Charney DS, Murrough JW. Neuropeptide Y, resilience, and PTSD therapeutics. *Neurosci Lett.* 2017;649:164–69.

13. Bolsinger J, Seifritz E, Kleim B, Manoliu A. Neuroimaging correlates of resilience to traumatic events—a comprehensive review. *Front Psychiatry.* 2018;9:693.

14. Pino O, Pelosi A, Artoni V, Mari M. Post-traumatic outcomes among survivors of the earthquake in central Italy of August 24, 2016. A study of PTSD risk and vulnerability factors. *Psychiatr Q.* 2021;92:1489–511.

15. Bush G, Luu P, Posner MI. Cognitive and emotional influences in anterior cingulate cortex. *Trends Cogn Sci.*2000;4:215–22.

16. Boldrini M, Galfalvy H, Dwork AJ, et al. Resilience is associated with a larger dentate gyrus, while suicide decedents with major depressive disorder have fewer granule neurons. *Biol Psychiatry.* 2019;85:850–62.

17. Cathomas F, Murrough JW, Nestler EJ, et al. Neurobiology of resilience: interface between mind and body. *Biol Psychiatry.* 2019;86:410–20.

18. Chen MC, Hamilton JP, Gotlib IH. Decreased hippocampal volume in healthy girls at risk of depression. *Arch Gen Psychiatry.* 2010;67:270–76.

19. Tashjian SM, Galván A. The role of mesolimbic circuitry in buffering election-related distress. *J Neurosci.* 2018;38:2887–98.

20. van der Werff SJA, van den Berg SM, Pannekoek JN, et al. Neuroimaging resilience to stress: a review. *Front Behav Neurosci.* 2013;7:39.

21. Cutuli D. Cognitive reappraisal and expressive suppression strategies role in the emotional regulation: an overview on their modulatory effects and neural correlates. *Front Syst Neurosci.* 2014;8:175.

22. Su Y, D'Arcy C, Yuan S, Meng X. How does childhood maltreatment influence ensuing cognitive functioning among people with the exposure of childhood maltreatment? A systematic review of prospective cohort studies. *J Affect Disord.* 2019;252:278–93.

23. Silveira S, Shah R, Nooner KB, et al. Impact of childhood trauma on executive function in adolescence-mediating functional brain networks and prediction of high-risk drinking. *Biol Psychiatry Cogn Neurosci Neuroimaging.* 2020;5:499–509.

24. Vythilingam M, Nelson EE, Scaramozza M, et al. Reward circuitry in resilience to severe trauma: an fMRI investigation of resilient special forces soldiers. *Psychiatry Res.* 2009;172:75–77.

25. Shallcross J, Wu L, Wilkinson CS, et al. Increased mGlu5 mRNA expression in BLA glutamate neurons facilitates resilience to the long-term effects of a single predator scent stress exposure. *Brain Struct Funct.* 2021;226:2279–93.

26. Stein MB, Choi KW, Jain S, et al. Genome-wide analyses of psychological resilience in U.S. Army soldiers. *Am J Med Genet B Neuropsychiatr Genet.* 2019;180:310–19.

27. Maul S, Giegling I, Fabbri C, et al. Genetics of resilience: implication from genome-wide association studies and candidate genes of the stress response system in posttraumatic stress disorder and depression. *Am J Med Genet B Neuropsychiatr Genet.* 2019;183:77–94.

28. Grimm S, Wirth K, Fan Y, et al. The interaction of the corticotropin-releasing hormone receptor gene and early life stress on emotional empathy. *Behav Brain Res.* 2017;329:180–85.

29. James LM, Engdahl BE, Georgopoulos, AP. Apolipoprotein E: the resilience gene. *Exp Brain Res.* 2017;6:1853–59.

30. Caspi A, Sugden K, Moffitt TE, et al. Influence of life stress on depression: moderation by a polymorphism in the 5-HTT gene. *Science.* 2003;301:386–89.

31. Kang JI, Kim SJ, Song YY, et al. Genetic influence of COMT and

Bibliography

BDNF gene polymorphisms on reslience in healthy college students. *Neuropsychobiology*. 2013;68:174–80.

32. Post RM. Myriad of implications of acetyl-l-carnitine deficits in depression. *Proc Natl Acad Sci USA*. 2018;115:8475–77.

33. Hernández-Díaz Y, González-Castro TB, Tovilla-Zárate CA, et al. Association between FKBP5 polymorphisms and depressive disorders or suicidal behavior: a systematic review and meta-analysis study. *Psychiatry Res*. 2019;271:658–68.

34. Frey BN, Stanley JA, Nery FG, et al. Abnormal cellular energy and phospholipid metabolism in the left dorsolateral prefrontal cortex of medication-free individuals with bipolar disorder: an in vivo 1H MRS study. *Bipolar Disord*. 2007;9 Suppl 1:119–27.

35. Nasca C. L-acetylcarnitine causes rapid antidepressant effects through the epigenetic induction of mGlu2 receptors. *Proc Natl Acad Sci USA*. 2013;110:4804–9.

36. Nasca C, Bigio B, Lee FS, et al. Acetyl-l-carnitine deficiency in patients with major depressive disorder. *Proc Natl Acad Sci USA*. 2018;115:8627–32.

37. Brachman RA, McGowan JC, Perusini JN, et al. Ketamine as a prophylactic against stress-induced depressive-like behavior. *Biol Psychiatry*. 2016;79:776–86.

38. Price RB. From mice to men: can ketamine enhance resilience to stress? *Biol Psychiatry*. 2016;79:e57–59.

39. Enman NM, Sabban EL, McGonigle P, Van Bockstaele EJ. Targeting the neuropeptide Y system in stress-related psychiatric disorders. *Neurobiol Stress*. 2015;1:33–43.

INDEX

[Index TK—hold 12 pages]

Index

Index

Index

Index

Index

Index

Index

Index

Index

Index

Index

ABOUT THE AUTHOR

Dr. Philip Gold is one of the world's leading researchers of depressive illness. Since 1974, he has worked at the National Institutes of Health, where he has served as Chief of Neuroendocrine Research and Senior Investigator in the National Institute of Mental Health Intramural Research Program, and Chief of the Section on Neuroendocrinology. For more than twenty years, he headed one of the country's leading clinical research laboratories, consisting of thirty individuals, at the National Institutes of Health Clinical Center in the study of the biological basis of depressive illness.